ARTISTS &
ACTIVISTS
Making Culture in New York's Capital Region

ARTISTS & ACTIVISTS

Making Culture in New York's Capital Region

To Gene —
with many thanks
for a great event at the
Albany Public Library.

Joseph Dalton
4/23/09

JOSEPH DALTON

Forward by Marion Roach

To order additional copies of this title, contact your favorite local bookstore or visit
www.tbmbooks.com

Cover photo by Renée MacAllister of Almost Foodies.
Author photo by Timothy Cahill.
Book Design by Melissa Mykal Batalin.

The Troy Book Makers. Troy, NY. www.thetroybookmakers.com

www.josephdalton.net

ISBN: 978-1-933994-727

Foreword: Art is Here

BY MARION ROACH

It's long been my hope that someone will fund a campaign in New York's Capital Region that not only reminds us how much art there is here, but also behooves us to see it, as it is everywhere. Maybe this would be best done in the form of billboards or bottle caps, I don't know – but my idea has always been that in small window signs, along the sides of buildings, on the bumpers of cars and the backs of t-shirts appear the words, "Art is Here."

Sometimes we forget that.

In fact, art is in the propinquities that architecture allows, as well as in the choices made by gallery directors, the musings of the conductor, the program planning of the regional arts center, in the planting of trees, the story-boarding of film and the quick flick of a dancer's heel. Art is here and it buoys what we do, infuses how we think, and propels us in courses we might not otherwise pursue. Art is like that, and we can always use the reminder of its presence since without that, we might mistakenly think that art is only to be found elsewhere.

Since 2002 Joseph Dalton has been reminding readers of the ubiquity of art here in the capital of the greatest state of America by focusing on those people who make that art. It's a broad definition that he employs to identify those who make art, rightfully encompassing percussionists as well as patrons alongside movie producers and violin makers, and including them in what we might consider the more traditional artistic pursuits of filmmaker, theater director, composer, pianist, painter, and photographer.

A prize-winning writer, Dalton is right in the way he defines an artist, and in doing so pushes us to define more broadly and to see more clearly the art that surrounds us as we live our lives. His is the voice we want to hear, and he invites us to go along with him as he talks with the artists whose works heighten our lives.

Read in sequence, what these pages provide is the reassurance that amid this crazy, every-shifting world, the one common currency we hold is art; that the ineluctable bond that brings us back to each other, that describes and defines and marks our time here on earth is art. And that's nice, but something more is at work here, as we are reminded where it is that art truly lives. It is not only someplace else. It *surrounds* us, holding us in its thrall, and at its best harmonizing the sometimes discordant sounds of living our lives.

Reading through these pages you will make studio visits and gallery stops, sit in the wings and watch the dailies. In doing so, see if you don't uplift your sights, and do as the pages demand: Drop the idea thinking of yourself as a mere listener, viewer, an audience of any kind, and instead get in touch with the living proof that art is, in fact, here.

Marion Roach is an author and teacher who lives in New York's Capital Region.

TABLE OF CONTENTS

Chapter Two: The Activists

Chapter Three: Visiting Artists

INTRODUCTION

Typical overviews of the arts in New York's Capital Region look at the biggest buildings and the oldest institutions. And that's not such a bad place to start. Consider just three examples: the Albany Institute of History and Art, founded in 1791, is one of the oldest museums in the nation; the Troy Savings Bank Music Hall is a Victorian gem with world renown acoustics; and the more newly minted, concrete clad Empire State Plaza Center for the Performing Arts, popularly known as The Egg, is surely one of the weirdest looking major structures on the east coast (as nearly every guest artist there seems to remark).

Yet it's not bricks and mortar nor organizational longevity that makes for a vital cultural life. It's the people – the persevering artists, the inquisitive audiences, and the producers and patrons who assure that the artists and audiences can find each other.

Throughout the Hudson Valley the very soil is alive with creativity. Just scratch the surface and all manner of vibrant art forms will greet and awaken your senses. It's been my great fortune over the past six years to be able to dig deep into this cultural landscape and get paid, modestly, to do so. As sometimes happens in my life, I was in the right place at the right time and my background in classical music led to writing for the Times Union. Soon the chance to cover a wider swath of the local scene opened up and I've relished the regular opportunities to sit down and chat with people who have the uncanny ability to grab beauty out of the earth or the ether and present it as a gift to the rest of us.

Yet dreamy inspiration has never been my focus. Production and hard work is where it's at. Most artists, I've learned, hate quantitative questions. Like, how long did it take you to write that string quartet? How many paintings do you complete in a year? And worst of all: How do you make a living? When something becomes measurable it is more understandable and it's my goal to give readers, sitting with a cup of coffee and the paper on a Sunday morning, a firmer grip on local art and those who make it.

By no means is this collection intended as a definitive guide to the cultural powerhouses in the Capital Region. Rather, it's a sampling of those who were doing something captivating at any given moment and who happened to catch my attention, either with the right kind of pitch or press release (which seldom work), or through some good word of mouth in the community (an effective but elusive barometer), or by producing and showing a high quality work that repeatedly grabbed hold of my imagination (always the most reliable standard).

Whether you read these profiles from start to finish or you jump around the pages – just as the most valuable kind of arts-goers bounce from an opening in a tiny gallery, to a lavish theatrical production, and on to a blockbuster movie, always with equal measures of gusto and discernment – you'll surely catch on to some of my own tastes and pro-clivities. These include artists who've taken circuitous routes to their chosen fields, individuals who excel at more than one field of creativity, and couples who are partners in both life and art.

There's also more than a handful of gay and lesbians here, which should not come as a surprise. We're talking about artists, after all. Yet I remember within the first year or so my contributing to the T.U., an editor remarked, "We've had a lot more gay people lately." What I think was actually happening is that someone had simply begun telling the rest of the story. Back when I was solely a consumer and not also a pro-ducer of arts journalism, I remember plenty of otherwise insightful and well rounded newspaper profiles (sometimes even entire biographies) that took a giant silent step around the matter of a middle-aged man's personal life – unless he was dying – where a wife and children might have otherwise merited a sentence or two.

Of course, I've not been a totally free agent over the years but have focused on at least a couple of "beats" – trade lingo for the field or ter-rain that a journalist keeps a steady eye on, not unlike a cop repeatedly walking around a neighborhood watching for new and curious activity. Classical music has been primary, and my coverage is mostly through reviews. If only I could actually walk that beat, but there's a veritable explosion of activity every summer and everything involves a drive – north to the Saratoga Performing Arts Center, east to Tanglewood and the rest of the Berkshires, south to the increasingly important Fisher Center for the Performing Arts at Bard College, and west to Glimmerglass Opera in Cooperstown. (I once thought I could use the time in the car to catch up on listening to new CDs, but I've learned that my ears are already too full and fatigued.)

There's plenty during the rest of the season as well. The Union College Concert Series in Scenectady is a regular stopover for top soloists and chamber ensembles on their way to bookings in Manhattan. And the Albany Symphony Orchestra consistently provides good fodder for stories, usually because of its advocacy of American composers but also for its tightrope act of performing at a higher level and producing a greater quantity of events than its modest budget and audiences would lead one to expect.

Shortly after my arrival in the area, I almost literally stumbled upon another area of pursuit – the quirky visual art scene that began to blossom in venues that were decidedly non-artistic but also distinctly right. Living a block off Lark Street at the time, I was drawn toward a psychedelic happening taking place within a tiny storefront on an otherwise sleepy weeknight. More such events kept being staged over the coming months and I like to think that my chronicling of it all played a part in the surging attendance.

The attention and insight of a sympathetic journalist and critic is a sometimes overlooked – and increasingly endangered – link between artists and audiences that can be crucial to the quality of life in a region. Really all of us involved in the arts are activists, no matter whether we're creating, producing, critiquing or simply buying tickets. Let's keep acting up.

My thanks go to all those who have supported me in my sometimes perilous career, initially as an administrator and more recently as a writer. Especially to my mom, for being my first writing instructor and for early-on making me stand up, articulate and defend the value and essentialness of a life immersed in the arts. To my friends, especially Gabriel Clark, Gwen Deely, Gerald Busby, Lynn Stone, Connie Beckley, David Del Tredici, Eileen Macholl, Judy White, Mary Ellen Cohn and Valerie Gillenwater. To Gloria Mazure and Lyrysa Smith for their advice and support in getting this book done. To my succession of editors at the Times Union, Steve Barnes, Casey Seiler, Susan Mehalick and Mike Janairo, as well as Rex Smith and Marion Roach. And finally, a loving dedication to my partner Richard, who I'm so happy to have walking with me in life – as well as sitting beside me at all the shows.

CHAPTER ONE
The Artists

KEVIN BRUCE

PAINTER/DRAG QUEEN

Beneath layers of paint, the persona of an artist

"You've decided what you're going to do, and it's all you can think about. Everything else is a bother. Going to work is a bother. Going out to get something to eat is a bother."

Albany artist Kevin Bruce is describing his feelings when in the midst of creating.

"You can spend a whole day painting and not eat and suddenly feel really faint and nauseous and dizzy and sick," he says. "And you'll still be like 'Oh, I have to work on this more.' And then you'll force yourself to go and take care of your body. You really are just getting nutty. That's how it's always been with every painting I've ever done."

The need to create might be a common denominator to the more than 70 artists who, like Bruce, will be exhibiting their work at Saturday's Art on Lark. But if his work habits are typical of the artistic mentality, Bruce's subject matter is unique – at least in Albany.

Through paintings, drawings and comic books, Bruce depicts what he knows well – mostly drag queens and other slices of gay life. More than an observer, Bruce is himself part of the local drag scene. His persona, named Patti Kettleton, is as colorful and fantastic as his visual art.

"His drag is art as well," says a fellow Albany drag performer who wishes to be known only by his drag name, Frieda Munchon. "Once you see him talk or perform you realize there's something there under all the paint."

"I made a decision before I moved here that I wanted to pursue art at any cost," says Bruce, 38, who came to Albany in 1998 after a year in Waterbury, Conn.

After being here about a year, Bruce began curating art shows in the modest gallery on the top floor of the Capital District Gay and

Lesbian Community Council. It became his passageway into the local community, as well as into a new creative pursuit.

During his two-year tenure, each show was an opportunity to help other emerging artists, and each opening a platform for his emerging drag persona.

"That's how I started doing drag, at the openings," says Bruce. He recalls saying to himself, "I'm going to wear makeup and crazy hats, 'cause I'm the curator. ... I'll dress up for all the openings, and they'll know I'm important cause I'm nutty-looking."

It didn't take long for Bruce to become part of the more traditional drag scene, which is centered at Albany bars like The Phoenix and Fuze Box. But he's always looking for new and unexpected venues for his friendly style of performance.

About a year ago, for example, he led a monthly bingo night at the now defunct Mama Rosa's Pasta Cafe on Albany's Lark Street. But rather than call it "Bitch Bingom: as such events are known in New York City, he gave it the name "Queenie Bingo." "People won't want to eat there if there's some evil drag queen cutting them to ribbons," says Bruce.

Coming up with fresh outfits for Patti sometimes interferes with time for Bruce's painting. But both pursuits emerge from the same source – the need to create.

"He can take a burlap bag and make it artistic and beautiful," says Munchon, whose own getups benefit from Bruce's imagination. "He made a dress out of Altoids ads, and it was amazing."

Drag may be a world of fantasy and play, but in the mind of Kevin Bruce and the character of Patti Kettleton it is also an art of expansion and possibility.

"You can turn an event from everyone socializing and being quiet into people being willing to let their wilder side come out, because somebody (else) already did," says Bruce. "I've taken the first step for them. Nobody is worried about being the biggest fool anymore – because I'm here!"

Big hair, ruby-red lips, black leather, rippling muscles and oversized angel wings populate Bruce's paintings. His elongated forms are backed by brick walls, cyclone fences or abandoned docks: a potent mixture of dream figures and urban reality.

Bruce is well schooled in fantasy art. His former mentor is the widely known graphic artist Greg Hildebrandt, who is best known for the original "Star Wars" poster from the 1970s and a popular series of "Lord of the Rings" calendars published during the 1980s.

In the late 1980s, Bruce studied at the Joe Kubert School of Cartoon and Graphic Art in Dover, N.J., where Hildebrandt was a faculty member. But Bruce actually came to know the older artist through Hildebrandt's two daughters, Mary and Laura, who also were studying at the school. Bruce became a regular presence at the Hildebrandt household.

"His daughters would never get up until noon, so I had all these hours to discuss art with Greg, and we'd pore over art books," says Bruce. "And he said (for example) 'I suggest you look at Botticelli ... to learn how to draw elegant hands.' He (also) introduced me to art of Paul Cadmus, who's one of my real heroes." Cadmus, who died in 1999 at age 94, was known for his virtuosic figurative style and often homoerotic subject matter.

When Bruce was living in Waterbury about eight years later, he developed another student-teacher relationship with the late painter Jules Moison. Where Hildebrandt taught craft and professionalism, Moison passed on something more personal.

"He didn't do the whole art-theory thing so much," says Bruce. "His was more about what I could bring to art spiritually as a gay man."

In Albany's ever-changing grass-roots art scene, Bruce has become an old-timer.

"I've never been to an art opening where I've not seen him," says painter and photographer Shaina Marron, who has made Patti Kettleton a subject of some of her own works. "He's been around a long time and seen the changes ... and the galleries that come and go."

And the traditionalist leanings of Bruce's painting style are not lost on his colleagues.

"Kevin is actually quite classical and does a great deal with highlighting and painstaking detail to make his paintings vibrant," says Albany artist Stephen Mead. The two met several years ago when Mead's work appeared in one of Bruce's shows at the gay and lesbian center.

Most any weeknight, Bruce can be found in the center's little coffee bar, or out on Lark Street chatting with friends. "I know everybody," he says.

But not everybody may recognize him if they've only met the flamboyant Patti. On a normal day, he embodies an entirely different archetype – the nerd.

Large dusty glasses, drab T-shirts and slouchy jeans adorn a slight frame and pronounced belly: a sharp contrast to the colorful and shapely figures of Bruce's painting. Yet his sparkling eyes and easy, hearty laughter, as well as the friends that often surround him, suggest there's more beneath the surface.

"Kevin is a free spirit," says Munchon. "He's crazy, but that's good. His outlook is different than anybody else's."

Bruce is also admired for his generosity. He regularly donates paintings to benefit auctions – seven sold at last fall's "Art for AIDS" – and an illustration of his is on the cover of this year's "Pride Guide" program for this month's gay pride events.

"Beyond his unique performance flair and sense of humor is a deeply serious and thoughtful man committed both to his art and to the betterment of his community," says Mead.

GERALD COBLE & ROBERT NUNNELLEY

JULY 4, 2003   ARTISTS

A collage of studios, art forms and lives

It's easy to drive right past the town without even noticing it. A smattering of old buildings on Route 29 northeast of Greenwich in Washington County, Battenville sits beside the Batten Kill and was briefly the home of Susan B. Anthony, who taught school there in 1826.

In 1971, artists Robert Nunnelley and Gerald Coble bought an 18th-century house to serve as their country home and studio. Since then, the two men – now in their 70s and a couple for more than four decades – have slowly made the town into their personal arts colony.

First, they restored their four-bedroom house to its original simplicity by removing layers of wallpaper, dropped ceilings and linoleum floors. They filled the rooms with period furniture and choice works of art – mostly their own. Then came the gardens, the clearing of trees to allow a view of the river, and the planting of new pines to serve as a shield from the road. As the years have gone by, they also acquired several smaller neighboring houses, which have been put to use as painting studios or rental properties.

They hardly act like land barons. Retired from active careers, they are quiet gentlemen who spend the days tending their gardens, caring for their Siamese cat, and producing deeply personal works of art that regularly draw collectors and other artists to sleepy little Battenville.

Nunnelley's colorful canvases are exuberant, but the artist himself is the opposite of effusive: His wrinkled face and brilliant blue eyes light up when he's asked about art, but he doesn't volunteer much. Coble is the more talkative of the pair, although his own art is more wistful, almost somber.

"I liked what they did from the word go," said Solange Herter, an art dealer who has lived directly across the river from the two artists for decades. "Yet, I've never seen anything in their work that in the remotest way shows that they even know each other."

11

Like Coble, Nunnelley came from the South. A native of Birmingham, Ala., he moved to New York City in 1957 as a protege of the sculptor David Smith. Nunnelley studied with Robert Motherwell and was associated with other greats of the abstract expressionist movement, including Willem de Kooning and Franz Kline.

"I came to be with that group, but late," Nunnelley says.

Settling in Manhattan's Greenwich Village, he became a professor of fine arts at Fairleigh Dickinson University in Teaneck, N.J., in the mid-'60s; he retired in 1996. While his teaching career remained stable, his art took some turns.

"Abstraction was emotionally demanding," he says. "It's a kind of involvement where you don't know what you're doing, and yet you have to structure it."

"It was very unsettling because it took a long time to find another tradition to belong to," he says. Eventually, Nunnelley found inspiration in the work of Matisse. His recent works share the French artist's vivid sense of color and bold lines, but there remain hints of his roots in abstraction.

Although he mostly paints still life compositions, his canvases are large – four feet by six feet, or bigger. The pieces are worked out in advance in a black-and-white calligraphic style (reminiscent of Smith, his initial mentor). Nunnelley frequently spends years on a canvas, returning again and again to get light and shadow just right.

After working in a variety of studios around the property, Nunnelley seems particularly happy with his current space, which occupies the entire second floor of a historic barn that was converted into a tavern a century ago. After eyeing the property for years, he and Coble bought it in 2000.

A self-taught artist, Coble was living in his native North Carolina when he met Nunnelley, who was visiting friends there in the early 1960s. Within a year, Coble relocated to New York. When they bought the Battenville house, he began staying in the country while Nunnelley spent part of each week teaching in New Jersey.

"Collage construction" is the term Coble uses to describe his work. Within a large white field surrounded by a simple frame, he places seemingly random objects – broken crucifixes, old postcards and magazine clippings, antique clothing. Although the works are sparse, they are also highly evocative.

Coble often works on a theme inspired by the life and work of artists as diverse as Walt Whitman, Marcel Proust and Ava Gardner. The materials have been gathered, he says, "over a lifetime of obsessions."

His work is sometimes compared to that of the American assemblage artist Joseph Cornell, but Coble cites no influences other than the Italian countryside, where the couple has often vacationed.

It was, in fact, the way the unspoiled countryside and gentle hills of Washington Country reminded them of Italy that drew them to the area. Not surprisingly, Coble's studio at the back of the main house looks out on the river.

Although their dining room table can seat 12, Coble and Nunnelley are typically modest about their social life, as well as their prominence as artists. It's a viewpoint that seems to fit with the simplicity of their lives, and the focused clarity of their art.

"The older one gets," says Coble, "the more one seeks to get to the essential and to remove clutter."

CHRIS DeMARCO

PHOTOGRAPHER/UPHOLSTERER   OCTOBER 5, 2003

Finding beauty amid chaos

Friends and colleagues of Chris DeMarco call her a perfectionist. It's an apt description for the keen eye and exacting standards that she applies to her art – photography – and to her craft – upholstery. But what captures her eye is the imperfect.

Natural landscapes marred by abandoned man-made structures, or decaying architecture that's slowly being reclaimed by nature are the kind of subjects that become beautiful, even luminous, through her photographic lens. And there's something similar in her careful, trans-forming approach to old furniture.

"She's pensive," says David Brickman, a fellow local photographer, "and really looks at things."

And what she sees is beauty in the broken down.

DeMarco, who is also the proprietor of The National Upholstering in Albany, an old family business that she's transformed into an art and design shop on Lark Street, has a new photographic obsession: unusual and elaborate displays at grave sites.

DeMarco's obsession is currently on display in "Remembrances," an exhibit at the Arts Center of the Capital Region in Troy. The dozen or so recent photos show colorful displays of flags, trinkets and memora-bilia in cemeteries.

The photographic series started during a visit last winter to North Carolina, where DeMarco's only daughter attends college. During a drive after an unusually strong storm left some 8 inches of snow on the ground, a cemetery caught DeMarco's attention.

"I noticed bits of color sticking up in the snow," she recalls. The following day, she returned, camera in hand. Her pursuit of the subject has continued at grave sites in the Northeast as well.

"I can't wait to see what some of them do for Halloween," she says.

Set against melting snow and dead grass, bright natural light falls on the elaborate compositions of pinwheels, stuffed animals, angel statues and fake flowers. They are curious combinations of the patriotic, religious and kitschy. The effect is not so much about graves and death but about consumerism and the blurring of the spiritual and commercial.

"I think of them as folk-art still lifes," says DeMarco.

Indeed, she treats the private memorials with the exacting detail of a painter. The color prints on the gallery wall were all made by DeMarco herself and selected after dozens of attempts were rejected.

"She'll print the photos over and over," says Iona Mirsky, an old friend and neighbor, "to get them just right."

DeMarco's need for exactness might be a gift from her late father, who trained her as a teenager in the craft of upholstery.

R. Vincent DeMarco founded National Upholstering on Washington Avenue in 1942. His daughter took over the business in 1980 and has evolved it in a few different directions over the years. For a time, she sold antiques out of the original large storefront and also had a team of upholstery assistants. Through it all, the standards have remained high.

"I started with her father, and I've used her for years," says Mary Tracy, an interior designer who has worked in Albany for 30 years. "She brings her artistic discipline to the work. You get perfection from her."

Changes in the furniture industry have made reupholstering a business less in demand and ever-more specialized. And the demands of being a boss as well as a landlord, since the original building included rental apartments, wore on DeMarco.

"I felt like a social worker," she says of her many experiences with difficult tenants. But through the unpleasantness of managing a building, she again found something captivating, if not entirely beautiful: "I once won an award for a photo of an apartment trashed by a tenant."

About a year and a half ago, after nearly closing the entire business, DeMarco instead relocated it to Lark Street. The shop is now one-sixth the size of the original and just around the corner from the townhouse where she has lived since 1976. "I kept the name for sentimental reasons," she says. "But my mother always hated it."

A portion of the shop is her work area, and a large walk-in closet contains thousands of fabric samples. The rest is filled with displays of photos, paintings, prints and knickknacks created by local artists and craftspeople.

DeMarco gives little prominence to her own photos, just as she usually hesitates to talk much about them. But she can become passionate about local artists in general.

"For the cost of a Thomas Kinkade print in a fancy frame," says DeMarco, referring to the California artist whose works have gone mass market, "people could have two or three pieces of (original) art by regional artists."

Her approach to the combination of art and home design is inscribed on a T-shirt: "Good art won't match your sofa."

Creating art is nothing new to DeMarco, who earned a master's of fine art degree from the Pratt Institute, where her thesis project was a collection of wall sculptures made of upholstered and painted fabric. She first worked with a camera as an undergraduate art student at the Rochester Institute of Technology.

"It was a required course," she recalls, "but I just kept taking pictures after the class ended." Yet another aspect of DeMarco's artistic vision shows up in her photos of decaying Southern architecture. "They are pictures of change and decay," says Brickman, "but a natural decay, maybe also an economic decay as well."

Some of Brickman's own photos are carried in DeMarco's shop, but his appreciation of her work comes from a kindered spirit who has built a reputation for photos that record and remark on aging architecture.

"There's a poignancy, a sense of loss, a haunted nature of these places" that she shoots, says Brickman, who also says that the fact that she prints her own color photographs is rare.

"She strives for quality; that's why her stuff stands out," he says. "You can't upholster a chair and leave a wrinkle."

ANN JON

SCULPTOR

Showing the art and politics of nature

When Ann Jon was scouting for a site for her next sculpture show, she got in her kayak.

"I've been in the Berkshires for years, and of course I knew there was a river here called the Housatonic. But once I got the kayak, I *discovered* this river, and it's so beautiful," she says.

Long before Jon started kayaking on the Housatonic – a nearly daily practice for the past year, weather and ice permitting – she pursued beauty on land.

Jon has been an artist for 40 of her 60 years, often working with the very stuff of the Earth, such as marble and granite. For the past five years, she's also been director of the western Massachusetts collective Sculpture Now.

When the potential for a collaboration with the Housatonic River Summer 2004 – a summer-long festival of cultural and recreation activities came along – Jon saw the opportunity to combine her two passions. The resulting show, "Sculpture In & By the River," is on two riverside locations and features nearly 30 works inspired by the river.

"There are two reasons for focusing on the Housatonic," Jon says, speaking of her own interests as well as the inspiration for the 27 other participating sculptors. "One is the beauty of it and the history, starting with the Mahicans who lived here and the many artists who have painted it over the years. But the other reason is it's really polluted."

"When it first started, it was wide open. Where on the river were we going to do this (show)? And that's when I got in my kayak. I probably found a dozen sites and had to select from those," Jon says. Concessions had to be made for safety and for access by nonaquatic transportation devices (i.e., automobiles).

She settled on two locations: a large wild field adjacent to the Norman Rockwell Museum in Stockbridge and a more manicured lot beside a bakery in the center of Housatonic. Participating artists were chosen by a jury from about 70 submissions.

The hard part was installing elaborate and often weighty sculptures amid the flora and fauna, fish and fowl. Some of the pieces were designed to be in the river itself. In Wendy Klemperer's "River Elk," a series of massive four-legged figures extends from the bank into the river. The pieces are made of recycled steel cables and were put in place by a crane.

A more fragile sculpture for the river is Gary Orlinsky's "Dwelling," a skeletal dome made of reeds. Jon attempted to deliver it by tying it to the back of her kayak and paddling upstream.

"The draw was so heavy that I kept getting swept downstream. ... We had three people running as well as they could through the brush on the bank trying to catch me and the sculpture," recalls Jon, laughing. "I knew I could handle the kayak, but I was afraid the sculpture would crash. So I finally got into shore and we carried it through brush, over our heads."

Jon's fondness for the Housatonic River has helped her take the show's complications in stride. Among her peers, she's long been known as hardworking and reliable.

"She certainly has to be very patient, getting installations done and accommodating everyone's schedule," says Allen Williams, of East Otis, a fellow sculptor and board member of Sculpture Now who has known Jon for about 30 years.

Whether it's coordinating a show of artists from around the world, realizing an artistic work or competing in a kayak race, Jon has a certain single-mindedness.

"She's a get-things-done kind of person," says Peter Barrett, a artist from Egremont who has a sculpture, "Plant Life," in the Housatonic show. "It's easy to start a piece and let it take a life of its own and let it evolve to a place where you had no intention of it going. But (Ann is) more disciplined than that."

After a period of large-scale architectural works, Jon is entering a new artistic phase. "What's interesting me more and more ... are issues beyond aesthetic and sculptural issues. ... I want to connect to something more than just myself and my subject."

Jon says this as she's driving through Berkshire County in her small pickup truck, a new Kevlar kayak mounted on a rack on top. It's the second kayak she's bought in less than a year.

The follow-up question is obvious: What does kayaking have to do with artistic direction?

"The politics of nature," she says. "It means there is a political issue with nature and I see that, and I want to connect with that so that I can connect with nature in the way that I would like to. I would like to go swimming in that river. I would like to see people go down there and catch their food. I would like to take my dog down there and not worry about him getting contaminated soil on his feet."

The 148-mile-long Housatonic River stretches from upper Berkshire County to the Long Island Sound in western Connecticut. Like the Hudson, it has inspired generations of artists. But also like the Hudson, it is contaminated by PCBs, the result of General Electric's legal dumping of industrial waste from 1932 to 1977 at its plant in Pittsfield near the river's headwaters. A partial cleanup in the immediate vicinity of the GE plant is in progress. In April, American Rivers, a Washington, D.C.-based advocacy group, named the Housatonic one of America's 10 most endangered rivers.

Jon's sculpture is one of the more somber contributions to the show. "The Fish That Cried Its Eyes Out," hangs from a bridge above the Housatonic. A stylized silver fish appears to be made of metal but is actually Styrofoam. "It's very light, probably 5 pounds," says Jon.

Hanging from the figure is a series of reflective lenses, as might be in a traffic light. "They're tears," Jon says. "They're also yellow (for) warning and red (for) stop."

HAROLD LOHNER

ARTIST   DECEMBER 3, 2006

Drawin' men

Every month Harold Lohner flips through the new issue of Art Calendar, a magazine that provides copious listings of exhibitions and other opportunities for artists. He regularly finds calls for submissions to shows of female artists and occasionally of gay artists. "I'm gay and an artist, but I don't want to be a practitioner of gay art. It's like you don't have to be very good," says Lohner, 48, who has been in a committed relationship for 10 years. Even in the gay community, gay art is a vague term that can encompass any art focusing on the male form or any art created by a gay man.

Like most artists, who almost by definition are individualists, Lohner sometimes wonders where he and his work fit in. A printmaker who's been on the faculty of the Sage Colleges for 25 years, Lohner creates works on paper that focus almost exclusively on the male form.

"There's lot of women who make art only about women. It's a way of studying yourself," says Lohner. "The prints are about men and me."

A wide array of recent monoprints by Lohner is on view at Albany Center Galleries in the exhibition, "Translations Lost and Found."

Most of his works depict faces, though "Atlas," one of four artist books included in the show, features reclining bodies in the greens and blues of a map. And in the series of prints titled "Column 1" and "Column 2" there's a tangle of male body parts.

Lohner views his current work as speaking of and to men, both gay and straight. "Sometimes men think what is interesting to them is interesting to everyone," he says. "But men have (their own) body issues and health issues ... overlapping issues and affinities."

There are piles upon piles of men's faces in Lohner's "Gate," a collage of 105 monoprints attached to a wall in an arched shape that suggests a passage or doorway. Most of them have open mouths, suggesting speech or laughter or perhaps even pain. In contrast, the dozen faces in

"Coins," a horizontal succession of circular prints, are more restrained, closemouthed and solemn. Ask Lohner the identity of any individual figure and he'll give you the same response.

"It's a portrait of Joe Blow, that's who it is," he says. "They're not real people ... just drawings."

Seldom do the figures have clothing or eyeglasses, because that would suggest a particular time or place. And while many of the faces appear to have African features, Lohner pleads ignorance of their heritage. "It's more about angle, gestures, shadow, texture, than age or race," he says. "I want my pieces to be timeless."

Nevertheless, Lohner doesn't pull the faces out of the ether. A self-described "pack rat," he collects reams of photographs from magazines and Web sites and uses them as guides to suggest the anonymous faces that populate his art. Working directly on the plate of a printing press, he draws with his finger in a sock.

"I begin with a putty knife, then a comb, then draw by hand, creating streaks that look like brush strokes," says Lohner. "(Photographs) are just to have a place to start."

"In scraping ink off of the plate, Harold makes a really bold mark. ... He's free-handing, not taking a rest, not using a guide, which is unusual," says Ed Atkeson, an artist and friend, who put on a show of Lohner's work in 2003 at the now-shuttered Firlefanz Gallery in Albany.

Occasionally, Lohner also lays objects onto the printing plate, thus leaving their impressions on the paper. For example, tools of the carpenter – rulers and T-squares – show up in a series of six prints called "Builders" that are also part of the current exhibit. Confetti, cassette tape and textured linoleum have been used in other pieces.

"It's a kind of magic you don't get if you're not walking out onto the limb," says Atkeson.

While the daring and experimentation of Lohner's prints are mostly in the process of creation, there's an obvious whimsy and playfulness in his other body of work – typefaces.

About eight years ago, Lohner began constructing original fonts, a painstakingly detailed computerized process. Today he has an inventory of several hundred original typefaces that are available at the Web site

Harold's Fonts. They include "Melody Maker," "Rice Cakes," "Queer Theory," "Bride of the Monster" and "Rubaiyat," to name a few.

"I make more money on fonts than I ever did on art," says Lohner. "My art is so important, it's like I squeeze it out of my soul, but strangers send me money for these fonts. It's like I do crossword puzzles and make money from it."

In the late 1990s, Lohner took almost four years off from creating and exhibiting art. The Firlefanz show in the spring of 2004 was his first in five years. The self-imposed exile was the result of an accumulation of frustrations with the art scene that will be familiar to most any artist in search of an audience.

"I thought avoiding the (hassles) of trying to get people to pay attention would be good, but not doing the work was depressing," recalls Lohner. "It made me realize I really do the work for myself. Even if I put it all away. I need to do it."

Lohner creates in the printmaking studio at the Sage College of Albany where he also teaches. And he likes to spread out, saying, "I'm such a hog, I use every table in the room." Thus, he works hardest during the school's winter and spring breaks and the summer vacation, when he can have the entire space to himself. Calling the intensive periods his "retreats," he says he emerges from them renewed.

"I have a friend who runs marathons. He has no hope of ever winning ... but he enjoys it and seems to need to do it," Lohner says. "It's the same thing with me and my art – there it is, if someone wants to see it."

CHRISTIAN STEINER

SEPTEMBER 5, 2004

PHOTOGRAPHER/
PIANIST/IMPRESARIO

Insightful eye, elegant touch

Christian Steiner can't move even a piece of paper without style and grace.

Best known as a photographer, he's been shooting portraits of the biggest stars in classical music – Perlman, Callas, Von Karajan – for more than 30 years. Also a formidable pianist, Steiner is the guiding force of the music series at Tannery Pond in New Lebanon.

It was during a Tannery Pond concert last month that he stepped up to the task of being a page-turner at the last minute.

"It's a rather lowly job for the artistic director to do, but he was so lovely and so discreet that he helped me to play better," says pianist Ken Noda, who was performing that night. "He had such good vibes and he just turned the pages so elegantly. He's like a count, or royalty."

Born in Germany of what he calls "a dynasty of musicians," the 66-year-old Steiner still speaks with a bit of an accent. On the phone, his deep and purposeful voice evokes images of a dark, well-fed baron. But in person, Steiner is trim and fair. His fashionably cut hair is as white as his sneakers, which he wears with bluejeans and a black polo shirt. His inviting, bright blue eyes always seem to say "yes."

Steiner may have agreed to turning pages for Noda on short notice, but don't ask him to sit down at the piano bench himself unless he has had plenty of rehearsal time.

"I play at the most two (concerts a year), and it stands to reason that when you play that rarely your nerves are unbelievably stressed," says Steiner. "I played this season once, which I hadn't expected."

The Borromeo String Quartet was booked for a July concert at Tannery Pond, which included two pieces with mezzo-soprano Margaret Lattimore. One of them, Ernest Chausson's "Chanson perpetuelle," also required a pianist.

Steiner normally sets the lights and microphones during rehearsals, and for the Borromeo date in July he also was asked by a board member to bring some flowers from his country home in Spencertown, farther south in Columbia County. But is duties ended with floral supply, or so he thought.

"I walk in (to the rehearsal) with a huge bunch of flowers, my arms full, and there was this piano sitting there," recalls Steiner. "And I said, 'Why is the piano on stage?' They said, 'You're playing.' I honestly thought they were pulling my leg."

Steiner had just returned from Europe and swears that he never knew the long-planned concert needed a pianist. After repeatedly trying to demure, he relented after realizing that dropping the piece would mean that Lattimore had traveled from Colorado for only 15 minutes of singing.

"So I walked onstage and looked at (the music), and they all said 'Yes, you can do it!' I stumbled through the first reading. ... We did it a couple of times, just the quartet and I. Then once more with Maggie. ... By then it was probably 12:30 (p.m.), and then I sat here until probably five o'clock," says Steiner, pointing at the small stage in the barn-turned-concert hall.

An entire afternoon may seem excessive practice for seven minutes of music, but it speaks to his high standards. It also allowed Steiner to move past the notes, to get himself out of the way and to allow the music itself to take the spotlight.

"He's a very humble man, and that shows through in his music," says cellist Daniel Gasford, a friend and occasional recital partner. "Where sometimes you get the feeling that there's a certain amount of narcissism going on onstage – 'Look at me and my incredible gifts' – you never get that with Christian. He's an incredible giver."

Steiner's generous and genial nature is a trademark of his photo sessions, the results of which have graced hundreds of record covers and concert programs.

"The fact is that I photograph musicians and I am one myself, and we have everything to talk about. ... It's just a fun session. ... While we're talking, I'll say, 'Stop,' and take a picture, or if they're listening to me and looking at me intently, I quickly snap a picture," he says.

As with his rehearsal time, Steiner is thoroughgoing in his photo shoots. "The sessions are long – the minimum time is three hours. But I have photographed up to six hours," he says. In a normal sitting Steiner will take 150 to 200 shots in order to yield one image. Steiner selects the final print in consultation with the subject. A session generally costs $1,250 for a publicity shot, slightly more for a record cover.

Often a subject will end up performing for Steiner and his camera. But on one occasion, it was Steiner who was asked to play – by the legendary pianist Vladimir Horowitz.

"As we were talking, he realized I knew more than an ordinary photographer," recalls Steiner of the first of three sessions with the pianist. "In his little voice he said, 'You play the piano! Play something.' ...I wasn't about to sit down and play in front of Horowitz."

The master wasn't put off by Steiner's emphatic "No," and volunteered to give him a lesson. That amazing offer was politely refused as well.

A less congenial subject was Leonard Bernstein, though they too ultimately worked together a number of times.

"The first time (Bernstein) came to me, he was so uptight that this good-looking man looked ugly," says Steiner, adding that Bernstein stopped by on his way to a concert and left his limousine waiting outside.

"I could turn it around by getting his sympathy (and) telling him how nervous I was for his arrival," says the photographer. "And then all of sudden he melted and said, 'I'm not that way,' and he relaxed, and I got some good pictures."

Giving a status report on his latest endeavor – what he modestly refers to as "an exercise" others would call an autobiography – Steiner says, "I've just come to America."

His last published collection of photos came out in 1982. The idea of a new book originally centered on his many anecdotes about celebrity musicians. But Steiner's own story is rich.

"I'm doing an exercise of writing about the beginning of my life, which I think wasn't all that dull since Berlin was being bombed. ... We were in the middle of the war then," he says.

Steiner's lineage includes a father who played in the Deutsche Opera Berlin and two brothers who were members of the Berlin Philharmonic.

As a promising young pianist, the family's youngest child came to New York in 1958 and has remained ever since.

Recently, Steiner and his companion of 25 years, Frank Heller, sold their spacious Central Park West co-op "3,200 square feet with terrace" and moved to a smaller apartment on West 72nd Street. Peak real estate prices coinciding with cutbacks at major record labels, once a primary income source for Steiner, made the timing right.

"The record companies are doing much less ... (and) I have outlived all the art directors I worked with. The record covers I do now are for the youngsters," says Steiner, who has no agent and relies on word of mouth.

Musicians do continue to pay for an audience with Steiner and his camera enough so that Steiner is able to expand and renovate his home in Spencertown. Hardly a country retreat, it includes his woodworking equipment – furniture-building being yet another pursuit at which he has excelled. And it's a short drive to the renovated barn at Tannery Pond where Steiner presents emerging and famous artists in concerts for small audiences, about seven times a year.

"Everything he does is so finished and sensual and beautiful, whether he's taking photographs, hanging photographs or setting the lights for the show," says Brenda Archer Adams, president of the board of Concerts at Tannery Pond. "He sets a standard that we all aspire to."

REINHARD STRAUB

SEPTEMBER 5. 2003   PAINTER

Primal urges

During the late summer, a wasps' nest outside the Albany home of Reinhard Straub and his family became an annoyance. The 53-year-old artist and musician attempted to combat it.

"I was trying to kill it and I put fire on it," he says. "I came back two hours later and 200 wasps were circling it. ... That's life. You can't control it."

There have been a lot of fires in Straub's life both literal and figurative. He's survived them all. Each experience serves as fuel for his art, which is something easier to control.

Straub's life has been a series of whip-lashing reversals: The son of a harsh father who was once a member of the Panzer divisions of the SS, Straub is now himself a father of three. Trained as a classical violinist, he turned to rock 'n' roll after attending the original Woodstock festival. But that scene ultimately led him to battles with drugs and alcohol. From there, he became a successful substance-abuse counselor.

Last year, Straub left that career to pursue painting full time. His first solo show, "A Fragile Universe," is currently on view at DeJohn's Restaurant and Pub. The exhibit's vivid abstract paintings provide more than a glimpse at his dramatic life.

The wrenching transitions that have characterized Straub's life began early – as an infant he was a European refugee. His Hungarian father was only a teenager when he signed on to Hitler's elite fighting force. Ultimately captured and tortured by Russians, the elder Straub escaped prison, took an Austrian wife and fled Europe to begin a new life in Burlington, Vt.

In the European tradition, his son was given classical music instruction at an early age. Reinhard Straub studied as a violinist at Syracuse University but dropped out to join the hippie movement, bringing his instrument with him into rock music.

"I was one of the first to electrify a violin," he recalls. Straub performed across the Northeast with the band Wail, including an extended stint as the opening act for a group of up-and-comers called Aerosmith.

"Rino had a following of his own," says Robert Murray, Wail's lead singer. Referring to Straub by his youthful nickname, Murray recalls him "on the floor, on his back, wearing a tuxedo and playing the violin. ... He was a great entertainer."

Music led Straub to New York in the early 1980s, where he was a session musician. He also hung out with some of the hippest characters of the day, including author and "Easy Rider" screenwriter Terry Southern.

"I was in the scene," says Straub. "I partied and played with all those guys."

Once he was established in the city, Straub began creating visual art. "I would just lock myself in a room with drugs and alcohol and do stuff. ... I would stay awake for days," he says. "It gave my life meaning as I moved toward a spiritual death or bottom."

Over a three-year period, Straub produced approximately 300 drawings, primarily using calligraphy pens. He sold around 80 of the works, though today he possesses only approximately two dozen pieces from the period.

While some of the drawings have faded, the creator's hallucinatory imagination and obsession with detail are still obvious. Though they are figural – distorted faces, alien creatures, insect forms – the bright colors and large scale of the pieces point toward Straub's current work.

The artistic results notwithstanding, Straub ultimately could not sustain the substance-fueled life.

"I had to bail out," he says.

His immersion in recovery led to a career in mental health. Also early in his newfound sobriety, he met Laurie Miner, the woman who would become his wife; they settled in Albany in 1987.

In May 1991, Straub was in a small plane being piloted by his father when it crashed on takeoff near Lake Champlain. A hole in the fuselage allowed Straub and his wife to escape, but his father remained trapped and unconscious as the plane was consumed by flames.

"It took two hours to get my father out," says Straub. "Not many people see their father burn to death. ... It altered me for all time."

"Ground Pilot," which Straub completed in 2000, was the artist's first work on canvas. The collage combines oil paint and newspaper clippings. A black-and-white photo is partially obscured, but a headline is bold and clear: "Pilot dies in fiery crash."

A year prior to completing "Pilot," Straub had already returned to visual art using oils on masonite. But the piece marks a turning point, for it brings to the surface the link between his dramatic life and his intense art. The power of that connection was not lost on Straub.

"I found myself at work (at the counseling center) and could hardly wait to get home and paint," he says. "And I'd do it until two or three in the morning, long after my kids were in bed."

The renewed call to create, combined with some new personal struggles, prompted Straub to leave his counseling career in 1999. Today he is a part-time house husband and full-time painter, while his wife works part time as a physical therapist. The large basement of the family's home is Straub's studio; the living room has become a de facto gallery.

In contrast to the detail-driven drawings from the 1980s, Straub's newest works employ broad gestures and a nontraditional tools. Copious amounts of paint are poured, splattered, smeared with his fingers or struck with wooden sticks.

"The paint talks to me," he says. "I don't like dabbling in the corner (of a canvas) the actual painting is my palette. The only time I ever mix (paints) externally is to maybe make a big jar of a color."

Many of Straub's works also incorporate decidedly nontraditional elements. Small pliers and wrenches, or even toy soldiers, might be glued on the canvases. They add a distinctly technological element to the washes of color and amorphous forms that Straub describes as "primordial."

The new work "is vintage Rino," says Murray. Straub's former bandmate is the CEO of Rel Comm, a telecommunications company based in Rochester. For his company's offices, Murray has purchased five of Straub's paintings, which he views as "Rino's abstract view of the real world."

"Reinhard's not trained," says Virginia Cantarella, a local artist and illustrator. "He didn't go to art school but he expresses himself. I find him remarkably willing to take big risks and put everything of his mind and heart and soul into it."

With 150 works completed since 1999, Straub remains productive. He is also finding patrons, having sold 50 pieces in the last six months. While an income from art is welcome and a little surprising, Straub's focus remains on the process of transferring life experiences onto his oversized canvases.

"A big part of doing art is that grinding feeling in your chest about how it's going to come out," he says. "I get right into it. I'm a mess when I'm done."

LEIGH WEN

PAINTER

Elemental art

Albany artist Leigh Wen was about six years old when her mother went to an I Ching master – the local shaman in Taiwan skilled in reading the ancient oracles – to learn of her daughter's fate in life. "She was told that I am a person who has to stay away from water," explains Wen, "and so I never could swim because I was protected from water, and it's a fear I can't get over. Once water comes to my chest I get nervous."

Though Wen's paintings focus on all four elements of life – earth, air, fire and water – she is probably best known for depictions of the oceans and the seas on vast canvases devoid of any horizons or shorelines.

Perhaps such figurative immersion in water is her way of warding off the real thing.

In a similar manner, a couple who collect art and live in a mansion high in the parched hills of California recently bought from Wen one of her large fire painting, viewing it as a protective measure.

"My fire paintings are actually more popular in Asia," says Wen. "Fire is a symbol of energy and warmth and power. For a new business, people will want something fire related to evoke that kind of energy."

Wen may be cognizant of the metaphysical powers of art and the elements, but she generally doesn't take time to ponder such things on a day to day basis. As a full time artist represented by galleries in New York, Washington, Los Angeles and San Diego, she's too busy producing new work. She estimates that she finishes up to 12 paintings a year, while also occasionally working in ceramics.

Her characteristic style involves a meticulously detailed layering of lines and etchings spread over huge canvases. A typical painting might measure six feet in height by 20 feet in length. Her largest work to date measured 10 feet by 50 feet. And that's a record that will probably hold, since 50 feet is the length of her studio adjacent to her home in Loudonville.

Wen's most recently completed major piece is "Hudson," a triptych that currently fills three windows of the Albany Center Galleries on

31

Columbia Street facing Tricentennial Park and is a part of the Summer in the Streets sculpture show sponsored by the Downtown BID.

"Hudson" does loosely qualify as sculpture since it includes LED lighting mounted in the windowpanes. When viewed at night, the lights' slowly shifting colors subtly change the feel of the blue and white wave formations.

Working with lighting, including learning how to program the LED controls, was something new for Wen. So too was cutting a painting into pieces, since "Hudson" originated as one large canvas.

"This piece has simple elements but very complicated construction," said Wen as the piece was being prepare for travel and installation in June.

Wen's large painting are never rolled, but must be transported on their stretched frames. Despite such logistical difficulties, they've become favorites for American embassies around the world.

The artist recalls being approached rather out of the blue about 10 years ago for a painting to go in the U.S. embassy in Amman, Jordan. "I think they saw my work in some art magazine," recalls Wen. "The embassy didn't have a budget for purchases. They wanted me to make something and loan it to them. I was okay with that and was excited to be included."

Since that first contact Wen has loaned some dozen pieces to the U. S. State Department for placement in embassies, including in Malaysia, the Philippines, Hong Kong, Singapore and Barbados, and she's learned about art's place in the cycles of diplomacy.

According to Wen, an embassy is actually just offices while formal diplomacy, receptions and the like all happen in the ambassador's residence. And every time there's a new ambassador, the place gets redecorated. "When an ambassador is done with a tenure, all the painting come down, and the new ambassador picks (his or her) own art work," explains Wen.

Making new works for long term loan has not been burdensome to Wen because every piece of hers placed in an embassy has sold. A memorable example was the painting shown at the American embassy in the Philippines, which was purchased by an economic advisor to that country's president.

"He had lunch with the ambassador once a week in front of the large painting," recalls Wen. "A week or two after the ambassador's departure, he called me and said, 'I miss the painting.'" He subsequently took the piece along when he became the Philippine's ambassador to France.

Wen has visited surprisingly few of the embassies where her work has been displayed, citing the art as the ambassador and not her. But this past spring, she did travel at the behest of the State Department as a cultural envoy to the Republic of Botswana, a landlocked nation in southern Africa.

For one week, Wen worked in the capital of Gaborone with 15 of the country's top artists, who ranged in age from their 20s to their 70s. She taught them her signature techniques, gave informal lectures on the trends in the American scene, and encouraged them to persevere in their work as printmakers, sculptors and potters.

"The art scene is very quiet, there is only one university in the entire country and no art department," says Wen. "They are very poor, there is no industry to support art and not many patrons. Most have no cars. They hitchhiked and got rides to my classes. No ever showed up at the same time. It made me feel very grateful for my situation."

One evening the U.S. ambassador Katherine H. Canavan threw a lavish reception in Wen's honor. "She invited 300 high powered people. It blew my mind away," says Wen, adding that all of the artists from her workshops were thrilled to also be included as guests.

Wen says she has no idea how she was chosen for the Botswana assignment, though she does have a painting – of water – hanging in the ambassador's home.

"In Botswana, water is 'pula,' which also means good fortune and money," says Wen. "It's also the name of their currency. Everything in about water."

YACUB ADDY

COMPOSER/PERCUSSIONIST   APRIL 29, 2005

Carrying the language of the drums

There will be many things to delight the senses at tonight's performance by Yacub Addy and his musical collaborators at The Egg in
Albany. There will be music ranging from lively African drumming to
contemporary jazz, and a small group of dancers clad in colorful costumes drawn from the culture of Addy's native Ghana.

But what sometimes concerns the 74-year-old drummer and composer are the invisible things, the silent things. "The music you play
invites things your eyes cannot see," says Addy. "Genies, spirits we
can't see them. They're around us, and they come to you when you play
music. The dangerous part is you don't know if they're good or bad."

Addy learned of the spirit realm from his father, who was a wonche – a
shaman or medicine man – in the Ga ethnic group of Ghana. Addy says
that his father had an intimate relationship with the djinn, or spirits.

"I was a kid, and sometimes I'm walking with him and then we stop
there's nobody there," Addy recalls. His father, he believes, was also
frequently possessed by the spirits: "When you are with him, you have
to be careful, watch him. His personality changed every two to three
hours."

Though Addy abandoned his father's religion and became a Muslim
while still a young man (and with his father's blessing) it's no surprise
that the beliefs of Addy's ancestors still inform his world view. It is,
after all, the music of his ancestors that Addy has carried around the
world. Since leaving Ghana in the early 1970s, he has become the leading ambassador of Ghanaian music and culture. After living in London,
Seattle and Washington, D.C., he's been a resident of the Capital
Region since 1993. Addy currently teaches weekly drumming classes at
Skidmore College in Saratoga Springs, and at Rensselaer Polytechnic
Institute in Troy.

"There's nothing like having a master Ghanaian drummer right here in the Capital District," says Peter Lesser, The Egg's director.

Tonight's concert features Addy and his ensemble Odadaa! in a program that mixes traditional Ghanaian folk music and dance with new compositions by Addy. Among the guest artists will be the acclaimed young vibraphonist Stefon Harris, a native of the Capital Region. "It's rare to come across a musician who has such a complete understanding of art," says Harris. "For Yacub, music is not only an intellectual undertaking, but is a social, historical and spiritual experience as well."

Another jazz luminary to fall under Addy's spell is trumpeter Wynton Marsalis, who has presented Addy's band at Jazz at Lincoln Center, a program Marsalis runs. Next year, Marsalis and Addy will collaborate on a new project, "Congo Square," a tribute to the music of New Orleans.

"When you come into another country, walk on your toes, not on your heels."

It's a bit of folk wisdom Addy learned from his people: Don't draw attention to yourself, be quiet and observe.

It's a rather ironic lesson for somebody who plays enormous, booming drums. But away from his instruments Addy can be cagey, even guarded, at least in the presence of a reporter.

In comparison, Amina Addy, his wife of 28 years, is downright effusive. During a recent conversation in their Latham apartment, when Yacub leaves a sentence unfinished and takes a slow drag on his cigarette, Amina fills in the silence.

"You need to get a sense of how far he's traveled culturally," she says. "When he was 16 years old, he became the first Muslim in his family. He did not go with his father's way of life. He plays the music of that tradition, but he doesn't use it to invoke the djinn."

Along with functioning as Addy's manager, press agent and annotator, Amina has also written lyrics for two new songs for The Egg program. "Babalomia or Onion Trouble" is about the sting of prejudice, while "Cashew Blue" is a reflection on Ghanian life of an earlier era. In addition, husband and wife have collaborated on a poem "Alhamdu li llah (All Thanks to God)," which is set to new music by Addy and Harris.

Amina Addy says that the entire program, titled "Kolo" (translates at "colonial") deals with the struggle for freedom. There will be traditional pieces like "Asafo Atsere" and "Odododiodio," which accompany fighting games in the Ga tribe, plus "Kolomashi" (literally "colonialists get out"), which was a popular processional piece for protest marches during Ghana's independence struggle in the 1940s and '50s.

"Sometimes I feel at home here," says Addy. "Sometimes I feel ... "

"Homesick," offers Amina.

"But I want to be African," continues Addy. "I don't want to change my life."

He says these words while sitting in a Naugahyde recliner. Cigarettes and coffee are to his side, while in front of him is a large TV. A single framed photo sits above the set: Addy at 8 years old, standing between the legs of his majestically garbed father. A portrait of his grandmother hangs above Addy's chair.

As the conversation winds down, Amina fetches her husband a drum, and he begins to finally speak more freely.

"I love to perform. If I don't perform, I get sick," says Addy.

"I'm a witness to this," says Amina.

He nods to the instrument in his hands. "I have a drum that belongs to my father, and it has a language," he says. "You have to learn that language before you play on the drum."

Addy may well know the rhythms of Ghana better than anyone alive today. But even at 74, he wishes he could receive still more lessons from his father.

"I wish he was still alive," Addy says, "because there's a lot of things I didn't learn."

WILHELMINA AMYOT

DECEMBER 2, 2007   PIANIST/PATRON

A fan for all seasons

A highlight of the Albany Symphony Orchestra's performance Nov. 16 at the Troy Savings Bank Music Hall was the brash performance of the Grieg Piano Concerto by the 20-year-old Adam Golka. But another memorable part of the evening was meeting Wilhelmina Amyot, a 90-year-old Cohoes resident who was seated immediately behind me in the dress circle.

Amyot (nee Mossey), in attendance with her daughter, Diane, volunteered that she herself appeared as a piano soloist with a local orchestra also at age 20. The year was 1938 and she was finishing her studies in music and English at The College of Saint Rose when she performed the Liszt Second Concerto in E-flat Major in downtown Albany. That may have been the high point of Amyot's career onstage, but her long life has been filled with music and service to the local performing arts scene.

Upon completing her college studies, Amyot gave private piano lessons and taught general music classes in three different local schools. She also later taught third grade for five years at St. Clare's School in Colonie. After marrying Bruno Amyot (now deceased) in 1942, the focus was on child-rearing. But each of the couple's five children got piano lessons at home before being enrolled in the now-shuttered Cohoes Conservatory of Music, which is where Amyot received her earliest training as well.

As the Capital Region's cultural life grew, Amyot did her part, serving on the board of the Albany Symphony Vanguard and the women's committee of the Saratoga Performing Arts Center. During her tenure as president of the Cohoes Music Hall in the 1970s, she even went to Washington to lobby Congressman Sam Stratton for funding.

Hearing Vladimir Horowitz at the Troy Music Hall and watching Eugene Ormandy in rehearsal with the Philadelphia Orchestra at SPAC are some of her favorite memories at local venues. But the center of Amyot's musical existence has long been the 1898 Steinway grand piano that was passed on from her mother-in-law. Failing vision has lately robbed her of the ability to sight read through scores, which was long a favorite pastime. But the piles of tattered editions of Beethoven, Bach and other masters that sit beside her piano give ample testimony to her dedication.

For all of Amyot's experiences, a landmark event for every classical concertgoer came only in October: her first trip to Carnegie Hall. While the performance of Beethoven Sonatas by Andras Schiff inspired her, Amyot was even more enthusiastic on how much alike are the auditoriums of Carnegie and the Troy Music Hall. Now, there's one faithful Capital Region music lover.

JOHN ANTONIO

MUSIC TEACHER/PERCUSSIONIST

Waking up sleepy musicians, inspiring young lives

Every Monday and Wednesday at Albany's William S. Hackett Middle School, about 50 students arrive at 8 a.m. 40 minutes before classes begin. Toting flutes, clarinets, trombones and oboes in hard plastic cases, they cram into a basement classroom where the walls are a dingy aqua green and half the fluorescent lights have burned out.

Mozart and Beethoven, Miles Davis and Stevie Wonder look on benevolently from aging, unframed posters while John Antonio coaxes music out of the half-asleep players. As the band works on pieces by Tchaikovsky and Gliere, Antonio is at once conductor and teacher, cheerleader and taskmaster. And friend.

A graduate of Hackett himself, as well as of Albany High School and the College of Saint Rose, Antonio led his final concert on May 13 after 33 years as a teacher in the Albany City School District. A youthful 54 years old, he's hardly going into retirement in any traditional sense. He'll continue teaching through his work as a percussion coach with the Empire State Youth Orchestra, plans to devote time to hiking and camping, and hopes to get his own chops as a percussionist back into shape.

But for several generations of students, some of whom have gone on to careers as performers or teachers, and for colleagues seemingly unanimous in their admiration, it's the end of an era.

"You can't replace a man like that," says James Gaudette, principal of Hackett for the past six years. "John has such excitement and passion that the kids just develop under his tutelage."

"He brings us to life," says eighth-grade clarinetist Katie Moy-Santos.

Antonio's most famous student is the percussionist and jazz composer Stefon Harris, who, during a recent call from Los Angeles, says, "He's had a tremendous impact in my life and introduced me to something that's really given my life focus and a direction. ... And certainly the fact that he was a percussionist had a big impact on why I would choose to be a percussionist."

Morning rehearsal may end at 8:35, but a pulse continues in the band room throughout the day. Each class period, students return in small groups for further rehearsal and coaching.

Working with three trumpeters, two boys and a girl, Antonio sits with them, on their side of the music stand. Pointing at a spot in their music, he claps to the count. "Two-and-three-and-four-and-go!" he says, gesturing a downbeat.

The distinctive bounce of the "1812 Overture" comes through despite some rhythmic stumbles and a few sour notes. Antonio winces and grins at the same time.

"You're relaxed, and it sounds relaxed," he says. "Be up and energetic." The students straighten their backs and plant their feet on flat on the floor. Briefly.

Antonio has a large repertoire of ways to combat teenage slouch.

"Ninety-nine percent of intonation is posture," he says at one point.

"I always have a coffee joke," he says later, between lessons. Today's perk-up was "Go to Professor Java's and get some Sumatra blend ... "

"Sometimes I make 'em stand up and scream," he adds.

Within the interlocking series of relationships that binds local teachers, administrators and former students who go on to be teachers, John Antonio is beloved.

"John is John, a wonderful human being," says David McGuire, another institution in Albany education. McGuire was a teacher at Hackett when Antonio was a student. And when Antonio returned as a faculty member, McGuire was principal, eventually taking the same post at Albany High School.

"He's no different as an adult than he was as a student," says McGuire, now principal of Christian Brothers Academy in Colonie. "He put his heart and soul into it and did an excellent job with the instrumental program at Hackett. I wanted him to come to Albany High, but he wanted no part of it."

Antonio offers several reasons for his steadfast presence at Hackett. "I've had a sound from that band for the past 20 to 25 years," he explains with the pride that made him reluctant to leave. "Middle-school kids are crazy, and they have kept me vibrant and jumping."

Another close observer is Michele Rooney, who has taught general music at Hackett for 20 years. She began her career as a student teacher under Antonio's wife, Beth, who teaches music at Ichabod Crane Primary School in Valatie. The Antonios have two sons, both percussionists: Alex, 19, is a student at the Berkelee College of Music in Boston; 22-year-old Ian recently graduated from the Manhattan School of Music.

Says Rooney, "(John's) great, easygoing, never a complaint in the world. He takes everything in stride and always gets the optimum sound from these middle school students."

Last fall, Hackett Middle School was one of 12 Capital Region schools flagged for poor performance under the federal No Child Left Behind Act. Although more math and science is the common answer to improving the schools, Hackett maintains four music teachers three full-time and one part-time.

"You have to look at the totality of the programs (including) music, sports, visual arts" to evaluate a school, says Gaudette, Hackett's principal. "We have a variety of opportunities for kids to excel, and the more they do that, the better they will do in life."

Gaudette regularly uses the Hackett music ensembles as a showcase for the school, asking them to perform for student assemblies. A few years ago, Antonio even led the band at a meeting of the city school board.

"I don't mind having a focus on math and English," says Gaudette. "I just think when you lose sight of the other kinds of experiences kids can have ... it becomes problematic for kids and schools."

Not that Antonio has problem kids. Indeed, it's been the opposite. "I've been able to maintain the highest quality of students in this building," says Antonio. A good music program also has subtle and long-term benefits for an entire student body.

"If we had one of the kids acting up in the classroom, we'd take him out," recalls McGuire of his days running Hackett, "and rather than

41

have them waste time in the office, we would have John take them in, hoping they'd get interested in something positive."

"There's a calming influence about the band room." says Antonio. "Something about the music or the teacher, and your cares melt away."

Having worked in – indeed created – an atmosphere like that, it's no wonder he says, finally, "I've always enjoyed every day I've been in this building."

ANN-MARIE
BARKER SCHWARTZ

OCTOBER 16, 2003   VIOLINIST

Reprising Albany's musical history

Violinist Ann-Marie Barker Schwartz may be one of the busiest musicians in the Capital Region – she's founder and director of Musicians
of Ma'alwyck, teaches at the University of Albany, plays in the orchestra at Glimmerglass Opera every summer (among other free-lancing
gigs) and does production work for Dorian Recordings. She's also a
mother of two.

That's a fairly busy present for a woman who, in a certain sense,
lives in the past.

A few years ago, Schwartz came up with the idea of re-creating
concerts that might have happened in Albany in the late 1700s or
early 1800s. She's now immersed in the era and the circumstances of
Albany's musical life at the time, and has made it the subject of her
graduate school thesis. She's also presenting the results of her research
in concerts by the Musicians of Ma'alwyck.

Two centuries ago, "Legislators loved music, and it was the sophisticated thing to do," says Schwartz. "It showed you were cultured if you
attended (concerts) and also played music."

Schwartz discovered a window into the past through the life of one
of Albany's first great socialites, Blandina Bleecker Dudley (1783-1863).
Daughter of one of the state's founding fathers, Rutger Bleecker, she
was married to Charles E. Dudley, who served as Albany's mayor twice
during the 1820s and went on to a career as a U.S. senator and an organizer of Martin Van Buren's presidential campaign. (The Dudley Obser-
vatory in Schenectady is a part of the couple's legacy in the region.)

His wife's archives, housed at the New York State Library, are full of
musical scores and ephemera that have captivated Schwartz.

"Blandina would attend concerts in New York and buy the music
right afterward. ... The pieces have fingerings (written in)," Schwartz

43

says, referring to Dudley's performance notations in the scores. "So they were obviously played."

Having ventured downstate to hear musical works newly arrived from Europe, Dudley would then present them to Albany audiences. But the musical events bear only a faint resemblance to what we think of as concerts today.

The individual programs "would be at least nine pieces, sometimes up to 11," says Schwartz. "There was dancing afterward, and theater was often integrated. ... It would start at 5 or 6 p.m. and run until 1 or 2 a.m. And events happened every night." (Don't worry. Schultz isn't planning to emulate such marathon programming.)

Despite the breadth of activities, there were no printed programs, only advance announcements. And the emphasis was on the performers – their full names were listed, with only scant mention of the composers. The practice has made Schwartz's work a challenge: "You have to pull together one little fact here and another there."

The further Schwartz has gotten into this research, especially concerning Blandina Bleecker Dudley, the more she seems connected to the past. And not just its music: In a remarkable coincidence, she recently learned that her family's country house near Cooperstown is on land once owned by Dudley.

"I've had a blast doing this," she says.

WILLIAM CARRAGAN

MAY 4, 2008   MUSICIAN/SCHOLAR

Ear for music, mind for everything else

Finishing up where great composers left off is one of the many specialties of William Carragan of Troy, a genuine Renaissance man who recently turned 70. The Schubert Symphony No. 8 "Unfinished" and the Bruckner Symphony No. 9 are just two of the heftier scores that were left incomplete by their composers and to which Carragan applied a thorough study before coming up with meticulously detailed and "finished" scores, based on what he believes to the composers' intentions.

A related talent is re-envisioning masterpieces for new and surprising instrumental textures. Just this past season, he gave local ensemble Musicians of Ma'awlyck chamber-sized arrangements of two popular orchestral pieces, Saint-Saens' "Danse Macabre" and Strauss' Four Last Songs. And some years back for the defunct St. Cecilia Chamber Orchestra, he rescored wind band marches of John Philip Sousa for piccolo and strings.

Carragan also plays music, usually on one of his four harpsichords. Over the coming months, he'll be appearing in a series of concerts of Renaissance and Baroque music around the Capital Region.

A nearly lifelong resident of Troy, Carragan's first musical studies were with his mother, Martha Beck Carragan, a composer and educator who founded the Friends of Chamber Music, which presents a chamber music series in Troy at Emma Willard School's Kiggins Hall. He also received instruction from another late titan of the Capital Region music scene, pianist Stanley Hummel.

But music is just one area of his expertise. Carragan holds science degrees from Haverford College and Rensselaer Polytechnic Institute, and in 2001 he retired from a 36-year career teaching physics at Hudson Valley Community College. While there he wrote, illustrated and published his own 1,000-page textbook, "Elementary Quantum Mechanics."

"Not that there's anything elementary about quantum mechanics," jokes Carragan, "it's bobsledlike, just really moves." The same could be said about a conversation with Carragan, who is a storehouse of information on a seemingly endless number of topics.

But it's his thorough knowledge of music history and keen listening abilities that have made him a go-to guy for certain local musicians.

"He is my closest musical confidant and friend, and when I am going to prepare a program I play it for him first," says Carragan's generational peer, the pianist Findlay Cockrell. "He also knows a lot about religion and theology, geology and astronomy, gastronomy and food. In fact, there's very little that he doesn't know something about. He'll take you through a whole subject, like jalapeno peppers or certain philosophers."

Carragan's authority is internationally known when it comes to the music of Anton Bruckner. In addition to his 1983 completion of the composer's Ninth Symphony, Carragan has published 10 scholarly articles on aspects of the composer's music and also made new performing editions of the first and second symphonies. Both of the latter are available from the International Bruckner Society in Vienna, and have been recorded on Naxos. According to Carragan, the recordings have sold 50,000 and 80,000 copies respectively.

There's a weight behind Carragan's work in this area because of his application of scientific rigor to musicological pursuits. "I'm interested in the nuts-and-bolts analysis of things," he says.

To reconstruct a new score of the Second Symphony from 1872 that would more accurately reflect the composer's original intents, Carragan gathered manuscripts, sketches and the earliest published versions and, most crucially, the parts that the original orchestra used for the premiere. Like the assembly of a puzzle, he then put back together – all 1,058 pages of material.

"I used classic research techniques in paleography, established a relationship of sources – and found where the dismembered fragments fit in," explains Carragan, who spent a year at the effort. To be near the libraries housing the materials, he spent much of that time in Austria near Vienna, staying in a monastery and sleeping in the same room where Bruckner once stayed.

"I feel a great deal of humility and kinship," says Carragan. "Bruckner did all the sinful things I do, like going out and drinking and smoking cigars."

In addition to the reconstruction of certain scores, Carragan has made "longitudinal performance studies" of all the symphonies. In other words, he's charted and compared the performance times of nearly all extant recordings – there are some 2,100 Bruckner CDs in his library – and made conclusions about the most successful tempos.

Armed with such knowledge, Carragan easily gains the ears of conductors. When the acclaimed Italian maestro Riccardo Chailly was at Proctors with the Gewandhaus Orchestra in February 2007, Carragan went backstage after the concert and gave the conductor a copy of his Bruckner Second. Within the year, Chailly had Carragan with him in Leipzig, Germany, advising on a performance, and also on a panel discussion in Chicago.

When the Albany Symphony Orchestra was preparing a performance of the Bruckner Seventh in November 2000, conductor David Alan Miller didn't have to go far to get a load of background material.

"He gave me an article he wrote comparing some 30 recordings, and he made me a composite CD with different movements he thought were particularly successful to show his argument made sense," recalls Miller. "Such a deep awareness of these pieces is fabulously helpful."

'It has to sound good'

Beyond the countless details of an orchestral score or the minute subtleties of performance tempos, Carragan is also attuned to the expressive and emotional side of music.

"Bill understands aesthetics and helped me appreciate Bruckner's connection to Schubert, which informed my performance with a much more light, lyric approach," says Miller.

Where Carragan's musicological work focuses on the Romantic ear, he performs from the body of literature that's become known as Early Music. It's a field that can often seem consumed with historic instruments and fussy tunings, but here again Carragan is ultimately interested in the music itself.

"Authenticity doesn't lie in just doing this or that," he says. "It has to sound good."

Pressed to only pick one composer to spend the rest of his life with, Carragan would probably chose Bach. There's the deep catalog, the consummate craft and the open heart – at least when Carragan plays it.

Sitting at a harpsichord and luxuriating in the slow movement of Bach's Fourth Partita, he observes, "It's as good as music gets. It's as if someone puts their arms around you and says, 'It's going to be all right.'"

HELEN CHA-PYO

CONDUCTOR

Directing students toward greatness

When Helen Cha-Pyo began her tenure as music director of the Empire State Youth Orchestra six years ago, she set her sights high and has encouraged every member of the orchestra she conducts to do likewise.

Each fall, she has the teenagers write on index cards their goals as musicians during the year. Sometimes Cha-Pyo even has students write down goals and subsequent evaluations for their individual performances during a two-hour rehearsal session.

"The lesson I tell them over and over is that something great will happen, and you have to expect it and if you don't expect it, we aren't tapping into the possibilities," says Cha-Pyo.

On Saturday, something great will happen and ESYO has been getting ready for it for months. In the Troy Savings Bank Music Hall, each of ESYO's nine ensembles – two orchestras, two jazz ensembles, plus string, wind and percussion groups – will perform for the first time in sequence on the same stage in a single concert. The program will be a succession of world premiere works written expressly for each ensemble.

"Commissioning music is collaboration that's not one plus one equals two," Cha-Pyo says. "When a composer and musicians come together, that's a synergetic combination. ... And when we are onstage, it's going to be something greater than we ever imagined."

"New Music for a New Generation" is the name of the project, which encompasses the commissioned works as well as a full day of activities: a family concert and workshops with the nine composers in the afternoon, followed by the evening of premieres.

The entire undertaking is made possible through a 2006 grant of $100,000 - the largest in ESYO's 29-year history – from the New York State Music Fund, which was established by the state attorney general's office with money collected as penalties from major record labels and radio stations for their payola ("pay for play") practices. (Full disclosure: This writer was an adviser to the fund.)

49

"Some organizations might have divided this festival into the jazz and percussion ensembles at a different venue and time and not mixing it with the orchestra," says Cha-Pyo. While acknowledging the considerable logistical challenges of shuffling more than 300 young musicians and their instruments on and off the stage, she adds, "I wanted everybody to come together. We need to get the image out there that ESYO is about all kinds of music."

Terms for each commission included that the composer attend two rehearsals, so that students have an opportunity to work with a professional composer and also that the realization of the piece is authentic and accurate to the composer's expectations.

Among the participating composers is Samuel Adler, a faculty member of the Juilliard School, who will turn 80 this week and who has written a new 16-minute piece for the orchestra, to be conducted by Cha-Pyo. Other recent Adler pieces were composed for the Dallas Symphony and the Cleveland Orchestra.

Also a conductor, Adler has led 39 student orchestras and bands at various festivals and competitions over the years. Since he knows more than a thing or two about youth orchestras, Adler does not write "down" for them.

"When I write a piece, I don't write for youth orchestra. I write a piece," says Adler. "I know what these kids are capable of. And I have to tell you, this is *not* an easy piece."

Cha-Pyo was a student of Adler's at the Eastman School in Rochester and had long wanted to commission him. When it came time to discuss particular aspects of the new work, she encouraged him to write some difficult parts for the first-chair players.

"I told our principals that Sam Adler wrote this for you," says Cha-Pyo. "It's personal, and they feel special. In that sense, it's an unforgettable experience for our orchestra."

It's not just the students who have enjoyed the recent rehearsals together. Recalls Adler: "One kid came up to me and said, 'You know, Mr. Adler, you wrote a damn hard piece, but it's cool.' They're working hard and enjoying it and that's all you can ask."

In the realm of contemporary music, premieres are the easy part; they can get lots of attention for everyone involved. The crucial part for a composer, though, is whether the piece has a future life.

For Adler's new work, ESYO already has that covered. The orchestra will take the piece on its European tour in April as part of a program that also features an overture by Samuel Barber and Dvorak's Symphony No. 8. The nine-day tour includes concerts in the German cities of Eisenach and Ilmenau, at Dvorak Hall in Prague, Czech Republic, and at the Mozarteum in Salzburg, Austria. Adler will accompany the group on the trip.

Knowing in advance of the plans for a tour, Adler incorporated into his composition both American and Czech folk material. And to highlight that music is an international language that crosses generations and nationalities, he named it "A Bridge to Understanding."

For Cha-Pyo, the title also connects with her imagining something greater than just another spring concert. "The legacy of creating nine different new pieces ...," she says, "(is) a golden opportunity to make a bigger contribution to the state and to the world."

FINDLAY COCKRELL

PIANIST   MARCH 12, 2006

Keyboard showman and icon

He's a pianist who needs just one name: Findlay. A singular personality
and an inescapable presence in the Capital Region's music scene for four
decades, Findlay Cockrell is as peripatetic as he is dedicated. If he's not
on stage at a concert, dashing off some Bach or Mozart, show tunes or
ragtime, then he's probably in the audience with his wife, Marcia.

Although he's designated this year as his "40th and farewell season,"
Cockrell, 70, has hardly slackened his pace. He's been surveying his
most beloved classical repertoire in monthly recitals at the University
at Albany, where he'll become a professor emeritus at the end of the
spring semester. He'll also appear with the Albany Symphony Orchestra
on Saturday at the Troy Savings Bank Music Hall as soloist in Morton
Gould's "Interplay."

"I'm a huge fan," says ASO conductor David Alan Miller. "He has
such an insatiable appetite for music and plays with great sophistication and elegance."

Cockrell has a natural flare for works like Gould's jazz-infused
"Interplay" and is especially known for Gershwin. But Miller views him
as more than a specialist or merely a hometown talent.

"It would be too simple to say that he's an American-style pianist,
even knowing what an American gregarious guy he is. He's an all-around
wonderful pianist and musician," says Miller. "Because he happens to
be local and to have done so much here, we in the music community
run the danger of taking musicians like him for granted."

Certainly Cockrell's talents have been seen and heard outside upstate
New York. A native of Berkeley, Calif., he was performing solo in the
Bay Area by his early teens. His flare for theatrics was recognized
early on, notably when he was asked to be the opening performer in
the first Junior Bach Festival, a Berkeley tradition that has continued
for 53 years since.

"The gal who created the thing wanted to start with a bang," recalls Cockrell, who was a high school senior at the time. He launched the proceedings with Bach's Toccata and Fugue in D Minor, the grand and halting tune popularly associated with Halloween.

Cockrell went on to study music at Harvard, where he took a class with composer Randall Thompson and also sang in the Bach B Minor Mass with the Boston Symphony Orchestra under conductor Charles Munch. Studies at the Juilliard School with pianist Edward Steuermann followed.

In spring 1965, Cockrell made his New York City debut at Town Hall, playing Bach, Chopin and Liszt in a recital presented under the auspices of Concert Artists Guild. That was the same season he was a contestant in the Chopin Competition in Warsaw, Poland. Marcia Cockrell recalls it as both a triumph and low point of Cockrell's career.

"Warsaw Hails U.S. Pianist," proclaimed a small wire report in the Feb. 24, 1965, edition of The New York Times. The notice prompted telegrams of congratulations from family, but Cockrell was devastated to be eliminated after the first round.

Just as his teachers had warned him, the politics of the Cold War infiltrated the judging process and none of the Americans made it past the first cut. "He played beautifully, but it didn't matter what you did," says Marcia. "They chose the right winner though." The Argentinean pianist Martha Argerich ultimately triumphed.

"I applied for (only) one college job," recalls Cockrell. It was for a faculty position at the newly established music department at the modern uptown campus of the University at Albany. With their newborn daughter, Dorothy, the couple had felt settled on Manhattan's Upper West Side, Marcia with a secretarial job and Findlay with private students scattered across the city. But something drew them up the Hudson. A visit to the future campus sealed the deal.

"Washington Avenue was dirt just beyond Brevator Street, but I saw fabulous architecture," recalls Cockrell, who arrived at UAlbany in 1966, though the university's Performing Arts Center wasn't completed until 1969.

An early pleasant chore for the university was going shopping at Steinway Piano on Long Island to select the instruments that are still in use by faculty and students. After pointing out the half-dozen or so grands that pleased him, Cockrell recalls adding, with a flick of the wrist, "and throw in 12 uprights."

Throughout it all, Marcia has been a faithful supporter, yet not just of Findlay's sundry enterprises but of the greater cultural scene. Currently she's an active board member of both the Albany Symphony and its support wing Vanguard, as well as the Albany-Tula Russia Alliance and the Friends of Chamber Music.

"They are at the epicenter of Albany's musical life," says the ASO's Miller.

Helping to christen the halls at UAlbany as well as at The Egg and broadcasting a 28-hour radio series, "Keyboard Masters," on public radio station WAMC were some of the ways that Cockrell made himself known to the larger community. He also started a series of noontime concerts, first at the Empire State Plaza, later at the Troy Savings Bank Music Hall.

For three seasons Cockrell even ran his own ensemble, the Amadeus Chamber Orchestra. "I needed it," he says. "I wanted to play those Mozart Concertos."

While his industry was obvious, it took longer for his mischievous side to show through. After a Gershwin recital in the early 1970s, there was no turning back.

For the finale, "I Got Rhythm," Cockrell recorded the second verse in advance and hid speakers behind the curtains. "I played the first chorus live, then got up and did a soft shoe around the piano (to the taped accompaniment)," recalls Cockrell with glee, "and ended with a kick from behind the curtain."

According to Marcia, Findlay wasn't faking the steps. He'd been going to New York to study tap with the great Sandman Sims after being wowed by a Sims performance at The Egg.

Energy and good-natured antics are now a typical part of Cockrell's daily life, especially at UAlbany, where he has taught both private lessons and courses in the rudiments of music. He's known for riding to campus on a scooter in good weather and for bursting into practice rooms when he's impressed by what he hears from the hall.

"People think he's crazy, but they recognize him as an authority," says Jared Shepard, a senior majoring in music and economics, who studies privately with Cockrell. "He's given to whims, and that's part of his personality."

That's not to say the affects of his teaching are transitory.

"I found what he had to say about music and playing often more valuable than (what I got from) more weighty teachers I had at the Curtis Institute," says Matt Herskowitz, who studied with Cockrell from ages 9 through 12.

Today Herskowitz, 37, is based in Montreal and balances a career in both classical and jazz. Cockrell's own wide embrace of music provided him an early example. He remembers Cockrell showing him "an almost obvious common sense of music that a lot of teachers don't get."

Although retirement is just around the corner, the Cockrells have been too busy to really discuss what's ahead, besides an early summer trip to Greece and Germany with their daughter and granddaughter.

Duties at the university will come to an end, but Findlay will continue giving private lessons and he'll doubtlessly pop up on concert stages.

"My life completely centers around the Capital Region," Findlay says. "I'm a regional artist, and I really like that term."

Marcia is confident that he won't slow down. She still observes in her husband the same characteristics she saw when they first met as teenagers at a church social: "A love of life and enthusiasm and naivete," she says. "It's strange for man of his age but I don't think he'll ever grow up."

JOSEPH FENNIMORE

COMPOSER/PIANIST   OCTOBER 22, 2004

Listening for sensual satisfaction

With typical brevity and wit, Joseph Fennimore has already composed his own epitaph: "Often wrong. Never in doubt."

It speaks well to the contradictions and apparent folly of Fennimore's livelihood. In a society where high art is little valued, he's a driven and earnest composer who refers to his pieces as "ditties." Also a virtuoso pianist who studied with the legendary teacher Rosina Lhevinne – as did Van Cliburn, Misha Dichter and John Browning – Fennimore's performances these days are heard mostly on CD.

True artists will identify with Fennimore's all-consuming motivation, even if he expresses it in an inimitable fashion.

"With music, it has to be a deep-within emotional need and some sort of genetic predisposition for sensual satisfaction through the ears," says Fennimore, 64. "Maybe some sexual nerve endings are in the ears instead of somewhere else."

Born in New York City and raised in Ballston Spa and Colonie, Fennimore, a current Albany resident, made his debut with the Schenectady Symphony Orchestra as a seventh-grader in 1953, playing Hadyn's D Major Piano Concerto. "I still have a tape (of the concert) – it's not laughable," he says.

His latest debut is also with the SSO. The new Tenor Concerto for trombone and orchestra will receive its world premiere Sunday at Proctor's Theatre in Schenectady with soloist Andrew Pollack and conductor Charles Schneider.

"He's one of the finest and most underappreciated American composers today, as well as a phenomenal pianist," says Washington Post culture critic Philip Kennicott. A Schenectady native and former piano student of Fennimore, Kennicott also has been a music critic for Newsday and the St. Louis Post-Dispatch.

"I find in his music, qualities that are really rare to be well managed within the same piece, like melancholy and playfulness, lyricism and unpredictability. His music makes me think of composers as diverse as Poulenc, Brahms and Faure, and it deserves a wider audience," says Kennicott.

"Joe's stuff is very special and unique, and that makes him very important to the area," says conductor Charles Schneider, who also conducted the SSO in a double-header of Fennimore's two short piano concertos, with the composer as soloist in 1998.

"We have lots of laughs, yet he's very serious about his music," say Schneider, who describes Fennimore's typical sound as "a French elegance."

It's a style that comes to the forefront in one of Fennimore's best known works, "Berlitz: Introduction to French," a light-hearted setting of the classic language guide. The song cycle was recorded by mezzo-soprano Joyce Castle, accompanied by Fennimore at the piano. It's on one of five discs on Albany Records that showcase Fennimore as composer and pianist.

Although he has composed music since childhood, when Fennimore left the Capital Region after high school, he set off to be a pianist. But it didn't take long for others to notice his compositional abilities.

At the Eastman School of Music in Rochester, he received the first concert performance of his music. It was by fellow student Ronald McKay who also happened to be a native of the Capital Region. The son of longtime Albany Democratic committeeman and party stalwart Emil McKay, he took the stage name Yvar Mikhashoff. He went on to great notoriety as a pianist, composer and impresario before he died of AIDS in 1993 at age 52.

Also at Eastman, Fennimore met another pianist, Gordon Hibberd, who has been his companion since 1958. After Eastman, the two moved to New York City so that Fennimore could begin studies with Lhevinne at The Juilliard School. And in the early 1970s, they took one of the first apartments in the Westbeth Artists Community, a massive building in Greenwich Village that once served as a research center for Bell Telephone Laboratories. In the mid-1960s, it was redesigned by architect Richard Meier for artist housing.

Composer Gerald Busby, a longtime Manhattan resident, recalls attending many intimate evening dinner parties during which Fennimore would dash off performances of major works like the complete Chopin Etudes.

"Joe is quietly flamboyant and intellectual, and he likes to impress you," says Busby. "He knows obscure, arcane novelists of 19th-century England and wants to be a memorable character himself – and he is, there's no question about it."

Fennimore and Hibberd left New York City in the early 1980s. In explaining the departure, Fennimore cites the specter of AIDS, which killed scores of his friends. "The cream of a generation was wiped out," he says.

And Fennimore's charm, which can work so well in intimate settings, never translated to the schmoozing and self-promotion needed to get his music heard by a wider audience. "I didn't play the game well," he says.

For more than 20 years, Fennimore and Hibberd have lived and worked across the street from Lincoln Park in Albany in a house they bought from Emil McKay. As with any pair of artists, the couple has had their financial ups and downs over the years – "I can make a penny scream," says Fennimore. But today, the two-family house is paid off, and they occupy both floors.

While Hibberd is in demand across the region as an accompanist, Fennimore teaches piano in the house's first-floor music room, which is crowded with two grand pianos and a harpsichord.

Over the years, three of his proteges have, like their teacher, played with the Schenectady Symphony. But Fennimore has outpriced himself for most parents to send their children. He currently charges $50 an hour which attracts more dedicated students and he seems the happier for it, though motivating adults can be challenging, too.

"I make them love me – that's how I get then to work. ... They've got to satisfy somebody," explains Fennimore.

A longtime observer of the local music scene, Fennimore finds great encouragement in the work of the Empire State Youth Orchestra. And it was through ESYO that Hibberd accompanied trombonist Andrew Pollack and steered him to Fennimore's music.

Fennimore explains that the new Tenor Concerto began at least a decade ago as a cello concerto but was never completed. Although the musical ideas finally came together for the sound of a trombone, he envisions rescoring it for a number of different instruments all in the tenor range, including French horn, tenor sax and cello.

Fennimore also just likes the name.

"'Trombone Concerto' doesn't have any panache, no glitz or cachet. Who would remember the title?" muses Fennimore. "Whereas 'Tenor Concerto' pricks people's curiosity because they'll think there's a singer in it, though there isn't."

Pollack says the piece is challenging but rewarding.

"A lot of the current trombone literature is regrettable – they don't take advantage of all the trombone has to offer. Joe's concerto takes no prisoners and makes you work for everything," says Pollack, who recently completed an engineering degree at Harvard and is currently enrolled in a graduate program at Cornell University.

He also suggests that most enticing possibility for any composer – future performances. "All of my friends would love to play the piece, I'm sure. I won't hide this from the trombone community," he says.

As for Fennimore, after a bow on stage this afternoon at Proctor's, he'll return to giving lessons and writing on the occasional commission. A solo harpsichord piece is next on the agenda.

"I just try to stay interested," he says, with total deadpan. "I'm not tired of eating, I'm not tired of music, I'm not tired of sex. Those are the most important things."

MARY JANE LEACH

COMPOSER   JUNE 11, 2006

At home in a sanctuary for music

Ceilings 30 feet high, 4,500 square feet of space, seating for 300, a century-old working pipe organ and a bell tower. It's a place with a history of community and transcendence. Composer Mary Jane Leach just calls it home.

The site is the former Our Lady of Good Counsel Catholic Church in Valley Falls, a Rensselaer County hamlet of 500 residents that lies just north and across the Hoosick River from Schaghticoke.

After Leach purchased the property from the Albany Diocese in May 2003, she spent her first nights sleeping in the choir loft. Since then, she has turned that area into her studio and made a comfortable living space for herself and two cats in the spacious basement. The sanctuary itself is on its way to becoming a concert hall.

"I was just looking for a small quiet place to live," says Leach, 56, who had lived in Manhattan since 1977. "But how could I not get it?"

Leach's property search gradually led her up the Hudson to the rural perimeters of the Capital Region. After a real estate agent suggested they check out a church, Leach spent a night dreaming of the possibilities.

She recalls saying to herself, "If it has an organ it would have to be a real dump for me not to want it."

The next morning, the agent volunteered, "You know it has a working organ."

"It turned out better than we could believe," says Leach.

Located just off Route 67 at the corner of Emily and State streets, the sturdy red brick structure dwarfs the surrounding houses. Its prominent cornerstone reads, "1883 OSA."

The founders, the Order of St. Augustine, also ran St. John the Baptist in Schaghticoke, where the priests for both parishes lived. Thus there is no rectory on Leach's one-acre lot. After the Augustinians left in 1997, the Albany Diocese finally closed Our Lady of Good Counsel in 2001.

"It remained available for a while, because you can't get a mortgage for a place like this," explains Leach, who sold her co-op apartment in Manhattan's Morningside Heights in order to pay cash for the full asking price of $69,900.

"Everybody wanted to know who was the lady that was moving into the church?" recalls Karen Carlson, who has lived across the street for 10 years. "Who in their right mind would buy a church and live in it?"

The natural answer, of course, is a musician, since churches and musicians have always been in each others' orbit.

Leach is no exception. Growing up in Vermont, her mother was a church organist. "We were in and out of church all the time," she recalls. And though she does not write sacred music, Leach was also an artist-in-residence at a Jesuit church in Cologne, Germany, for two years in the mid-1990s. There, she lived a few steps from the vestibule. Now, her bedroom is beneath a former high altar.

"Musicians are used to going into churches and just playing (a concert)," says Leach. Nevertheless, she's in the process of removing most of the furnishings and ornaments left behind. Taking down the Stations of the Cross will eliminate most of the remaining iconography, while selling the pews will allow for a more versatile use of the space.

Some items are finding new uses. A wooden cabinet with numerous shallow drawers was once used for liturgical vestments. Now located in the choir loft, it serves as an ideal cabinet for oversized scores.

As a member of the East Coast contemporary music scene, Leach has no shortage of friends and colleagues to invite for a performance and sleepover. (She's thinking of making one of the small rooms off the main altar area into a guest bedroom.) So far, the guest artists have come away not only admiring her chutzpah for staking claim on the space, but also praising the acoustics.

"It's got an intimacy and a resonance ... without the tubbiness that afflicts (the sound in) so many church spaces," says composer Dennis Bathory-Kitsz of Northfield, Vt. He participated in the space's inaugural concert in fall 2004.

An experienced producer, Leach collaborated during the 1990s with another composer, Phil Niblock, in running the XI label, a recording offshoot of Experimental Intermedia, Niblock's own combination residence and performance space. Says Niblock: "It was time for her to leave the city, and it's the perfect thing for her ... a place where you can do acoustic music, small ensembles or soloists very well."

Traditional repertoire is already finding a home in the space as well. "I love the space; it's ideal for Bach," says cellist David Gibson, a faculty member at Rensselaer Polytechnic Institute in Troy, who will be performing three of Bach's Unaccompanied Cello Suites this afternoon. After hearing Gibson's first installment of the Bach cycle last month at her venue, Leach says, "It's like you were in the middle of the cello."

Long before she found such a richly reverberant space to call her own, acoustics were an important element in Leach's compositions, which are primarily vocal.

"An abandoned church is about ideal for the kind of music she does, which is voices in space and how they reverberate against each other," says Frank J. Oteri, editor of the online contemporary music magazine New Music Box. Mark Stryker of the Detroit Free Press heard an ethereal aspect in Leach's music, saying it "offers a spiritual recharge without the banalities of the new mysticism."

Now in progress from Leach is an evening-length feminist revisioning of the ancient Greek myth of Ariadne. Portions of it were recorded on an all-Leach disc issued by New World Records in 1998. But a local performance is not in the immediate offing, since bringing in a full chorus to Valley Falls would get expensive.

Leach is more focused on events that bring together local audiences with contemporary music. For example, at a recent concert composer Daniel Goode performed a piece that draws on the calls of Northeastern birds. Leach said the sounds intrigued a neighbor, and that she wants to have more contemporary music programming of "things that aren't threatening or make people feel stupid."

For now, the space itself may be enough of a draw for audiences.

"I remember the first time she had a concert," recalls neighbor Karen Carlson. "It was eclectic music and modern and I was wondering who would attend ... but there was a huge cross-section of people there, who were interested in supporting her or just interested in the music."

JAMES LEVINE

CONDUCTOR   JULY 13, 2006

So many scores, so little time

During a curtain call at Boston's Symphony Hall on March 1, conductor James Levine took a serious onstage spill that caused a tear to his rotator cuff – a major impairment for a conductor.

As Levine spent the subsequent four months recovering from surgery, the Boston Symphony Orchestra and the Metropolitan Opera – the renowned musical organizations he leads – scrambled for substitute conductors, and the larger musical world waited and wondered about his long-term prognosis.

Levine got back in the saddle, so to speak, just last week, when he led the BSO in Friday's opening night at Tanglewood. He returns again Friday with Schoenberg's massive oratorio "Gurrelieder" with the BSO; Saturday, he leads the Tanglewood Music Center Orchestra in a concert performance of Strauss' explosive opera "Elektra."

Such ambitious programs on back-to-back nights were set in place long before Levine's hiatus from musical life, but they nevertheless are ideal tests of Levine's recovery and stamina. In all, Levine's July schedule at Tanglewood includes nine performances, including an appearance at "Tanglewood on Parade" and the American-staged debut of Elliott Carter's one-act opera "What Next?"

During a conversation in the Tanglewood greenroom late last month, the conductor was raring to go.

"I'm wonderful well and rested and the shoulder is amazing," Levine said. "(But) it was really a massive tear. They had to repair it and also cut a bone spur that was in there acting as a razor blade against the tendon."

Along with physical therapy and rest, Levine also took the opportunity to focus on his diet. "I lost 35 pounds," he said. "I won't really be through (until) I lose 50. You know, you can't make a change like that on top of performing and rehearsing where you eat in a hurry and you eat at the wrong times of day."

Levine's real appetite, of course, is for music. Though he was forbidden to conduct or even play piano during his forced sabbatical, he still devoured music, reading and studying up to 50 different scores.

He's a voracious consumer of music, on paper and otherwise: "I always have with me the scores I'm about to do, the scores that I've planned to do and scores that I'm studying that don't have anything to do with the current conducting plan," he said.

To prepare for a performance of any single work, Levine may study up to 10 other scores by the same composer.

"I'm much more comfortable with doing a work by a composer if I know as much of the rest of his work as possible," he said. "This is so I can gradually see what a composer is really doing, so I can bring it to bear on what I'm doing."

Before and after his surgery, much of Levine's focus has been the music of two composers in particular: the ever-popular Beethoven and the still forbidding Schoenberg. The BSO is in the middle of a two-year immersion in which Levine places the two men's music on concerts together. And as happens most seasons, the highlights are reappearing at Tanglewood.

The opening night program featured Schoenberg's Chamber Symphony No. 1 and Beethoven's Symphony No. 9 "Choral." By coincidence, it was the very same program played on the night of Levine's accident.

"Mostly, I am not a fan of thematic programming, but once in a while there's an idea that's organic and exciting," said Levine.

For this project, the central idea was one of connection between these two composers, born nearly a century apart.

"The things that Beethoven did to develop music in every respect didn't really find their consequent until Schoenberg," said Levine, who lists "everything that happened in between" such as the work of Mendelssohn, Schumann, Brahms and Wagner as a failure to live up to the promise of innovations such as those expressed in Beethoven's Grossa Fuga, Missa Solemnis or the first movement of his Ninth Symphony.

For almost a century after Beethoven's death, his late excursions beyond the boundaries of traditional harmony were viewed as pure lunacy by critics and scholars. But eventually the genius showed through. While nobody seriously accuses Schoenberg of being insane, his music still isn't embraced like that of Beethoven.

Acknowledging this, Levine nevertheless seems undaunted, perhaps even emboldened.

"There must be some people who, when they see Schoenberg's name for a whole program, say 'I'll put that on my must-miss list,' he said. "(But) I find the audience responding marvelously. There's no doubt that this juxtaposition makes the listener more involved with both composers, and involved in new ways."

As Levine's re-entry into concert life intensifies, listeners shouldn't expect bold departures into new musical territories. Though he hinted at a couple of surprising composers that were in his stack of study scores – namely Olivier Messiaen and Gyorgi Ligeti – his period of rest and reflection seems to have only solidified his existing views of what suits him as a conductor.

"I turned 63 last week," he said, "and I've never conducted a Bruckner symphony, and I've never conducted (Mussorgsky's) 'Boris Gudunov.'"

And he probably never will: By way of illustration, Levine told the story of his final season at the Ravinia Festival, the Chicago Symphony Orchestra's summer home where he was music director from 1973 to 1993. Management hoped that during his farewell he'd finally conduct a Bruckner symphony.

"I said, 'OK, which one? The ninth? OK,' recalled Levine. "I went home, took the score off the shelf, started again. And when I was finished, I was here (on the couch) and the score was over there (in the far corner of the room)."

"I swear it has nothing to do with not responding to (the music). It has to do with not arriving with any certainty that I can reach a point of view of how it should be and persuade an orchestra to do that," he said. "Another example is ... (Janecek's) 'Jenufa.' I'd so much rather sit in the house and listen than get anywhere near it (as a conductor)."

Such an attitude might be viewed as obstinacy toward certain avenues of the repertory, but it can also be considered the mark of that rare conductor who is willing to acknowledge that he simply can't do everything.

In the music world, this year is all about birthdays, chief among them Mozart's 350th and Shostakovich's centennial. At Tanglewood, Levine is digging into Mozart with three programs, which include nothing less than a concert performance of "Don Giovanni" plus the Requiem, a symphony and a piano concerto.

But he's happy to hand over the job of honoring Shostakovich to guest conductors.

"When it's something that I don't do, I look around for people who will do it and fortunately, there are a great many where Shostakovich is concerned," he said.

It's this single-mindedness of purpose that infuses Levine's performances with clarity and precision as well as insight and revealing detail. While the conductor says that after the coming season in Boston there won't be any more Schoenberg for a while, he is already building enthusiasm for honoring Elliott Carter on his 100th birthday in 2008.

"All I can do," Levine said, "is give (the audience) what we do the best, what I believe in the most, what fulfills my responsibility and my exhilaration at it."

MAX LIFCHITZ

COMPOSER   JANUARY 29, 2004

Pushing music, sometimes his own

To make it as a composer, you usually need a certain amount of hubris. But Max Lifchitz is a humble guy.

Sure, he's tenacious enough to run a New York City concert series since 1980 and an independent record label since 1992. But the pianist lacks the self-promotion gene, and seldom gives much prominence to his own music in the concerts he conducts or in the many CDs he produces.

That's why this Sunday's all-Lifchitz concert in the Recital Hall at the University of Albany's Performing Arts Center will be a special event. It's not an anniversary or a birthday; the event was first scheduled as an installment in Lifchitz's annual series of piano recitals. But instead of playing his own works, he's allowed seven of the university's top faculty musicians to give a mini-retrospective of his musical trajectory. Lifchitz will also perform at the keyboard.

"I don't like to push my own music. Maybe I should," says Lifchitz, 55, during a recent conversation in his UAlbany office. He speaks fast and fluent English but with a distinct Latin accent.

Born in Mexico City, Lifchitz has lived in the United States since 1966. After joining the UAlbany faculty in 1986, he continued to keep a base of activity in New York City. In both locales, he devotes his efforts as performer, producer and teacher to building musical bridges between the Americas.

"I started my group (to perform) music that was unjustly neglected," he says of the origin of the ensemble, which is aptly named North/South Consonance. "Hardly any groups played Latin American music. (It) was a blind spot."

Lifchitz has been widely recognized for filling that void. In 1982, he was presented the United Nations Peace Medal by U.N. General Secretary Javier Perez de Cuellar for work on behalf of Latin American music.

Nevertheless, Lifchitz's programs have remained below the radar of musical politics and trends. As the aesthetic battles between "uptown" intellectual music and "downtown" experimentation raged through the '80s and '90s, Lifchitz never took sides.

"I thought I was from out of town," he says. Instead, he just kept giving concerts.

The North/South ensemble, which occasionally performs in Albany, has premiered more than 700 new works, while the North/South record label has released 36 discs. Amid all this activity, there's music of almost every style and a liberal mix of Latin and American composers. And occasionally a piece or two by one Max Lifchitz.

Asked to describe his own music, Lifchitz tends to be affable and talkative but not terribly specific. Similar to his inclusive programming of music by colleagues, his own compositions can go in different directions.

It's partly a result of the state of musical flux in his homeland during his student days.

"In Mexico, there was an unspoken assumption you had to make nationalistic art and music," he says. But his teachers' generation began to break that mold, and by the time Lifchitz began composing, "you had to make a choice between being a nationalist or an internationalist."

With former mentors like the Italian Luciano Berio and the American Leon Kirchner, Lifchitz is fluent in the international style – more commonly known as serialism. But he also knows how to work with a folk tune, a key to a nationalistic style. Lifchitz' most popular piece, "Mosaico Latinoamericano," which will be performed on Sunday, is full of Latin dances including the *merengue* and the *huapango*.

"I never made a choice," Lifchitz finally admits. "I've always been an eclectic at heart."

Among Lifchitz's nearly 100 compositions, "Yellow Ribbons" is a series of pieces that manages to straddle nationalism and serialism. The composer began it in the 1970s during the Iranian hostage crisis and picked it up again after Sept. 11. He's completed 39 "Yellow Ribbons" pieces so far and six will be performed on Sunday.

"Everyone asks me, but I don't use the 'Yellow Rose of Texas' song," says Lifchitz, explaining that each piece in the long series utilizes the same tone-row or series of pitches. "They share rhythms and general shape and a counterpoint of tempos (which is) each instrument moving in its own tempo."

In other words, the substance of "Yellow Ribbons" is in the international style. But the idea is more nationalistic.

"The first time I saw yellow ribbons, I thought of them as a sign of solidarity," says Lifchitz, who calls the series "a celebration of political freedom and the freedom of expression we have."

BART & PRISCILLA McLEAN

JANUARY 16, 2005   COMPOSERS

Following the rhythms of the
road, the sound of the earth

The McLean Mix world tour is about to begin. First stop: Poughkeepsie.

The tour's booking agents, road crew, stage managers and star performers are Barton and Priscilla McLean. Their caravan is a 2003 Toyota Matrix.

For most of the year the McLeans are quiet residents of Petersburgh, Rensselaer County, where they've lived for 20 years. But each spring, they earn their livelihood by taking to the road and presenting their homegrown, avant-garde music at institutions like Tulane University in New Orleans or Texas' Abilene Christian University, both stops on this year's trip.

The McLeans' music is based in an admiration for nature, but it's created using the most advanced electronic tools available. The combination is thus primitive and highly sophisticated at the same time.

One critic described the experience of a McLean Mix concert as "getting close to the inner forces and rhythms of the Earth."

In today's larger musical scene, the McLeans are as rare as a banjo in symphonic orchestra. Their music is as unique as the way they lead their career, which is with a remarkably low level of ego-driven ambition.

"They follow their own star," says composer Joel Chadabe, who runs the Electronic Music Foundation in Albany. "Within the world of electronic music, there are definitely conventions and norms. ... They don't fit (any of) them easily."

The McLeans' music is characterized by an austere, often macabre resonance. The boundary between reality and the cyber world becomes slippery.

In works like "In the Beginning" by Priscilla and "Dawn Chorus" by Barton, such an effect is the result of both an artistic vision and certain musical techniques.

They often work in a form known as electro-acoustic wherein a live, or acoustic, instrument is accompanied by electronic effects. And their electronic sounds frequently come out of the technique of *musique concrete,* in which a raw or natural sound, like a bird call or Priscilla's singing voice, is manipulated using electronic tools.

The sounds of nature seep in and out of the music, and its themes are prominent in titles like "Earth Music" and "Visions of a Summer Night."

After another Hudson Valley appearance in New Paltz on March 1, the road show begins in earnest with six dates in the South, a couple of appearances in Texas and a final swing through the Midwest. In all there will be 12 concerts, two residencies and approximately 10,000 miles of highway travel.

"They believe in their creative work, and that work defines their life," says composer Edmund Campion, who has presented the McLean Mix at the University of California at Berkeley, where he teaches. "They are total artists, not compromised by university or commercial constraints. That is what I call a big success."

Among American composers, it's often considered a badge of honor to earn a living from music without having to teach. Although the McLeans today carry that distinction, they always have been part of the academic orbit.

It was while earning graduate degrees in composition at the University of Indiana that they met. "We married three months after we started going together. Once you know, you may as well do it," says Priscilla.

"Also a matter of economics," chimes in Bart, during a recent discussion.

"He's so practical," replies his wife. But she adds, "I'm the one who initiated it."

Exchanging vows in 1967, the couple felt a part of the progressive spirit of the times. But the universities where they studied and later worked were slow to embrace change.

The first lesson of institutional resistance came at Indiana, where they weren't allowed access to Iannis Xenakis, the visionary but self-taught composer and theorist who was a visiting scholar.

"He was such a threat to the (traditional) music people that they just put him in a hall and did not allow him any contact with students," says Bart McLean, recalling how they got to know Xenakis' music through recordings that they bought off-campus.

In their own version of free-form "happenings," which they dubbed "fiascoes," the McLeans and their circle would come together to perform, improvise and play recordings of Xenakis and other renegades like Edgar Varese. "All the music the professors were ignoring," says Priscilla.

Another grating aspect of academia were the opportunities given to Bart but denied Priscilla. "I was not allowed to teach in any of the departments Bart taught in, ever," she says.

Recalling their days in Austin, where Bart was on the University of Texas faculty from 1976 to 1983, Priscilla says that she was refused access to department's underutilized electronic music studio. It was even suggested that she apply as a student. "I was so incensed by that (that) I never worked in the studio," says McLean. "I just took pieces of it home."

"We exploded in 1982," says Bart of the launch of the McLeans' touring business. A string of recordings on the CRI and Folkways labels around the time also didn't hurt.

"In 1984 we had 15 concerts, which went all the way to California," says Priscilla.

"At that point we felt we had to leave the university, (because) the direction we were going was more professional than academic. We moved up here and decided to be starving artists and see how it went," concludes Bart, smiling a bit at the obvious happy ending. (They both look sufficiently nourished.)

But they still hustle. Every fall Bart begins cobbling together dates for the spring tour. Ten years ago, he would do a mailing of 4,000 brochures and typically get a 1 percent response. Today, it's all done by e-mail 1,100 messages were sent last year, some to old colleagues, many to new contacts.

"We'll get in touch with what we think is a cold contact and they'll say, 'We've been wanting to have you for 20 years,'" says Priscilla, who's recently completed a first draft of a memoir.

The McLeans' most widely known work from recent years is "Rainforest Images," an installation that allows visitors to sing, speak or play an instrument into a microphone that echoes throughout a dense electronic landscape. The Albany Center Galleries presented "Rainforest" several years ago, and the McLeans have also had installations at MASS MoCA in North Adams, Mass.

All of the McLeans' works from the last few years now also include visuals by Priscilla. It makes for more dynamic performances and further heightens the surreal. In "Autumn Requiem," for example, she uses computer technology to superimpose images of the New England landscape.

But the McLeans can celebrate as well as be reflective. They frequently entertain in their large old farmhouse, and Bart's piece "Happy Days" consists entirely of the sounds of music boxes, small percussion instruments and New Year's Eve noisemakers. It ends with a quote of "Auld Lang Syne." When they perform the piece, they don party hats.

"It's very seldom that two composers work it out as well as they have," says Karl Korte, a composer in Buskirk, Washington County, who has known the couple since the days when he and Bart McLean were both on the University of Texas faculty. Says Korte, "They're so supportive of one another."

MAUREEN O'FLYNN

No longer sneaking around

"I'm a Stockbridge girl," declares Maureen O'Flynn, the internationally known soprano who's currently appearing as Mimi in the Berkshire Opera production of Puccini's "La Boheme" at the Colonial Theatre in Pittsfield, Mass. "I grew up here when it was the quintessential New England town," she continues.

O'Flynn's Berkshire bona fides include having worked at the Norman Rockwell Museum when it was in its original location at the Old Corner House on Main Street in Stockbridge, Mass. She also used to sneak into Tanglewood performances through a hole in the fence. But in voicing that memory during a recent lunch in downtown Lenox, Mass., she seems to have surprised herself.

"It was only once or twice," she adds, with a rare bit of sheepishness.

O'Flynn has called Stockbridge home for most of her life, and not just in a fond-memory kind of way. Except for a few years of hustling for auditions in New York City, she's kept a home there. But the success of her career – she recently appeared in New York, Cincinnati, Portland, Ore., and Minneapolis – means that she's typically only in Stockbridge for two or three months out of the year.

Yet Berkshire residents have not forgotten the hometown girl. When O'Flynn made her debut at the Metropolitan Opera in 1998, "there were busloads of people who came down from the Berkshires," she recalls. Her role that night was the lead in Gounod's "Romeo and Juliet," a part that O'Flynn reprised there just this past year.

Then there's her long association with the Berkshire Opera, where she could be considered the company star. She performed in its first three seasons and returns on a regular, though not always annual, basis.

Her most recent appearances have been in Verdi's "Rigoletto" in 2004 and Handel's "Rinaldo" two years ago. But it was her searing portrayal of Violetta in Verdi's "La Traviata" at the Mahaiwe Theatre in Great Barrington, Mass., in 2003 that lingers in memory.

"People still talk to me about that, saying they've never been so moved," says O'Flynn.

For the Berkshire Opera's 2007 season, O'Flynn is not resting on her laurels. Although to opera audiences, "La Boheme" is about as familiar and popular as opera gets, for singers it's still serious work. And for O'Flynn the role of Mimi is new and starting to feel special.

"It has quite quickly become my favorite role. There's just something about the character," she says.

That enthusiasm continues for the whole piece. "I am unashamedly head-over-heels in love with this opera. It's the perfect opera, there's not a wasted note. It's not just about romance, but a portrayal of friendship and youth and the bohemian life."

O'Flynn is calling the Berkshire run her staged debut in the role, since she has performed it before. Earlier this month she was part of an outdoor concert version with the Minnesota Orchestra. But there's an earlier history with the piece as well.

"I sang the role once years ago when I had no business doing it," she admits, recalling a touring program with the Boston Opera some 17 years ago. "The years went by, and I did other repertoire and my voice matured ... This is coming home now, vocally and dramatically."

The soprano is also enthused about collaborating again with conductor Kathleen Kelly, the Berkshire Opera's music director since 2006. During lunch, O'Flynn mentions that it was at the Met where she and Kelly first worked together. (Kelly was on the music staff of the Met for eight years, and left in 2006 to become head of music staff for the Houston Grand Opera.)

"She was my prompter in 'Traviata,'" says O'Flynn.

Assuming that prompters were crutches for singers who didn't do their homework in learning a role, this seems a remarkable revelation. All the more so because of O'Flynn's extraordinary command of "Traviata."

"Everyone needs a prompter at the Met," replies O'Flynn. "It's so big, there are places on stage that you can't see the conductor or hear the orchestra.

"Kelly was phenomenal," she continues, "a great musician who knows singers."

Although there won't be a need for prompters during "La Boheme," the Colonial performances are nonetheless a step up to a larger venue for the Berkshire Opera, which has previously performed in the 680-seat Mahaiwe, and the 500-seat Boland Theater at Berkshire Community College.

Yet the Colonial's capacity of 800 still seems intimate for O'Flynn, who more than knows her way around the Met where a sell-out night is a crowd of 3,995.

"What a small company has to offer is the intimacy to invite the audience on stage with you," says O'Flynn. It's all the better when that audience consists, in part, of old friends and neighbors.

"I'm in the Berkshires and singing 'Boheme,'" says O'Flynn. "Life is good."

PAULINE OLIVEROS

COMPOSER/ACCORDIONIST   JUNE 8, 2007

Making conscious connections

In 1988, accordionist and composer Pauline Oliveros made a recording with a trombone player and a percussionist inside a 2 million-gallon empty cistern buried 14 feet below ground at Fort Worden, near Port Townsend, Wash. The resulting CD on New Albion Records was titled "Deep Listening," a play on the unusual location and also an apt description of the trio's meditative and reverberant improvisations.

Soon thereafter, Oliveros realized "Deep Listening" more broadly described the aesthetic approach to contemporary music she had been pursuing for 30 years. While it can seem abstract, Deep Listening might be described as "musical mindfulness," in which the composer or other artist approaches the work from a position of deep awareness.

Oliveros began using the term in her myriad activities as a performer and teacher, and started offering training and certification in Deep Listening techniques. A few years ago, she renamed her Kingston-based organization the Deep Listening Institute.

Deep listening is no longer underground. This weekend, three Hudson Valley locations will host concerts that mark the culmination of the Deep Listening Convergence, a coming-together of 45 musicians from across North America and Europe that began in January with online dialogues and rehearsals.

Yes, online rehearsals. Since the 1950s, when she experimented with the then-new medium of electronic tape, Oliveros, 74, has remained at the forefront of technology, and the Internet has long been one of her tools. Participants in the Deep Listening Convergence used the networking program Skype to improvise and rehearse new compositions. Like a telephone conference call, Skype allows up to 10 computers to give and receive audio and video information in real time.

"I was sitting here in my kitchen and hearing four people from different cities in Switzerland and four from Canada and others from the U.S.," said Oliveros last week from her home in Kingston. "It was great. They did a long and goofy improvisation."

Whether they are goofy or serious or a bit of both, a lot of Deep Listening compositions are in store this weekend. Each of the three concerts, at venues in Troy, Hudson and High Falls, will have a different program of new works, from solos to large ensemble pieces. The instruments at hand are also diverse, and will include traditional Western instruments, drums and folk instruments, plus electronics. Vocalizing and some movement will be part of the mix as well.

Among the new works is "Spiral Tap," by Sarah Weaver, 29, a trombonist and composer from Chicago. She composed the new work using Deep Listening techniques to explore the number sequences represented in the spirals of a seashell. It will be performed by six musicians playing conch shells.

"Everyone using the (Deep Listening) system is more in touch with their authentic selves and a new level of communication is available that's not there in other compositional systems," says Weaver, who's in the process of moving to New Paltz. She plans to become Oliveros' apprentice in Kingston and also start an ensemble in Manhattan.

Like most of the participants in the convergence, Weaver has completed a three-year training to become certified in Deep Listening. Over the years, Oliveros has spread the word – and the sound – of Deep Listening far and wide. Her institute offers a variety of special workshops and summer retreats, and Oliveros has been teaching Deep Listening at RPI for the past six years.

One method Oliveros uses to track the reach of Deep Listening is a "Google Alert," in which the search engine sends her a message every time it spots a new Web site using the term.

"I get alerts every day," says Oliveros. "The usage includes all kinds of musicians and it includes religious and spiritual groups. It's becoming very common."

CHARLES PELTZ

CONDUCTOR   SEPTEMBER 25, 2005

In tune with community

Eavesdrop on a board meeting of most any small to midsize arts organization and you'll hear one phrase repeated like a mantra: community outreach. Building new audiences and forging alliances with other nonprofit organizations has become a perpetual agenda item for artists and administrators during an era when the fine arts are increasingly marginalized.

Luckily for the Glens Falls Symphony Orchestra – a 28-year-old professional ensemble – proselytizing classical music is a natural calling for its music director Charles Peltz. "I want us to be part of the community in such a way that any member of the community can see in their life the value of the orchestra and what it does," Peltz says.

"People have responded very well to him," says Viviann Bergstedt, a former orchestra board member. "He's very energetic and a wonderful addition to the community." According to executive director Robert B. Rosoff, subscriptions to the orchestra's annual season of five concerts at the Glens Falls High School have increased 30 percent during Peltz's five-year tenure.

In addition to owning a contagious enthusiasm, Peltz knows how to turn concerts into events. Take, for example, the biggest undertaking yet in the orchestra's history: the Musicbridge Festival, a series of concerts, recitals and other happenings held in Glens Falls, Saratoga Springs and Queensbury through next weekend.

Peltz will conduct the final event, an orchestra concert featuring the world premiere of a new orchestral work by Joan Tower, one of today's most highly regarded composers. The Tower premiere is of national importance because the piece, "Made in America," has been co-commissioned by more than 50 other small orchestras around the country, which will all perform it during the next year.

After growing up in Hammondsport in the Finger Lakes Region and spending most of his career in upstate New York, it was no great stretch for Peltz, 46, to settle in Glens Falls. "I promised the board I'd own property and have my number in the phone book," he says.

Peltz and his wife, Kirstin, own a 1920s Arts and Craft house just blocks away from the town center. A tangible sign of the local conductor's commitment to the community, the place is also the site of semiannual parties where the sometimes disparate wings of the organization – namely orchestra members and trustees – come together.

But like any modern conductor, Peltz is often on the road. The same year he took the Glens Falls post, he also received an appointment to the faculty of the New England Conservatory in Boston, where he leads the program for wind players. Peltz had already mastered the balancing act of directing a part-time orchestra while holding down a faculty position during the 1990s, when he was at the State University at Buffalo and a staff conductor of the Syracuse Symphony.

Although Peltz takes in stride the drives from Glens Falls to Boston, the weeklong Musicbridge Festival will put the first blemish on a perfect five-year track record of never missing an obligation in Boston.

Peltz can still boast of his attendance at orchestra board meetings; he shows up by phone when out of town. Such heavy interaction with board members might be atypical for conductors, but Peltz says he does it "because I want to be questioned. My actions are able to be scrutinized, because they pay the bills."

"I have colleagues who would not do well here – the person interested (only) in conducting pieces for their growth or their career-building," says Peltz.

While aspects of the Musicbridge Festival encompass community outreach, the programming itself spotlights connections between music of the past and present.

"We're taking the role an art museum would take," explains Peltz, "putting artists of today next to artists of the past, just like the Hyde (Collection) does."

He points with special pride to Tuesday's concert at the Charles R. Wood Theater, featuring solo performances by three new orchestra members. Peltz asked each of them to play mainstream repertoire alongside contemporary pieces and to be prepared to describe how they relate.

"Charles e-mailed asking for suggestions of how to mate an 18th-century piece with a 20th-century piece," says James Platte, "It's the kind of (connection) that musicians make automatically." The cellist will perform J.S. Bach followed by Bright Sheng, and point out the bowing techniques and dance forms that both pieces share.

Platte, 28, says it's such unusual opportunities that keep him driving three-hours from his home in New Jersey to be part of the orchestra.

"A lot of younger conductors will be leery and not try things," he says of Peltz's initiatives. "But it always goes well with Charles, because he's so organized. I get the idea he's thought it through for years."

The so-called musical bridges present in next Sunday's orchestra concert will come from featured composer Joan Tower. She'll introduce the works by Beethoven, Barber and Stravinsky that will be performed alongside her new piece, "Made in America," and her "Fanfare for the Uncommon Woman."

"It's important for my audience to hear a composer share with them a love for music of the 18th and 19th centuries," explains Peltz. "When a lay person looks up and sees a composer who loves all the same music, a certain defense falls away. (It's as if they think) 'Anyone who loves Beethoven like I do can't be so bad.'"

NEIL ROLNICK

All circuits firing

Neil Rolnick has spent most of his career putting music and musical ideas into machines, and making them spit it back out again. But it's only in recent years that the composer and longtime Rensselaer Polytechnic Institute faculty member, who turned 60 last month, has found the unique musical voice inside himself and been able to embrace it.

"I have figured out what my music is about: material that grows organically out of little seeds and with instruments interacting with electronics, so that the electronics become magic. It's important for me to be able to hear the architecture of a piece," he said in a recent interview.

Rolnick's birthday and his music will be celebrated on Saturday evening in a concert produced by RPI's Experimental Media and Performing Arts Center in the university's Academy Hall. The program focuses on Rolnick's recent works and features a world premiere, but it also includes "Ever Livin' Rhythm," a 30-year-old piece for electronics and percussion.

Rolnick's first effort with electronics, "Rhythm" was written shortly before he moved to Paris to study at the famed IRCAM (Institut de Recherche et Coordination Acoustique/Musique), the center for advanced musical research headed by composer Pierre Boulez.

Rolnick made valuable contacts during his time there, but IRCAM is a place for dense thought and denser compositions – not such a good match for music that's as lively and playful as something called "Ever Livin' Rhythm."

"Pierre Boulez said you're too American, go back to America," recalls Rolnick, who took the advice. He later concluded: "If I'm a composer, then it's my job to write down what I hear. Why write difficult and complex stuff if that's not what I hear? I've always had a gift for melody. I used to be embarrassed by it."

As Saturday night's program will attest, Rolnick is no longer blushing at his inherent musical gifts. Says the composer, "Whatever it is I'm meant to do, I'm doing it now."

What Rolnick has also been doing for years, besides writing music, is building the arts programs at RPI. He began as a junior faculty member in January 1981, arriving in Troy, as he recalls, "with a kid, a wife, no money and a piano, which was pretty much my only possession."

"He was energetic, very smart, and very ambitious," says sculptor Larry Kagan, also a young faculty member at the time. "He saw the real possibilities of growing an arts program that relied on technology."

"I presumed it was going to be a temporary deal," Rolnick says of his early days teaching at RPI. "I'm a musician. I didn't see how I could be long term at an engineering school."

Despite such concerns, Rolnick got busy pulling together some semblance of an electronic music studio. At the time, composer Joel Chadabe was running the electronic music program at the University at Albany. He provided Rolnick with crucial advice as well as spare equipment.

"Joel told me to get anything I could working, and then ask for funding to expand it," says Rolnick.

The first major hardware was an IBM PDP 11/10, something that Chadabe no longer needed at UAlbany. "It was an old computer even then," says Rolnick, who describes it as measuring about 19 inches wide, 2 feet deep and 6 feet high. Together, the two musicians transported it across the Hudson in Rolnick's Volkswagen van.

Shortly after its installation, Rolnick put in a request to the higher-ups at RPI for an equipment upgrade. That, of course, is something he's done again and again over the years, as technology marches on. Lately though, the fact that every student owns a laptop computer has eased the pressure for ever-new equipment. "There are still things you need a studio for," explains Rolnick, "like space, microphones, and a video or sound stage."

Besides pushing for access to the latest tools, Rolnick has been a driving force in making the arts a prominent and respected part of the university. During his two nonconsecutive terms as chair of the arts department, he supervised the expansion of arts at RPI from being merely a variety of enrichment courses for students from other departments, to the offering of bachelor's and master's degrees in "integrated electronic arts."

Rolnick remembers during his early days hearing a now-retired arts faculty member tell him, "Our job is to interest engineers in the arts enough to be future board members and supporters of arts organizations." He still groans at such a limited mindset.

Growing bored with teaching introductory-level courses only, Rolnick and his colleagues decided to seek students who would be interested in the arts as a career by offering a master's of fine arts degree. The multidisciplinary ("integrated") focus made the program unique in the nation when it was first offered in 1987.

An undergraduate program, which began nine years later, was the most successful new undergrad program in RPI's history, according to Rolnick, with an enrollment that grew from 40 to 300 in four years.

"The timing was right, at the beginning of the tech boom," he says, adding that it was a good fit for "students who play video games and have various music and graphic programs on the computers and they would say, 'Can I really made a career of that?'"

The latest manifestation of arts and technology at RPI is the prominent glass building on the hill above downtown Troy – EMPAC, the Experimental Media and Performing Arts Center, a unique lavishly expensive facility scheduled to open next fall. Rolnick had a role in its genesis as well.

"The germ for EMPAC was an idea that Neil brought to me," says Faye Duchin, an RPI faculty member who was dean of the humanities and social sciences from 1996 to 2002. "I brought (the proposal) to a president's retreat with the deans, and (RPI President Shirley Jackson) loved the idea as soon as it was on the table."

"Neil basically prepared the ground for EMPAC at RPI," says Johannes Goebel, director of EMPAC. "So I think it is most appropriate for EMPAC to throw a birthday party in the form of a concert."

Among the half-dozen Rolnick works on Saturday's program is "Digits," a 2005 piece for piano and electronics. Earlier this year,

Anthony Tommasini of The New York Times caught a performance at the Juilliard School in New York City and described it as "an exhilarating interactive piece."

"Digits" was written for Kathleen Supove, a Brooklyn-based pianist who is known for tackling the most demanding contemporary scores. In the piece, computer programs sample and transform portions of the piano music as it unfolds live. Managing such electronic trickery is nothing new for Rolnick, which was a relief to Supove.

"I would put him at the top tier of people to work with. He knows a lot about the technology of the piece, and has made it easy for me to be able to do it," says Supove. "I've had some other pieces that are terrific, but the composer knew what he wanted but didn't have a clue how to realize it, and I had to go talk to an engineer and figure out how to set up."

Amid the virtuosity and technology, Rolnick's personality comes through.

"His music has lively tunes and rhythms, and is immediately understandable," says Chadabe. "And it is has a very good disposition, a sunny disposition, very much like Neil himself."

PETER SCHICKELE

DECEMBER 16, 2007   COMPOSER

The cadence of humor

To the relief of music historians and the dismay of musical satire fans, it has been 12 long years since the last CD release of music by P.D.Q. Bach, "the last and the least and certainly the oddest" of Johann Sebastian Bach's 20-odd children. But composer and professor Peter Schickele, the principal researcher into the almost-forgotten music of P.D.Q. Bach, has remained hard at work, reconstructing and bringing to life heretofore unknown masterpieces from his fictional alter ego, such as "The Next To Last Songs" and the String Quartet in F Major ("The Moose"), which includes the scintillating dance "Menuetto no sweato." These and other enduring treasures are contained in Telarc's new disc, "P.D.Q. Bach: The Jekyll & Hyde Tour."

Although he maintains an office/pied-a-terre in Manhattan, Schickele, 72, has been a longtime resident of Woodstock. Over coffee in one of the village's more chic establishments, he reminisced about 30-plus years in the music business, and showed that the good-natured humor infused in his music – whether published under the name P.D.Q. Bach or Peter Schickele – comes naturally and abundantly.

"I had no idea P.D.Q. Bach would go on this long. In April 1965, we were just trying to put it on the map. We borrowed money and rented (Manhattan's) Town Hall and put on a concert. It virtually sold out," recalls Schickele. "We'd already been performing at Juilliard and Aspen (Music Festival) for six years, so the music had a reputation. We got really good musicians and tried to put the debut concert on April first. That's his birthday, of course."

Vanguard Records soon showed interest, and another concert, to be recorded live, was quickly scheduled at Philharmonic Hall (now Avery Fisher Hall) for December 1965. "An Evening with P.D.Q. Bach (1807-1742)?" was issued on LP the following year and was followed by nine more recordings for Vanguard, all of which remain available on CD.

Of the six discs Schickele made for Telarc, four received Grammy Awards for best comedy recording. Following the concert at Philharmonic Hall, the holiday season in New York City has almost always included a concert of P.D.Q. Bach, sometimes with a pickup orchestra or a group of singers, but just as often under the auspices of major institutions including the New York Philharmonic, which presented last year's event.

Schickele himself produced the concerts in 2004 and 2005, but they lost money and with no new offers arriving, P.D.Q. Bach will be absent from Manhattan this holiday. A concert with the Westchester Philharmonic today at Purchase College is the nearest to the city he'll be spotted.

Still, there are numerous bookings ahead throughout the winter and spring of 2008, including performances of the "P.D.Q. Bach: The Vegas Years" with the Atlanta, Houston, Minnesota and Edmonton orchestras.

Says Schickele, "I love working with the top orchestras and most of the musicians know P.D.Q. Bach, so they approach it the right way, which is to play it well."

Until six months ago, Schickele had a weekly presence on the local radio airwaves, thanks to the WAMC-FM broadcast of "Schickele Mix," an engaging, often ingenious exploration of musical terms, theories and styles, written and narrated by the composer. The award-winning hour-long show was produced in Minnesota and syndicated through Public Radio International.

"A lot of people don't realize that we stopped making that show in 1999. Funding ran out, but PRI just keep distributing it," explains Schickele, who says the program was finally pulled from syndication in June.

Among the 169 shows that premiered between 1992 and 1999, program No. 29 provides as good an example as any of Schickele's wide embrace of music. Titled "Parental," it includes pieces about parent-child relations written by classical composers Mozart, Schubert and Ives, as well as rock star John Lennon, country music's Gene Autry and the 19th-century American songwriter Henry Clay Work.

All of the musical examples were drawn from Schickele's enormous record collection. "I love finding unusual pieces by unknown composers," says Schickele. "I wouldn't buy a Beethoven Fifth, that is, unless it was played on break drums or something."

Part of the mix in Schickele's career has always been his own concert music. Yet even here, in the "serious" side of Schickele, traces of comedy are easily found.

"I'm in the fortunate position of having as many commissions as I can handle," says Schickele, who's currently proofreading the score and parts to "Lincoln at Ease," a new piece written for a February premiere by the Louisville Symphony Orchestra, and conductor Jorge Mester, a longtime friend and collaborator. The piece includes parts for soprano and narrator, with texts by the late president.

"It concentrates on Lincoln's humor. He was a great joke-teller and punster," says Schickele. "The challenge is to write a piece that doesn't sound like Copland's 'Lincoln Portrait.'"

One can understand Schickele's difficulty in writing music that does not sound like something of the past, when P.D.Q. Bach is known for creating dead-on sendups of the classics. A short list of examples includes the oratorio "The Seasonings," the piano collection "Liebeslieder Polkas," the choral work "Oedipus Tex," and the opera "Hansel & Gretel & Ted & Alice."

But the ever-expanding and historically questionable oeuvre of P.D.Q. Bach is full of evidence of a brilliant musical mind and an intimate knowledge of what makes good music. And it's only a true friend who can tell the best jokes about someone.

"A music educator I won't name told a friend of mine, 'Peter makes fun of things some of us hold sacred,'" recounts Schickele, gently shaking his head as if to shed such a notion. "It's a satire of love, not a put-down."

HILARY TANN

COMPOSER   MAY 15, 2005

Sounds like now

If globalism were an artistic category, it might be a good fit for local composer Hilary Tann and her music, at least judging by the facts. "I'm a Welsh woman living in America with influences from Japan," she says.

But when Tann speaks, it's with a calm, thoughtful centeredness, a quality that also characterizes her music. And so Tann doesn't really bring to mind globalism with zipping and pinging electronic networks, frenzied free trade zones, and all that so much as she evokes the Earth itself.

"I can't write if I don't have the image. That's the seed," Tann says, and her imagery is almost always nature. For example, her large catalog of works includes orchestra pieces with titles such as "Adirondack Light," "The Open Field" and "Through the Echoing Timber."

Tann's latest work in the genre, "From the Feather to the Mountain," was commissioned and premiered by the Empire State Youth Orchestra in March and will be given an encore performance Saturday night at the Palace Theatre in Albany, where the ESYO performs on a program of the Albany Symphony Orchestra.

"From the Feather to the Mountain" was inspired by pen-and-ink drawings by the late local artist Arnold Bittleman. Both composer and artist communicate a breadth of perspective but also an immediacy of time and place.

"I really like the piece," says Helen Cha-Pyo, ESYO's music director and conductor, who approached Tann last year with the idea of a concerto for orchestra. "She really captured the essence of what *we* wanted, but she had enough freedom to imagine what *she* wanted."

The ESYO project is one of a series of recent and upcoming events in the Capital Region for Tann, who has been a faculty member of Union College in Schenectady for more than 20 years. Also in March, Max Lifchitz premiered her piano piece "Light from the Cliffs." And in May, the Meininger Trio of Germany will perform a concert at Union College featuring Tann's "The Gardens of Anna Maria Louisa de Medici" for flute, cello and piano. That concert will mark the release of the trio's new CD featuring four Tann works.

"I can only describe both her and her music as charming, kind and peaceful, and with a soulful inner depth," says flutist Christiane Meininger, who first approached Tann through her Web site. "I simply felt that a person with such a beautiful home page, a charming picture of herself with her dog, surrounded by nature ... could only write beautiful music. This turned out to be absolutely true."

When Tann speaks, she often uses her hands. As she describes the ESYO piece, its landscapes and mountains, she rolls her hands and arms in the space on either side of her body. When she gets to the clouds and mentions Debussy, her arms are extended high and her hands are gently, slowly turning.

"That sound of a single line, the landscaping of a single line," she says as a hand circles in the air.

Simplicity of expression is a fascination for Tann. It's rooted in her Celtic heritage – she was born in a coal-mining village in South Wales – and has found fulfillment in the culture of Japan, specifically the shakuhachi, a bamboo flute, and in haiku poetry. Both have become more than mere pastimes.

Tann took up the shakuhachi in 1984, and six years later went to Japan, where she taught traditional Japanese music. "She knows more about it than most Japanese, and that's no hyperbole," says David Bullard, Tann's husband of three years who is also a longtime student of Japanese language and culture.

As for haiku, the little poems take up a relatively large space in Tann's creativity. For almost 10 years, she has been part of the Route 9 Haiku Group, a collective of four poets that meets monthly at Tai Pan restaurant on Route 9 in Halfmoon. Their leisurely meetings usually last five to six hours; each member brings a dozen or more new haiku, which are read aloud and discussed. Food and fellowship are also part of the mix.

"Simplicity is a strong value in haiku," says John Stevenson, a member of Upstate Dim Sum, who is also editor of Frogpond, the journal of the Haiku Society of America. "Hilary's clarity of expression is very marked ... and she really focuses on the way the poems sound when they're recited," he says. Stevenson also edits Upstate Dim Sum , the semiannual journal of the Route 9 Haiku Group.

"Haiku keeps me in the moment," says Tann. "With composing, one is always projecting ahead. It pulls me back to the 'a-ha!' of the day."

In her office at Union College, Tann's desk and piano are covered in scores, recordings, student assignments and administrative paperwork. That's where she does business. But Tann's composition studio, located in the "Apple Cottage" behind her home in Schylerville, Washington County, is a model of order.

On the music rack of her upright piano where she composes are a half-dozen snapshots and postcards of Welsh landscapes and coastlines. The room is decorated with a mix of traditional Japanese and early American furnishings.

The swirl of nationalistic flavors continues in the property's main building. Known as the Marshall House, it was built in 1763 and is the vicinity's only surviving building that predates the Revolutionary War. It's been in the family of Tann's husband since 1930.

"The living room was a field hospital for the British during the revolution," says Tann. "As a Brit, I come over and have this idea that I know history ... but this house predates what we know of as America, and I have a sense of belonging to this house."

As she speaks, Tann perches on the bench of a small pipe organ in the living room. Displayed on the mantel are three fist-sized cannon balls that hit the house in battle. Bloodstains from wounded soldiers are said to be hidden by the rug.

"I think of the people that came over with hope and vision. ... When prayerful people wanted to establish a new land. ... I like being here. This land. This house," she says as she jabs her finger at the space in front of her.

GEORGE TSONTAKIS

COMPOSER

CHO-LIANG LIN

JANUARY 9, 2003   VIOLINIST

Time for a homerun

It wasn't in a concert hall or a practice room where composer George Tsontakis and violinist Cho-Liang (Jimmy) Lin first met. It was on a softball field.

That was more than 20 years ago, in the pastoral setting of the Aspen Music Festival, where the two have been regulars for years. It was only after they got to know each other's skills on the diamond that they got to know each other as artists, and began considering a collaboration.

Tsontakis wrote a violin concerto for Lin, which was premiered in 1998 with the Oregon Symphony and conductor James DePreist. Friday in Troy, the concerto will be premiered in a newly revised version by the Albany Symphony Orchestra. The story of how Tsontakis' substantial piece came to be reworked provides a rare glimpse at a composer who admits to striking out with a major work, but who's willing to step up to the plate and take another swing.

In separate interviews, Tsontakis and Lin spoke of their admiration for the original piece while expressing the belief that it could be improved. "I really liked the concerto," Tsontakis said, "but it wasn't successful."

In the realm of contemporary visual art, everybody's a critic and snap decisions on a painting's merit are common place. But when it comes to new music, phrases like "the work grows on the listener in repeated hearings" are all too often used to excuse a perplexing or unsatisfactory experience in the concert hall. So just how does a composer judge a piece – is there a standard?

"Composers take reactions of audience and performers in different degrees," Tsontakis says. "I take the reaction of the performers to heart; I like Jimmy Lin and care what he thinks about it."

"Once I learned the piece," Lin says of the 1998 version of Tsontakis' concerto, "I thought that there were certain challenges he could impose on the soloists even more – to make it harder, believe it or not. I guess I'm a masochist.

"After playing it with the orchestra, I realized that the first movement was more of a symphonic work than a violin concerto. So I asked him if he ever revises it, could he put in more violin so that I would do more playing? And George felt the last movement could have a better ending."

Tsontakis was happy to oblige, although "I don't do much revision," the composer says flatly. "I may take a few measures where orchestration was off-balance and re-orchestrate. But this is a concerto, and there's always something about a concerto that could be revised or tweaked or rewritten."

Concertos have become something of a specialty of Tsontakis. In addition to the work for Lin, he wrote a percussion concerto for Evelyn Glennie which was premiered by the National Symphony Orchestra, and a horn concerto for soloist David Jolley.

A new violin concerto is currently in the works, as is a piano concerto for Stephen Hough with a troika of orchestras including the Dallas Symphony.

Tsontakis was remarkably open about the hard work of composing on commission: "There's a deadline and the orchestra librarian is calling you for the parts and you've just got to cap the thing and get it done."

In the case of the violin concerto, the cap came a bit too soon.

"It's like taking a half a breath," says the composer. "I didn't take a full complete breath, and that's what I had to do."

The revived piece needed a willing conductor with an orchestra at the ready. It was Lin who suggested the work to the ASO's David Alan Miller, but the local connection of all the participants - Tsontakis lives in Shokan, Ulster County, and Lin has a new weekend place in Rhinebeck – cinched the deal. ("David's great," says Tsontakis. "Most conductors don't want your input at all – very strange.") It was the ASO's decision to call the performance the "world premiere of the revised version."

"Even though much of the music is the same, to me it's a major difference," said Tsontakis. "And it's the difference between success for me and failure. And I'm hoping it's successful."

"There's a lot more for the violin to do now," Lin says. "I'm very happy."

JOHN WILLIAMS

COMPOSER/CONDUCTOR   AUGUST 15, 2003

Not dead yet

Before John Williams ever writes a note of music for a Steven Spielberg film, he sits down alone in a private screening room to see the nearly completed movie. Such was the case with the Holocaust drama "Schindler's List." After watching the film through, Williams took a brief walk outdoors to collect himself before returning to talk with Spielberg.

His first comments to the director – with whom he'd already made such classics as "Jaws," "E.T." and the three "Indiana Jones" films – was, "Oh, Steven, that's such an amazing film. You really need a better composer than me to write the score."

"I know," replied Spielberg. "But they're all dead."

As Williams' fondness for the story reveals, he's the first to admit that he's not in the ranks of Beethoven and Mahler. "My professional life is Hollywood," he said in a recent phone conversation from his summer home in the Berkshires. "(My music) may not be at the level of Brahms, but it was never intended to be."

Whatever his intentions, Williams' resume of more than 100 film scores has made him today's most well known and widely heard living composer. And he couldn't have gotten there without a thorough grounding in classical music – a world in which he is increasingly active as a composer of concert works. This fall, Williams' compositions will be premiered by the Chicago Symphony Orchestra and the Los Angeles Philharmonic. And for his second appearance at Tanglewood this summer, Williams will conduct the Boston Symphony Orchestra with guest soloist Yo-Yo Ma in a program that includes his Elegy for Cello and Orchestra, which is based on themes from his score to the 1997 film "Seven Years in Tibet."

"I never thought of myself as a concert composer," says Williams, 71. "I've always written film music, and done concert pieces as a kind of respite from my other work."

It's an indication of the huge quantity of film music that Williams writes that his so-called part-time work as a concert composer has resulted in nine concertos, two symphonies and a slew of what he calls occasional pieces – fanfares, overtures and suites.

An example of the broad appeal of Williams' music is the genesis of his recently completed Horn Concerto. The Chicago Symphony Orchestra, seeking to honor its longtime first horn player, Dale Clevenger, decided to commission a piece for him. Clevenger picked Williams as the composer, though the two had never previously worked together.

"Film scores are a lot easier (to write) than 'absolute' music," says Williams. "Say the first scene has to be three minutes long. The first minute is soft because of dialogue, the second fast and loud and an abrupt change at two minutes, thirty seconds to fit some editorial piece of architecture. You can almost graph out the piece.

" ... Sit down to write a concerto, the given is it is an empty page."

"He lives in both worlds," says classical composer John Corigliano of Williams' balance between the realms of concert and film, "and that's getting to be more and more the case."

Corigliano also straddles both worlds: He wrote the scores to "Altered States" (1980) and won an Academy Award for 1998's "The Red Violin." As another example, Corigliano points to Elliot Goldenthal, who won the Academy Award for "Frida."

Decades ago, composers such as Erich Wolfgang Korngold (whose scores include "The Adventures of Robin Hood") would "have to leave the concert world ... and only write a piece every five years or so," says Corigliano. "Today, the barriers are breaking down – at least I hope so."

As some composers' careers become more broad, Williams points to a similar cross-pollination in art forms.

"Forty years ago, the only inspiration we had for incidental music for Hollywood was the art music of Europe from the 19th century," Williams says. "And it's reversed now when you have an art music composer like John Adams, who will seek inspiration not from the music of Europe, but the media racket of his own country. ... It's an aesthetic that's done a 180."

Adams, a Pulitzer-Prize winner, is only the most prominent member of a school of composers – including John Zorn, Julia Wolfe and Phil Kline – who draw musical and thematic inspiration from the drone of pop culture.

"Whether we like it or not, the future of art music is going to be more and more intimately connected to the future of media and film music," he says. "One of the biggest reasons is this visual addiction that all our children are growing up with."

"Most film music is not very good," says Williams. "Most concert music is not very good either. ... The best usually comes to the fore as a sort of natural-selection process."

Despite his well-honed dramatic sense, the composer has never turned his hand to opera or musicals. But that may soon change: He's currently in discussion with the Los Angeles Opera for what could ultimately be his first musical work for the stage.

"We've been talking about it – myself, (General Director) Placido Domingo and the management of the company," says Williams. "I'm warm to it if we can find the right notion, the right text and all the rest of it." (Williams declines to reveal any of the story ideas under discussion because of pending negotiations over rights.)

"I've written so much incidental and dramatic accompanimental music," says Williams, "that to a lot of people, (opera) seems to them a natural and an easy step for me. I'm not sure... It could be great fun, if the subject and the writing is sympathetic to what I can do."

In late October, the ears and eyes of the music world will settle on the Walt Disney Concert Hall, the Frank Gehry-designed new home of the Los Angeles Philharmonic.

Inspired by the building and his long association with the orchestra, Williams has created a new piece, "Soundings," which employs concepts and techniques borrowed from both avant-garde art and film editing.

"My idea was to have the audience sit in the theater and have the feeling that the building was singing to them," Williams says.

In homage to Gehry's signature curving steel structures, which he calls "sails," Williams commissioned an artisan to create curved steel plates which were suspended and bowed like a musical instrument.

"They make the most beautiful sound," says Williams.

The sounds were recorded and fed into a computer which will play them back through loudspeakers located around Disney Hall. But unlike a static tape part, that simply rolls while the orchestra plays, the computer also functions as a sort of digital duet partner, responding to notes played by the orchestra with ever-changing tones.

"It's a piece in five movements where the hall awakens, the hall glistens, the hall rejoices," says Williams. "How well it will come off, I don't know. We'll do our best."

NUTCRACKER AUDITIONS

SEPTEMBER 28, 2003

Forecasting snow (flakes)

Retailers aren't the only ones with Christmas already on their minds these days. Ballet companies are now focused on their annual productions of "The Nutcracker," some of which open in just two months.

"The Nutcracker," the story of a magical evening when a little girl is transported into a fantasy world of dancing snowflakes and sugarplum fairies, is more than just a holiday favorite – it's the Super Bowl of dance.

For area companies, the classic ballet set to Tchaikovsky's famous score is the most important and elaborate production of any season and the one piece that consistently draws nondance audiences. For aspiring dancers, it can be the launching pad to a career. And for young children, it is a doorway into great beauty and enchantment.

The long road to opening night begins with auditions, a grueling process that took place two weekends ago for each of the Capital Region's four ballet companies: Northeast Ballet, Malta Ballet, Capital Ballet and Albany Berkshire Ballet. Hundreds of nervous children, focused young dancers and anxious parents turned out in hopes of being part of the magic of "The Nutcracker."

"Auditions are very stressful for everyone involved," says Darlene Myers, artistic director of Northeast Ballet, which held its auditions on the stage of Proctor's Theatre in Schenectady. Its production will play in early December. "It is one of the most difficult weekends of my entire year."

"It's adorable and wild," says Madeline Cantarella Culpo, artistic director of Albany Berkshire Ballet.

In separate interviews, directors from each company expressed a common desire to make casting decisions that balance artistic considerations with concerns for the feelings of those who audition.

"We don't cut that many children," says Ginger Morris, Malta Ballet's artistic director. "We don't want to break their little hearts."

Each company's "Nutcracker" has slightly different children's parts, including gingerbreads, reindeer, angels, soldiers, dolls, clowns and mice. But in all cases, logistics place limits on the size of casts: There are only so many roles, costumes and performances.

The common practice of double- or even triple-casting allows for separate groups of children to play the same roles at different performances. It boosts participation, but complicates rehearsals.

More than 600 children are involved in the Albany Berkshire Ballet's annual "Nutcracker," which is performed in New York, Massachusetts, Vermont and New Hampshire, from late November through mid-December. At each of 12 venues, approximately 60 children are used.

"You get used to it," says Culpo. "It becomes routine."

It's Saturday morning at Proctor's Theatre and the large atrium is alive with children's voices. Little girls in tights and leotards cluster together or cling to their mothers. As the day progresses, older dancers arrive and the parents are fewer.

By the end of the weekend (a second audition call is held the next day in Saratoga Springs) Myers will have cast the Northeast Ballet's 16th annual "Nutcracker" at Proctor's. "I've learned that what's now is not what will be on stage in December," she says. Injuries, scheduling conflicts and other unexpected events will intervene.

Every hour, dancers move from the back of the darkened auditorium, down the long aisles and onto the large stage. First come the 5- and 6-year-olds at noon, followed by 6- to 12-year-olds, and then adults. Finally, at 3 p.m., are the trained dancers, the majority of whom are young women in pointe shoes.

Each prospective cast member is assigned a number that's pinned to his or her chest. On stage, they are addressed by their number: "Let me see more turnout, No. 12." Near the end of the day, a little boy arrives late with his mother and is assigned the day's final number: 131.

"That's a lot of legs and feet to look at," says Myers. "I could go blind."

After introducing herself to each group, she steps back to watch, flips through the applications and occasional resume, and mutters about the difficulty of the decisions ahead. Meanwhile, the dancers are led in movement by one or more of Myers' four energetic assistants, Jessica Miranda, Melissa Merrill, Marcus Rogers and William Spillane.

The littlest ones are asked to stand in first position – "toesies out" – bend from the knees and rise back up on the beat (*demi-plies*). Following direction and wearing a smile count.

"I look for poise, confidence, musicality, brains and beauty," says Myers.

Of the 20 hopefuls, 16 are chosen as gingerbread people. Myers is soft-spoken but direct to those who are dismissed.

"You did really good but we just don't have enough costumes," she says. "We may be calling you, but for now I'm going to say 'no.' I want you to go back to your dance schools, wherever they may be, and work harder."

A similar process happens with the 6- to 12-year-olds, but the dance steps are more complex, and the cut is harder. When tears come from a few, their mothers are waiting just outside the stage door.

"Tears just break my heart," says Myers later. "But this profession is very tough, and this is the real thing."

Parental involvement is an essential element to any "Nutcracker." Throughout the year, parents pay for dance classes and chauffeur the kids. On the morning of auditions, moms and dads – and it's usually moms – complete the application forms for their children and pay the audition fee, usually $10.

"The mothers and grandmothers get excited," says Jane McGrath, executive director of Capital Ballet. "The phone calls start in August."

Parents are banished from watching the actual auditions. They generally can attend rehearsals only if they are helping with the production. But volunteer opportunities are plentiful. For the smaller companies, help is needed backstage, in the box office and at intermission.

While anxiety may run higher in some parents than in their children, most parents stay out of the process. Myers is the only director who told of once being offered a bribe. Parents promised cash if she would cast their daughter in the lead role of Clara. "I said 'I'm sorry I'm not for sale,'" says Myers, who gave the child a role but not the lead. "That was seven or eight years ago, and I'm still getting over it!"

At Proctor's, the tension reaches its peak during the final auditions of the day. Determined dancers who have been studying for years give their all in hopes of landing parts in the variations, sometimes called the international or character dances.

Advanced moves are called out in French, the language of ballet: *fouette* and *pique* turns for girls, *tour en l'air* and *tour a la seconde* for boys.

"We're much more interested in how you come across, not if you mess up," shouts one of Myers' assistants. "Let's see where your head takes you with this."

Myers watches for technique, stamina and body types.

"Anatomy is destiny," she says quietly, "at least in this art form." As an example, she pointed with awe to a slim, long-limbed 11-year-old girl who she says has the classic look of a New York City Ballet dancer.

For a solid hour the stage is filled with movement, sweat and exertion. Then it is nearly dead-still as Myers makes her decisions. At the perimeter of the stage, dancers stand in a large semicircle and wait expectantly.

Myers groups dancers together for each variation to see how they complement one another in height and general look. Earlier in the day she had gently nudged the dancers into lines. Now, she snaps her fingers at them and points to where they are to stand. It's not until 5:30 p.m. that the final decisions are made.

The next day at Saratoga, from another 20 hopefuls that show up, a third cast of eight gingerbreads is taken. Also triple-cast was the role of Clara, to be played by Alena Bagoly, 10, Rosaire Benaquista, 9, and Jessica Lape, 11.

Through the course of the long audition weekend, Myers works like an artist, selecting the materials for a new piece that's to be made on the canvas of the historic Proctor's stage. At the rehearsals, which begin immediately, she becomes a sculptor, shaping and honing her dancers into this year's "Nutcracker." Christmas is just around the corner.

TYLER PECK

BALLET DANCER   JULY 23, 2005

Teen on a working vacation

Fast food, shoe shopping and hanging out by the water. Sounds like a reasonable summer to-do list for a 16-year-old girl, especially one who's got three weeks to spend in Saratoga Springs.

But Tyler Peck, the youngest member of the New York City Ballet (the average age for a dancer is 27), had to wedge these activities into an already packed schedule of dance rehearsals and performances.

Peck had barely arrived in town when she walked with other dancers in the Fourth of July Parade. There, the sights of downtown and the friendly smiles of pedestrians made a good first impression.

"I love it, it's so pretty. It reminds me of home," says Peck.

Despite having lived in New York City for almost two years now – for a year as a student at the School of American Ballet, then since March in the City Ballet corps – Peck still refers to home as Bakersfield in Southern California. That's where she started dance lessons at age 3 in a studio owned by her mom. Her first exposure to New York City was at age 11 when she spent a year performing in the Broadway revival of "The Music Man."

Although Saratoga is no longer the sleepy country town it was when City Ballet arrived 40 years ago for the opening of the Saratoga Performing Arts Center, it can still feel like a relief from the hectic pace of Manhattan life.

"Everybody looks at Saratoga as a vacation – well, until you have to dance," she says.

Tuesdays through Saturdays are workdays for City Ballet dancers. They report for class at 10:30 a.m. at SPAC; rehearsals fill most afternoons. Plus, there are five evening performances and two matinees every week.

Peck's first excursions beyond SPAC and her hotel were for quick bites at Subway and Wendy's. Since then, she has extended her culinary explorations to become a fan of turkey sandwiches at Putnam Market and a "really good salmon dinner" at Lillian's.

But Peck prepares most of her own meals in her hotel room, which she shares with dancer Rachel Piskin. They rely on light, healthful fare like fruit, sliced meats and English muffins. Gatorade is always on hand for home and for class, especially in the girls' favorite flavor, Cool Blue.

In addition to offering a kitchenette in the room and a nice pool for lounging, the hotel is near SPAC, where they spend most of their time.

Another bonus: "They make your bed," says Peck.

Packing for three weeks away from home was a challenge. Peck managed to take along enough clothes, in four bags, to avoid doing laundry. And though the public sees her mostly in pointe shoes, she also lugged about a dozen pairs of street shoes including four pairs made by Converse, culled from a total collection of about 40 pairs.

Shoes may be a typical young-female obsession, but for Peck, it's fed by having a professional dancer's salary. (Pay for City Ballet dancers starts at $956 a week)

"Getting paid? It's nice," says Peck. "You don't feel as bad as when you spend Mom's money."

Although her tight time schedule has pushed major shopping stints to a future season in Saratoga, Peck did find time for another favorite activity – bowling.

Twice after performances, which sometimes go as late as 11 p.m., Peck was part of a group of dancers who hit the Hi-Roc Lanes. "I broke 100 twice! It's the best I ever did," boasts Peck of her first night out.

And on one of the Mondays, Peck and about 20 other dancers, mostly from the corps, spent a day at Lake George.

"We all met at Dunkin' Donuts and carpooled up," Peck explains, adding that they also rented a motorboat. Although she passed on tubing because she was afraid of injury, Peck had a great time hanging out by the water for six hours.

A bit of romance even blossomed that afternoon between her and a young male dancer. More than a week after the fact, the day still brings a big grin to Peck's face, although she's not sharing details.

While getting to know Saratoga Springs, Peck has made some other friends as well.

"It's just like I knew everyone (in the company)," says Peck, "But you get to know everyone better because you're with them 24/7."

CELEBRATING 40 YEARS OF NEW YORK CITY BALLET

A deeply rooted dance community

It was early July 1965, just a few nights before the grand opening of the new Saratoga Performing Arts Center. New York City Ballet dancer Shaun O'Brien and his companion, Broadway actor Cris Alexander, were in a taxi on their way to a late supper at Hattie's Chicken Shack. The crusty cabdriver asked the two men what they were doing in town. O'Brien explained that he was with New York City Ballet, which was about to open the theater. The cabbie harrumphed.

"Saratoga's a horse town," he said. "Always has been and always will be."

As it turned out, the cabbie was half right. As SPAC celebrates its 40th season, Saratoga Springs still has plenty of horses. But for a few weeks every summer, it hosts another kind of thoroughbred – the New York City Ballet dancer.

As the annual influx of dancers has evolved from an oddity to a beloved fixture, the region has been transformed. Community leaders and figures from the dance world agree that NYCB's summer residencies have been an engine for the community's economic growth and quality of life, and a catalyst for a higher level of artistic achievement and appreciation throughout the region.

"If you look at Saratoga prior to the opening of SPAC, it was a one-horse town," says Joseph W. Dalton Jr., president of the Saratoga County Chamber of Commerce (and no relation to this writer). "It was a town that had harness racing most of the year and thoroughbred racing for a season. When SPAC opened up, it extended the season for at least two months, but it also extended Saratoga as a cultural capital for New York state."

Since SPAC's beginnings, the Philadelphia Orchestra has been an equal component of the annual seasons. But many major orchestras also have summer residencies away from their urban base. Because no other

American dance company compares in size to City Ballet – its annual budget is $45 million, about $10 million more than that of its closest competitor, American Ballet Theatre – it could be argued that there is no other regional center for dance like SPAC.

Point to almost any local dance studio or school, ballet or otherwise, and you're apt to find signs of the New York City Ballet's presence.

There are Saratoga's major summer ballet training programs, all of which have current or former City Ballet dancers on their faculties: the Briansky Saratoga Ballet Center, the ballet program of the New York State Summer School of the Arts and Ballet Regent. Then there are operations like Creative Dance Studio of Johnstown and eba Inc. in Albany, where most summer programs revolve around pilgrimages to SPAC.

Even a fitness studio, Total Body Trifecta in Saratoga, has been drawn into the City Ballet orbit. Trifecta's owner, Mary Anne Fantauzzi, teaches the "New York City Ballet Workout." Every July, she also recruits company dancers to lead workouts and classes in popular dance.

An entrepreneurial drive and a fondness for the Capital Region, born of the annual summer residencies, led two former City Ballet dancers to start ballet schools locally.

When Michael Steele began offering classes at Ballet Regent in 1979, nine years after retiring as a City Ballet principal, he found a base of students eager for what he had to offer.

"A whole slew of adults who all just adored the New York City Ballet wanted to know what makes that fascinating thing tick, so they came and took a class and brought their kids," says Steele.

In 1990, after his own career with NYCB came to a close, David Otto ceded Saratoga to Steele and went to Albany to start his school, the Albany Dance Academy.

"I came to Saratoga when I was 13, in 1973, and I pushed the bed for 'The Nutcracker,'" recalls Otto.

He views City Ballet's presence as a unique complement to his teaching. "I tell people all the time to go to the ballet. You need to see the real thing so you know where you're headed," Otto says.

Another school closely aligned with New York City Ballet is Myers Dance Studio of Schenectady. Its founder, Darlene Myers, was just 16 when she was accepted into the first summer classes of the School of American Ballet in Saratoga in 1967. (The program eventually became part of the New York State Summer School of the Arts.) Myers took classes in the Canfield Casino alongside future star Gelsey Kirkland.

"It was the first year, and no one knew what was going to happen. When Mr. Balanchine walked in with Suzanne Farrell on his arm, I knew it was going to be great," recalls Myers, who also leads Northeast Ballet, the resident company at Proctor's Theatre since 1991.

Other dance-related enterprises have also taken root in the Capital Region in the four decades since City Ballet's arrival. The National Museum of Dance and Hall of Fame, located adjacent to SPAC, was founded in 1986. Last summer, it staged exhibits on Balanchine that complemented the City Ballet's celebrations of the master's centennial.

Just a short walk off Broadway is the 15-year-old shop Saratoga Dance. Its owner is yet another NYCB alum, Leslie Roy. Her shop is the home of Bunheads, an internationally known line of dance accessories. (The line is named after the classic ballerina hairstyle.)

Dance Alliance, a service and funding organization founded in 1978, represents all forms of dance in the region. Organizations like it are increasingly rare, according to John Munger, director of research and information for Dance/USA of Washington, D.C.

"Dance service organizations have had a hard time of late, and several in major communities have gone down Chicago, Philadelphia and Minneapolis-St. Paul, to name three," says Munger. "I'm struck by the existence of one going back (more than) 20 years."

"I literally grew up with New York City Ballet," says Suzanne Delman of Lake George.

Delman was raised in Manhattan by a balletomane mom. Twelve years ago, she acquiesced to her husband's plans to relocate his dental practice from New York City to Chestertown only because every summer she could get her ballet fix at SPAC. When the NYCB's presence was threatened last year, Delman took to the barricades and joined the now-extinct group Save the Ballet.

"Never mess with ballet lovers," says Delman. "You just don't go there. They're passionate."

Norton Owen, the chairman of the dance panel for the New York State Council on the Arts, believes that a passion for dance or any art form grows in direct relation to one's experiences of great art.

"If people are exposed to art on the highest order, and I certainly classify NYCB in that realm, they can't help but have that be a force that becomes a part of their lives," says Norton, who works as director of preservation at Jacob's Pillow in Beckett, Mass.

"You carry that kind of consciousness around with you when you go to a museum or see a different dance performance or go to a concert," continues Owen. "It's an intangible thing that some of us have invested our whole lives in."

For further evidence of the Capital Region's investment in dance, there's the current situation of Shaun O'Brien. He's still in Saratoga and still taking taxis. O'Brien, 79, and Alexander, 85, bought a home just off Broadway in 1973 and have lived there full time since 1991, the year O'Brien retired.

O'Brien himself remarks at the difference in attitudes: "There's been an interest in ballet to the point where I'll get in a cab and (the driver) says, 'How's it going at the ballet?'"

PETER MARTINS

CHOREOGRAPHER/IMPRESARIO

Ballet for everyone

The ballet scene in America was forever changed after the fall of the Berlin Wall, according to Peter Martins, New York City Ballet's director. Ballet's heyday of popularity during the 1970s – when City Ballet's Saratoga Performing Arts Center shows were packed – was driven by news stories about figures such as Mikhail Baryshnikov defecting from behind the Iron Curtain.

"Once you didn't have to defect ... it became less interesting. Every ballet company in American has two or three Russians now," Martins said, speaking backstage at SPAC.

For example, tonight his troupe will dance an all-Russian program. Martins believes that at one time it would have caused a sensation because it includes "Russian Seasons," by Alexei Ratmansky, the 38-year-old director of the famed Bolshoi Ballet. "Now he just gets on a plane," Martins said.

"After the high of the Baryshnikov era ... there were all the naysayers (declaring) that ballet's finished," said Martins. The deaths of City Ballet's George Balanchine and Jerome Robbins, as well as of British choreographers Kenneth MacMillan and Frederick Ashton, contributed to the attitude of despair.

"But I knew it wasn't going to be over. (Because) there were still those of us who were able to make a difference."

Martins has been thinking a lot about programming lately, especially at SPAC, where he consults on the matter with Marcia White, SPAC president and executive director.

Audiences heading to see City Ballet for the first time this summer will notice that each program has a title thematically linking the scheduled ballets. The titles, such as "European Masters," "Americana" and "Now & Then," were written by Martins at the request of White.

Martins said he has a good relationship with White, who was appointed to her position two years ago after the long but troubled reign of Herb Chesbrough came to an abrupt end. "She does her thing, I do my thing," said Martins. "We talk periodically how to address this audience issue."

"I don't do things singly; I check with Marcia. It's a partnership," he said regarding programming. "I sweated blood coming up with these programs. Everything has been carefully considered to address what I think a public like the Capital Region would want to watch."

Martins strives each year for a balance of classic works by Balanchine and Robbins, plus some of his own ballets and other new works. There's also the need for full-length pieces, like "Swan Lake," which opened this year's season, and some pieces that include children, like tonight's "Firebird" and Wednesday's "Songs of the Auvergne."

For Saturday evening's gala, Martins decided to push the envelope with a lineup of four works from the Diamond Project, the company's initiative for the creation of new ballets.

"I thought, let's not be complacent and do the same old thing," he said, punching the air with a fist. "Normally I would schedule (Balanchine's) 'Vienna Waltzes' as the closing of a gala, but you get that on Friday night. ... If you come on Saturday night you're going to get blown away by where ballet is at this particular moment."

Among the pieces will be "Slice to Sharp" by Finnish choreographer Jorma Elo, who is known for a high-energy kinetic style of dance. Twelve curtain calls were given for its premiere last month at the New York State Theatre at Lincoln Center. "It blew the roof off. It was hugely successful," said Martins.

Audience response to ballets such as this lead Martins to believe a new resurgence in popularity for dance is ahead. "I think we're on an upswing. ... I'm seeing it and feeling it already. It hasn't manifested itself to the general public, but I think it will be there," he said.

Ultimately, ballet is for everyone, and Martins wants the message spread throughout the Capital Region. "As a lay person, if you want to encounter the arts, go to the ballet because you get a double dose," he said. "You get a great visual gratification and a great dose of wonderful music."

DANCES OF
UNIVERSAL PEACE

Stepping into prayer

Imagine a hymnal that includes Tibetan meditations, Hindu chants, the Jewish Kaddish and Christian songs to Jesus and Mary.

If the Dances of Universal Peace, a nearly 40-year-old practice of prayerful movement and song, had a standardized text, that's something of what it would contain. But instead, participants at "dance meetings" are taught to sing from memory short sacred phrases borrowed from or inspired by various traditions. And rather than being confined to church pews, they move about in circular patterns using simple steps akin to folk dancing.

"Some people call them walking meditations," says Farid Gruber, "even though some (dances) are joyful."

For the past six years, Gruber has led a monthly dance gathering at the First Unitarian Universalist Church in Albany. This month, the group is hosting a weekend conference at the National Museum of Dance & Hall of Fame in Saratoga Springs that will explore the life and work of Ruth St. Denis, the late modern dance pioneer. Affectionately known to her students and spiritual descendants as Miss Ruth, she is regarded as the godmother of the Dances of Universal Peace.

"'Spiritual' is a hard thing to put into words, but it's a genuine heart-felt experience," says Regina Dew of Albany, who for the past three years has been a regular participant in the Dances of Universal Peace. "It's a childlike glow that people get ... and you don't have to push hard for it."

A mix of Hindu, Jewish and Christian elements always has been at the heart of the Dances of Universal Peace, but they were born of Sufism. A mystical branch of Islam, Sufism is known for its distinctive practice of spinning male dancers known as whirling dervishes.

In the late 1960s, Samuel L. Lewis (1896-1971), an American Sufi master, created a body of some 50 participatory dances. They were the result of his in-depth study of world religions and his contact with Ruth St. Denis.

"Lewis' objective was to promote peace through the arts," says Gruber. "He said to Miss Ruth, 'I'm gonna solve the world's problems by teaching the children how to walk.'"

Originally known as Sufi Dances, they were re-christened in the 1970s with the more inclusive name, and an international organization was established to codify and teach them.

In the ensuing years, hundreds of new dances have been created by others, and the practice has spread around the globe. All the while, the dances' multicultural embrace has become wider.

"There's always a real diversity," says Dew of a typical evening of dance. "We'll do an American Indian dance, followed by something Russian, followed by something Mexican."

While there may be no hymnal as such, the music and the steps to many of the dances have been transcribed and are published. There is also a certification and mentorship program for dance leaders. Gruber and the other leaders of the Albany dance group, Frank A. Lombardo and Virginia Miller, all have received training.

"The Dances of Universal Peace are not intended to copy religions but to invoke their spirit and their intent," says Gruber. "The sacred phrases of some traditions are out there in the air already."

"I walked out of the dance and thought when can I do this again? Sign me up!" says Lombardo of his first dance gathering in Saratoga Springs more than 10 years ago. He now regularly plays guitar accompaniment for the monthly dances in Albany, and he also conceived and organized next weekend's conference.

"I like them as an alternative to what our culture seems to be saying, which is sit at home and watch the messages being transmitted to you," says Lombardo. "It's a challenge to come face to face with someone else ... and look at them as the reflection of the world around us."

Lombardo's sense of discovery is common among first-time participants.

"I was at this hippie gathering called the Rainbow Gathering and went to check it out," says Gruber of his first taste of the dances in 1984. "It was a eureka experience. It was, 'Throw away the drugs, here's a way to get high without chemicals.'"

Raised Jewish, Gruber considered himself an agnostic until the Dances of Universal Peace put him on a spiritual path. He is now a practicing Sufi and is affiliated with the Abode of the Message, a residential Sufi community in New Lebanon. Such a complete conversion may be exceptional, but the dances have proved beneficial on many levels.

"It would be particularly helpful for someone who has lost touch with their body," says the Rev. Sam Trumbore, minister at the First Unitarian Universalist Society. "There are other types of spiritual movement such as tai chi and yoga, but they don't have the same sense of community. Anybody who's depressed will get an easy-going uplifting connection."

JIM DE SEVE

Rushes for rights & rites

His husband.

Her wife.

The coupling of these words may cause your tongue to stumble, but for many people in committed gay or lesbian relationships, the terms are longed-for alternatives to euphemisms like partner, companion or lover.

Yet there's far more at stake in the cause of same-sex marriage than just better terminology. Filmmaker and Troy native Jim de Seve, whose documentary "Tying the Knot" opens today at the Spectrum 8 Theatres in Albany, named his 4-year-old production company 1,049 Films because that's the number of federal rights and privileges afforded to married couples.

"That number's now risen to 1,138," said de Seve, who will attend tonight's screenings. "There's Social Security benefits, hospital visitation rights, fishing licenses just a huge number of things. And because of the Defense of Marriage Act, gay couples get zero."

Between 2001, when De Seve began work on "Tying the Knot," and the film's debut at last year's Tribeca Film Festival, same-sex marriage went from the margins of public debate to become a fierce legal battle, a central issue in the most recent presidential election and an international cause. Since filming began, gay marriages have been sanctioned in Amsterdam, Canada and Massachusetts, while a countervailing movement has added "traditional" marriage definitions to several state constitutions.

De Seve and his collaborators "really just walked into this issue," the director said. "We were chasing footage on a couple of different levels. We wanted to include personal stories, but also have bits that would explain the history of marriage. We'd go on these 'marriage movements' where people go to city hall (for a marriage license) and get turned down. There are funny moments, because the clerks can't make heads or tails of a couple of women coming in together."

Like a Michael Moore for lavender audiences, de Seve uses both original and archival footage as well as humor to make his points. "Tying the Knot" makes the case that the precepts for marriage have changed dramatically over the centuries, and mixes in potent human drama.

"We tell the story of Sam, a rancher in Oklahoma, who was with his husband for 25 years," said de Seve. "When he died, a will said Sam should inherit everything – a huge farm, a barn and a house that they had built together." But relatives of the deceased man prevailed in court to deny Sam any inheritance.

Then there's the story of Lois and Mickie, a couple who were both police officers in Tampa, Fla. After they had been together for 10 years, Lois was killed during a bank robbery, the first woman ever killed in the line of duty in Tampa. "It was almost a state funeral," de Seve said. "Mickie sat in front, was handed a flag by the police chief, and was treated like a survivor in every way except the pension."

De Seve believes both couples had marriages based more on love than on laws. "I came to understand and believe that the real marriage happens in peoples' hearts, and if two people are entering into what they term a marriage, they are in fact married," he said. "In terms of having your marriage recognized by the state, that's the next level."

"Tying the Knot" played at more than 60 festivals before going into general release. When it screened at the Toronto International Film Festival last September, de Seve and Kian Tjong, his co-producer and partner of five years, took the occasion to tie their own knot. Tjong is Indonesian; the couple is acutely aware that if they were straight, Tjong could become a U.S. citizen.

"We're feeling it right now," said de Seve, referring to the lack of those 1,138 advantages to marriage. Tjong's father in Indonesia is seriously ill; even though he is in the United States legally, if he were to visit Indonesia he might not be able to re-enter America.

"Kian hasn't seen his father for seven years it's just really inhuman," said de Seve. "We pay the same taxes as everybody else."

Tjong helped raise the $250,000 budget for "Tying the Knot." The funds were cobbled together from a variety of investors and donors, including celebrities such as Liam Neeson and Yoko Ono. Tjong "went around and hand-delivered a small chrysanthemum with a fund-raising packet," said de Seve. "Yoko sent us a check for $5,000 with a picture. She signed it, 'Celebrate life. Love, Yoko.'"

Earlier this week, de Seve and Tjong sold their home in the Crown Heights section of Brooklyn in anticipation of a move to Troy, where they've already purchased two fixer-upper houses off Hoosick Street. "I love that I'm coming home," said de Seve. (Co-producer Stephen Pelletier and story consultant Amy Halloran are two other "Knot" participants with roots in the Capital Region.)

His mother, Geraldine de Seve, is looking forward to her son's return to the Capital Region and bringing along "his husband." The phrase seems to flow easily for her.

"I've been practicing for a long time," said Geraldine de Seve. "My daughter has a husband, and my son has a husband."

ISMAIL MERCHANT & JAMES IVORY

Collaborators across decades, continents

In the movie world, the name Merchant Ivory has for decades served as a dependable trademark for sumptuously photographed and dramatically intimate films like "A Room with a View," "Howard's End" and "The Remains of the Day." But Merchant and Ivory are also, of course, the names of two men: Ismail Merchant, who died in May, 2005 at age 68, and James Ivory, 80. Their collaboration in life and in work spanned 44 years and produced more than 30 films. When they weren't shooting films in exotic locations, they could be found at their Manhattan apartment or their restored farmhouse in Claverack, Columbia County. Following are edited transcripts of separate conversations with the filmmakers.

May, 2003

Merchant spoke from New York City about his involvement in promoting Bollywood – the catch-all phrase for the colorful and prolific Indian film industry that had its first flowering in his hometown of Bombay. "Bollywood Comes to the Hudson: A Half-Century of Indian Film" was a festival hosted by Merchant and presented by the Merchant Ivory Foundation and Time & Space Limited, an arts space in Hudson. It featured the acclaimed "Apu Trilogy" by legendary Indian director Satyajit Ray along with three Bollywood musicals, a photo exhibition and a discussion and reception. The following month, he introduced four evenings of Bollywood films on the cable network Turner Classic Movies.

Q. What exactly is Bollywood, and why has it begun to enter the American consciousness?

Merchant: The term Bollywood was brought into effect by the wonderful critic Derek Malcolm, who used to write for the Guardian.

After coming to the festivals in India for many years, he invented this thing called Bollywood. "Bolly" is Bombay, of course, and "-wood" is Hollywood.

Actually, people don't like to be called this, because India is a very rich country and there are about 850 films made a year and they're not all Bollywood films. Bollywood is maybe about 200 or 250 films, but the rest are in regional languages, because India has 18 languages.

Q. What makes Bollywood films unique?

Merchant: Bombay films are famous for musical numbers. Songs and dances are the preoccupation of these films. We have a very strong and rich culture of dance which has played a very important role in our lives; MTV started to see these wonderfully choreographed numbers in Bollywood films and they started copying Bollywood. Then Indian films and musicals started to improvise on MTV, hip-hop and rap. Now people like Madonna are looking at Bombay and incorporating it into their song and dance. Baz Luhrmann's film "Moulin Rouge" has taken everything from Indian musicals. The way the cuts are done and the way the dancers are choreographed are typical of Bollywood.

Q. Your Bollywood film festivals in Hudson and on TCM – are they all musicals?

Merchant: The one on TCM is a whole range of films made by different directors over the last 60 years. (The festival in Hudson) is focused on Satyajit Ray, the great director who won the Oscar for Lifetime Achievement in 1992 and died right after that. We were the ones who promoted the idea of him getting the Oscar, and we restored nine of his films with the help of the Academy.

His "Apu Trilogy" is one of the greatest movies ever made in the world. It's a real human drama that speaks the language of human emotions in the most clear terms – family, children, love of your roots, village life. All those are there.

Q. The term Bollywood is really coming to represent all of Indian film. Are you OK with that?

Merchant: Absolutely. It's like American hamburgers and McDonald's: Anywhere you go, you find McDonald's – and that is associated with America. And if Bollywood is to be associated with all of Indian culture, fine.

Q. How does it feel becoming the face of Bollywood for America?

Merchant: I'm happy to be a face for all of India. But if they want to just focus it on Bollywood, that's fine with me. India is a large country. We have over 1 billion people, and film is the basic entertainment we have. Not so much TV or anything else, but cinema. A person would give up his food to go to a film. That's why the movie stars are worshipped like gods and goddesses.

Q. How long have you lived in Columbia County?

Mechant: For 27 years. We restored this beautiful Federal house that was built in 1800, and we have the (Merchant Ivory) Foundation there, in the oldest mill in the country, the Red Mill, on Route 23. We have an exhibition there of photographs from Bollywood taken by this wonderful photographer, Jonathan Torgovnik. The exhibition is in the Mill adjacent to the house and will run for a whole month.

Q. How did you start working with Time & Space Limited?

Merchant: Our relationship goes back. ... This is our first full collaboration, and it's going very well. We've had so many people calling, I wish we had Madison Square Garden. The theater is only 150 seats – people should call in advance.

Q. In addition to your work in film, you've written a number of books, including several on food. Any chance you'll be preparing some specialities for the cocktail party on Saturday night?

Merchant: I don't think I'll have time, but I'll give my recipes to someone and they'll prepare it.

February, 2006

The following interview with Ivory occurred eight months after Merchant's death and shortly before the local opening of "The White Countess," their final collaboration. Set in 1930s Shanghai, it stars Ralph Fiennes as a blind diplomat who becomes entangled with a Russian emigre with dark family secrets, played by Natasha Richardson.

Q: Is "The White Countess" the end of an era?

Ivory: It's certainly the end of the era in which he was present, there's no denying that. But we have other projects we were working on. One of those is "The City of Final Destination." It's based on a book by Peter Cameron and is set in Uruguay. We'll probably make it in Argentina. It's a modern story – really a romance, I suppose.

Q: You were typically billed as director and Merchant as producer, which meant he gathered all the bucks. Are funds in place for this and future films?

Ivory: There was no one like him who could raise the money for various, sometimes quiet, complicated films. On the other hand, there are people we have been working with for many years who I think are capable of doing that, just perhaps not in the same style that he did it. But they must manage, and we will go forward for a while. I'm getting on.

Q: Do you foresee retirement?

Ivory: I don't know about retirement. There are always things you can do of interest in film, but the actual making of a feature film takes a lot out of you, physically. I'm now in my 70s and, sooner or later, I probably won't have the energy to do that. But I still do, and will go on as long as I can.

Q: Amidst the many demands of making films that were often shot at locations around the world, how did the two of you balance being professional colleagues and personal companions?

Ivory: We were most of the time in this country. He would go off quite frequently to England and occasionally to India. I tended to stay here more. Like any pair of friends there would be disagreements, and since we were working together as business partners, the disagreements were major ones. We had to find a way around them, and we did. They could be on some aspects of the film or some tiny thing, but the fight would be a fierce one.

Q: What would be a tiny thing?

Ivory: Gosh, it could be that I would think certain people who were part of a crew, if they were going to take a long flight, should be in first class or at least business class. And he's say "Nonsense, they don't have to be." Another good example of that kind of thing: You always invite your various movie stars to film festivals, and before you know it the agents of the movie stars have attached themselves to the trip. He would just flatly refuse to do that. Sometimes I thought it was undiplomatic and sometimes I agreed with him wholeheartedly.

Q: Was your domestic life relatively free of disagreement?

Ivory: It could be stormy also.

Q: Did you schedule downtime together, perhaps time at your place in Columbia County?

Ivory: We just automatically went up there on the weekends. But he really didn't like being up there as much as I did. He thought business matters would be going on in the city that he needed to be there for, doing the kinds of things that would advance a project or just life in general.

Q: Did he work too hard?

Ivory: Yes. But if there's somebody you think is working too hard, they're scarcely going to change. His work was what made him happy.

Q: Do you feel the two of you were perceived as a couple?

Ivory: I think we were perceived as the same person.

Q: Will the name Merchant Ivory remain on your films.

Ivory: Sure. Of course.

Q: "The White Countess" continues a theme that's in so many of your films: people looking for intimacy amid difficult times or foreign environments. Why do you think the public responds so well to that?

Ivory: It's one of the basic difficulties of life, isn't it? We all have to go through that. Maybe not as violently as the couple ripped apart by the destruction of Shanghai by the Japanese, but it's a common human state.

Q: During your 45-year collaboration and career, the world has changed in so many ways. Does your work reflect what's happening in the world?

Ivory: Our films aren't really about current events, but they reflect large ongoing things. With "The White Countess," you had the Russian family there because they were White Russians driven out by the Bolsheviks. You had, simultaneously going on, the invasion of China by Japan in the north and you had a civil war between the Chinese communists and the Chinese nationalists. All that is there in the film.

Q: Can the public relate those times to the turmoils of today's world?

Ivory: Well if they can't, they're awfully dumb.

Q: Are your films comforting to people?

Ivory: Well, this film has something of a happy ending. The couple that don't seem to want to be a couple finally do become a couple, and they are able to escape the mayhem that was coming.

Q: Do you like making movies with happy endings?

Ivory: Most of our films do have happy endings. We have had some which are a bit enigmatic at the end, but for the most part they have to have happy endings. (The next film) is a romance, and it ends happily I can promise you that.

JOHN FELDMAN
& SHEILA SILVER

JUNE 22, 2003 FILM MAKER & COMPOSER

His images, her sounds, their kid

If the combination of music and pictures tells a tale, then Sheila Silver and John Feldman together have a lifetime of stories to convey.

She's a composer; he's a filmmaker. Over the 15 years of their marriage, they've each achieved acclaim in their respective fields and have worked together on a few projects. But since they closed their New York City apartment and settled in Columbia County full time a year ago, they've deepened their collaborations on a variety of levels, from film, video and opera to homemaking and family life.

They've also each got important current projects of their own. Silver, 56, has a new CD arriving in stores this month featuring her large-scale Piano Concerto, and Feldman, 48, has recently completed his third feature film, "Who the Hell Is Bobby Roos?" But both would probably agree that their most important project is an ongoing collaboration, their 5-year-old adopted son, Victor.

The Silver/Feldman family lives on the side of a leafy green hill in the village of Spencertown. In what would be the master bedroom of their two-story house is Silver's studio. There's the black grand piano where she composes and the modern teak desk from which she applies for commissions and manages projects like her new recording. She seems equally confident at composing and at the business of being a composer.

"I think that every piece I write will be worthy of those before," she says with regard to her 1996 Piano Concerto. In the tradition of the genre, it is a grand and mighty work. It may not be as lavish as the concertos of Rachmaninoff, but it's just as expressive and challenging as those of Prokofiev and Shostakovich, composers who wrote in the midst of repression and war, a situation Silver relates to.

"The piece is very timely," says Silver. "The first movement uses images of a youthful invincibility, beating one's chest and marching off to war. ... In this climate of bullying politics, it's important to remember that war has repercussions."

Those consequences are depicted in the second and third movements, which deal, she says, with "coming to terms with mortality" and "continuing on, no matter what."

"The finale has an original Hasidic melody," says Silver. "It's the dance of life a kind of Zorba the Greek, 'Dance no matter what.'"

"I try to do that in my life as well," she says, referring to the periods of being discouraged that are an almost inevitable part of being a creative artist. At such times, having a spouse in the same general business also comes in handy.

"We boost each other when the morale is low," says Feldman, "and also in handling the political aspects of being an artist."

Politics and networking come easily to the energetic and talkative Silver, who was recently named composer-in-residence for the Columbia Festival Orchestra, based in nearby Chatham.

"We are honored to have somebody of her caliber in the area," says Gwen Gould, the orchestra's conductor. "She's aiding us in our programming, and we've brainstormed together many times."

Having already performed two Silver compositions, the orchestra will next spring present three pieces in the "MusicVision" series, which combine live chamber music by Silver and non-narrative video by Feldman.

"Our MusicVisions are conceived as a collaboration in which neither of us is the boss," says Feldman.

Across from the couple's main house is a two-car garage, above which is a new suite of rooms that Feldman himself built. Along with generous closet space and ample shelving, there's his state-of-the-art digital editing studio. In this space, Feldman single-handedly edited his newest feature film, "Who the Hell Is Bobby Roos?"

Winner of the New American Cinema Award at last year's Seattle International Film Festival, "Roos" explores the psyche of a gifted comic impersonator who begins to lose hold of his own personality. It's a natural follow-up to Feldman's previous films "Dead Funny"

(1995) and "Alligator Eyes" (1990), which explore dark comedy and comic suspense.

What is different about "Roos" is that it was shot without a script and is based on true life. The star, Roger Kabler, plays himself, the film's title notwithstanding.

"He becomes possessed by the characters he impersonates and it drives him mad," says Feldman. "It's as if (pianist) David Helfgott played himself in 'Shine.' There were times when I was afraid of what I might be getting myself into."

Early on in work on the film, Feldman decided that it should not have music.

"I pouted for a day," says Silver, who had written scores for her husband's previous films.

Feldman eventually came around.

"The character is not sympathetic, and we wanted to use music to draw sympathy to him," he says. "Music is the most powerful tool in the arsenal to get the audience in sync with where the film is headed."

Such appreciation of music may be unusual for most film directors, but Silver can speak with equal respect for Feldman's craft, and, as a secondary collaborator, she knows when to get out of the way. For example, when the producers of "Dead Funny" said there was too much music, she readily obliged and suggested which cues should be excised.

"People love it or hate it," Silver says of the new film. "But everybody who sees it is blown away by it. The actor is totally brilliant."

While "Roos" is "still on the trail of a distributor," according to Feldman, it will be shown in the fall at the Catskill Mountain Foundation in Hunter.

Besides pursuing new outlets for the film, Feldman is currently at work editing a DVD of Silver's opera "The Thief of Love," from live performances at its 2001 premiere by Stony Brook Opera on Long Island. He also earns income from producing industrial films for local corporations and nonprofit organizations.

Victor Silver Feldman is the name of the couple's most important collaboration. Born in Romania, the 5-year-old was adopted a little more than three years ago. While his toys and sundry playthings are often strewn about the house, Victor also has his own studio space.

On the wall of the child's bedroom, at eye level for a youngster, is a remarkable collection of miniature art works. There are small framed prints of 19th-century-style portraits and a few colorful abstract post-cards and prints. Where other children might play school, he seems to enjoy playing art gallery.

"He has a good visual sense," says Silver, who recalls bringing the child to their country home for the first time.

"After the long trip back from Romania, we got to our house and I held him up to the window and pointed to the mountains," Silver says. "I said 'Isn't it pretty?' and he said, 'Pretty.' It was his third word in English."

PLESANT DeSPAIN

Gentle journeys for rapt audiences

It was in the basement of a Seattle church in the early 1970s that Pleasant DeSpain knew for sure his commitment to becoming a professional storyteller was going to work out. "I had my hat by the door, and I told stories for two hours," he says. "At the end of that night, there was $27.68 in that hat. And rent for a decent apartment was $100 back then. I knew then that there was no turning back."

DeSpain has been telling stories to audiences large and small, old and young ever since. Next month, the Troy resident turns 60 and will have three new books released, drawing to a conclusion his nine-volume series for August House publishers titled "The Books of Nine Lives." The multicultural story collections will bring his published books to a total of 20.

In all of his stories, which he estimates total approximately 1,000, DeSpain has one central message.

"My main force in the telling and the writing is to point out in an entertaining way that we human beings are far more alike than we are different, no matter the culture, the time, the language, the religion," he says. "I search for stories that are a good yarn, that are suggestible with vivid feelings, events and actions and that have a soul or a consciousness without being preachy."

A 32-year career of speaking and writing has brought DeSpain into contact with thousands of listeners and countless readers. But it started with a leap of faith.

DeSpain decided that storytelling would be his life's work when he was 25 and sitting on a beach in Zihuatanejo, Mexico. That trip was the first of many world travels that have punctuated DeSpain's life and brought him new story material. But at the time, he was no itinerant.

DeSpain had earned advanced degrees in communication, literature and drama and seemed on the verge of a career in college teaching. A position at Seattle University soon brought him to the Northwest.

"I moved to Seattle and stayed for 27 years," he says, "but I left teaching after two years" to tell stories.

Coffeehouses were DeSpain's first regular venue, although his reputation grew quickly.

"It took a few years, (but) I became Seattle's resident storyteller (as) proclaimed by the mayor," he recalls. In 1977, the year of that designation, he also began a syndicated newspaper column and a television show, both called "Pleasant Journeys."

An old family name, "Pleasant" is also a nearly ideal moniker for a man who has a special way with audiences.

"He was wonderful," says Kim McMann, head of children's services for the Troy Public Library. In May, she organized a DeSpain performance for an audience of about 40 children and adults. "He told stories and wrapped everyone around his finger," she says. "We were on the edge of our seats."

To DeSpain, audiences are an essential component in his art.

"Three elements – story, listener, teller – must come together as one during the experience," he says. "If I'm doing my job, the audience is getting the story they deserve based on the quality of their listening."

The idea of storytelling can evoke intimate and nostalgic locales, like campfires or elementary school classrooms. But DeSpain performs in a wide variety of settings, including corporate offices, supper clubs and large conventions. His largest live audience 16,000 strong was at a storytelling conference 10 years ago in Louisville, Ky.

Last year, prior to an appearance at another large gathering in Boston, DeSpain invited some friends and neighbors to hear him rehearse. Jim Lewis, a Troy furniture designer and artist who had made a mask for DeSpain to use as a prop, was on hand for the run-through.

"He blew me away," says Lewis. "He had three interwoven stories and he would tell a bit of one, a bit of the next and then the other. They supported each other and had different takes on his theme. The effect was seamless and powerful."

"All of my writing is a result of my telling," says DeSpain. "When I write the story down I've probably (already) told it over the course of a year. You will be able to hear me in the reading, because my pauses and breaths, my rhythm, is contained in the prose."

Before adding a new story to his repertoire, DeSpain researches its origins and finds variations in written sources.

"I take the story apart, down to its skeleton," he says. "I put it back together, simply, purely. I go out and tell it. And then I learn how I tell it. And then I write it the way I told it."

DeSpain is almost as enthusiastic about sharing the art of storytelling as he is about the stories themselves. During residencies in schools, he follows up a performance by teaching children how to tell their own stories.

"We're all natural storytellers," he says. "Our lives are a story, and when we share them with each other, our lives are enriched."

CHAPTER TWO
The Activists
CREATING THE PLATFORM

JUDITH BARNES

ARTS PATRON

Fund-raiser? Laugh-raiser? Same to her

In June 2002, Judith Barnes was laid up in Albany Medical Center on a form of life support after undergoing surgery for an intestinal resectioning to repair a congenital abnormality that had become life-threatening. Although tubes down her throat prevented her from speaking, Barnes persisted in communicating through writing.

When one of her doctors explained the possibility of a permanent colostomy, Barnes wrote, "Bag must match shoes. Heh, heh."

As ill as she was, Barnes' laugh remained. It's omnipresent in any conversation personal or professional with her. Hearty, generous and sincere, Judy Barnes' laughter is the leaven that makes all of her projects rise.

And her endeavors are manifold. While running her own one-woman national consulting firm in marketing and communication for more than 30 years, Barnes, 56, also has been a leader and a yeoman for scores of arts, civic and educational institutions across the Capital Region. A co-founder of the Troy Savings Bank Music Hall Association, she designed the logo that's still in use. She's also been an officer or trustee for groups as diverse as the Historic Albany Foundation, Upper Hudson Planned Parenthood and the City of Troy Economic Development Corp.

"She's an absolutely good woman a dynamic persona and a loyal friend," says Shirley Jackson, president of Rensselaer Polytechnic Institute in Troy. Jackson describes Barnes as "well-rounded, intellectually agile and not afraid to try new things and reinvent oneself." Barnes received her Ph.D. in communications from RPI in 1984 and sat on the search committee that hired Jackson.

Today, Barnes is well ensconced in downtown Troy. She lives and works out of a large renovated townhouse on Washington Park that she has shared with architect Vincent Lepera for about 20 years.

But a life in the Collar City wasn't in the plans back in 1965, when her family pulled up to the little urban campus of Russell Sage College for a visit.

"I was going to go to Smith (College), and I didn't even want to get out of the car," even though an interview was scheduled with admission staff, says Barnes. "My father said, 'Young lady, you have obligations...'"

An hour or so later, Barnes returned to the car and announced that she'd signed up for early enrollment. She recalls saying to her incredulous parents, "I think I can make a difference."

Last year, as chair of the board of trustees of Sage, Barnes presided over the dedication of $30 million in capital improvements to the campus.

Sage President Jeanne Neff calls Barnes, whose term as board chair has since ended, her "close partner and fellow architect," and says that she was personally responsible for raising $5 million of the recent campaign.

"One of the things she accomplished was a board that functioned without factions," says Neff. "People were unified and had a common purpose and direction. Judy's energy and focus kept that on track."

"Even freshmen year, Judy always had the good ideas and was out doing artistic things and talking to people," says Sandra Gull, a classmate of Barnes' at Sage who remains a close friend.

Gull recruited Barnes as her campaign manager for student body president. Gull triumphed, while Barnes won the post of class president for three consecutive years.

"That's the same laugh I heard in 1966. That's the delight," says Gull. "She's giving, caring, clever and fun, and it's all those things wrapped up into one, and you never know which one is next."

"Subjects come alive under her leadership. ... There's accomplishments when Judy's in the room," says Alan Goldberg, the chairman and chief executive of First Albany who is also a noted arts patron. Goldberg and Barnes have served together on the boards of the Albany Institute and the Sage Colleges.

In the world of arts and academia, Barnes is the rarest of board members – she's unafraid of The Ask. "She can get people to step up to the plate," says Goldberg.

"I'm unafraid to ask for money for good causes, and a lot of people are," confirms Barnes.

During the capital campaign at Sage, Barnes was in touch with a West Coast patron, who came through with an initial gift of $250,000. With unexpected ease, Barnes leveraged it for far more.

"She had the capacity to give at least $1 million. I called her and said, 'This is absolutely wonderful, and I'm very grateful. I need $2 million. Can you help me get $2 million? You are the type of person I need to have this move forward, and there aren't a lot of you,'" Barnes recalls saying. "The next morning she called and said, 'I'll give you the $2 million.'"

Barnes' next call was to the grants office at Sage, where jaws hit the floor.

"She is so persuasive that people with resources trust her and her judgment and respond," says Raona Roy, president of the Arts Center of the Capital Region, who called on Barnes to help with another capital campaign several years ago that raised $5 million for the center's current home.

"My favorite line is, 'I don't do well in captivity,'"says Barnes, laughing again. Actually, she appears to have lots of favorite lines. Some of them are mounted in her basement office in Troy. A decorative pillow is embroidered thus: "No Whining."

The "don't fence me in" attitude is big for Barnes. It explains why she's turned down so many job offers over the years.

"I was being interviewed by IBM in 1971, and they were very interested in hiring women with technical communication backgrounds," recalls Barnes. "I remember sitting there and saying, 'I will not live through this interview, let alone a job here.' I just knew it."

Shortly thereafter, Barnes formed her own consulting firm.

"Even guys weren't consultants then. ... The term 'entrepreneur' wasn't in the lexicon," says Barnes.

Branding, marketing and public relations are among Barnes' business offerings, but basic communication skills are her specialty. She takes special pleasure in working with engineers and techies.

"I worked with General Motors for years. I was brought in by the heads of different divisions and would say, 'You know, communications is a system.' And once they heard the word system and realized I wasn't going to turn them into a gothic novelist, they began to relax," says Barnes.

"People are taken aback by her overt enthusiasm," says Clinton Ballinger, CEO of Evident Technologies, a Troy-based nanotechnology firm, who has engaged Barnes over the past year. "In a company where it used to be more quiet and reserved, they're shaken to the foundation when she comes around, and that's just fine."

Each fall, as she has for the last 20 years, Barnes gives an evening talk to a select group of undergrad students who are part of the Archer Leadership Program at RPI.

"The very first thing I thought of when she walked into the room," says Erick James, 28, a former member of the program, "was, 'Holy hair!'"

As bountiful as her laughter, Barnes' ample gray locks are high-lighted by two white streaks that frame her face.

James got past the hair and ended up lingering around the classroom afterward to have some extra time with Barnes. "I was struggling with my hockey and my studies and in a turbulent time. She was a beacon of stability and enthusiasm," says James, who after graduation became an amateur stand-up comic and magician locally. "I wouldn't be on stage in front of 150 people making 'em laugh if I hadn't met her," he says.

Now good friends, James and Barnes attended the Metallica with Godsmack concert at the Pepsi Arena in October. Barnes, it seems, is a particular fan of rock drumming.

"At the concert, I could see her attention to detail. She was really listening and noticing the nuances," says James. "That's what she does with people. She's cognizant."

ANTHONY CAFRITZ

OCTOBER 9, 2005 — SCULPTOR/ORGANIZER

Shaping a creative community

The village of Salem in Washington County, population 964, has a new skyline. On the hills just west of the town center are two 40-foot-tall orange steel sculptures by the internationally known artist Mark di Suvero. They're part of Salem Art Works, the 8-month-old arts center founded by the sculptor Anthony Cafritz. A graduate of Bennington College and faculty member at Castleton State College near Rutland Vt., Cafritz had long carried the desire to establish a haven for artists in the region. During his first tour of the shuttered farm just off Salem's main drag, he realized the time and place were at hand. "I felt God was on my shoulder," he says.

Cafritz made the down payment on the 119-acre property with his own money and has wasted no time in filling the buildings and pastures with like-minded creative folk and their wide-ranging art works. To date, more than 40 artists have held residencies, anywhere from a couple days to a month or more. Currently on display are several dozen large outdoor works, many created at SAW's makeshift barn studios.

"It fell out of the sky," says Al Budde, president of the Salem Chamber of Commerce, regrading SAW's dramatic arrival on the local scene. "An art colony enhances the landscape and adds to the culture of the community without despoiling the surroundings."

"You get a group of people together and the possibility of invention comes. That's the ethos of this place," explains Cafritz.

So far, the activity at SAW is mostly centered on sculpture, but Cafritz wants it to also be a place for writers and performers as well as all manner of visual artists. His model is the legendary Black Mountain College in southwestern North Carolina, which from 1933 to 1956 drew a dizzying array of now-iconic artists. The lineup of faculty and students included painters Willem de Kooning and Robert Rauschenberg, composers Lou Harrison and John Cage, choreographer Merce Cunningham and poet Robert Creeley.

"That place probably died because of egos," says Cafritz. "My hope is we have good checks and balances."

The legal process has begun to make SAW a nonprofit tax-exempt organization and Cafritz has drawn together a small board of artists and neighbors, while the temporal duties that keep the place going are shared.

Lisa Mordhorst, a 34-year-old multidisciplinary artist, lives in the Williamsburg section of Brooklyn but spent her summer weekends at SAW.

"This is the first time I've had a working space outside the city, but all of my work is landscape-based," says Mordhorst. "It's wonderful to be there to see what happens if I'm within a landscape when I'm doing (my art), as opposed to traveling back to the site."

When Mordhorst isn't working on sculpture and photography, she helps out with meals. As with other resident artists, both students and professionals, the arrangements are informal.

"There's no rules, just safety and personal responsibility," Cafritz says, pausing for a quick moment before adding: "It is pretty communal isn't it?"

Communities, partnerships, and artistic ideals seem to be favorite topics for Cafritz. But by the look of him you might expect to see the 42-year-old artist at a rock concert rather than at some New Age artists retreat.

Thick sideburns and a leather jacket give him a tough-guy exterior that's undermined by an artist's sensitivities. In what was once a sheep field, Cafritz points to scores of milkweed plants. He's hesitant to have them mowed, because he's heard they attract Monarch butterflies.

When he talks about his own artistic career, Cafritz sometimes reveals a tattoo on his left shoulder. It's a round logo from a 1963 Ford pickup. He got the ink in 1990, to boost him up as he prepared for his first solo sculpture show. Recalls Cafritz, "I'd look at it at 4 a.m. and it would give me power beyond coffee."

There's a connection, both graphic and emotional, between that tattoo and SAW's own logo – a circular saw.

"It's a bit aggressive, but it's perpetual sharp, not nullified," explains Cafritz. "It's about power and industry and intentionality."

Those qualities are obviously present in Cafritz himself.

"Sometimes he's an artist with a lot of ideas and you need to slow him down a touch," says Bruce Steinberg, 23, a stage designer who's been involved with SAW since June.

"It's rural and gritty," says Cafritz of Salem and its environs. "We don't want to gentrify the neighborhood at all, but perpetuate what's here, industry and agriculture."

Add to that art. But on the grounds of SAW, the difference between art and industry isn't always clear. Sometimes there's confusion on what's fresh creativity and what's agricultural detritus.

For example, out in a field are four round hay bales covered in white plastic. They turn out to be a work in progress by Cafritz. And off on a hillside there's a section of sagging fencing. That's Lisa Mordhorst's "Moving West 2."

What about those three old trailer homes rallied around a fire pit, perhaps an installation of some sort? Nope. Turns out, that's housing for interns.

While art inspired by the environment might become, over time, a unifying factor for SAW artists, it is the property itself that will surely be Cafritz's greatest creation. That is, if his many dreams continue to manifest.

He sees a future theater in an immense 1865 barn on the property. Another 8,000-square-foot building will, according to the Cafritz vision, have a dance studio and an exhibition space. A gently slopped and concaved hillside will serve, naturally, as an amphitheater. It will all be for the freedom of art.

"The idea is a place where you feel relaxed," says Cafritz. "No confines or sensibilities or politics or way of being that prevents your process."

JIM CHARLES
& TONY RIVERA

PERFORMERS/PRODUCERS   APRIL 29, 2007

Reviving musicals and a city

In 1969, the city of Cohoes purchased the abandoned National Bank Building at the northern end of Remsen Street for $1 to save the prominent 1874 edifice from imminent destruction. As city officials began examining the building's interior, they couldn't find any stairs to a third floor. Eventually, they broke through a ceiling panel, only to discover that hidden away in the top half of the building was a gem of a theater, complete with a small stage, a fly space for dropping in sets, and seating for 350 people, including a wrap-around balcony.

In the ensuing years, the space has been used for a variety of civic activities, and there have been attempts at having a resident organization, such as a professional repertory theater company, a community theater troupe and a folk music group. But since 2003, when Cohoes native and off-Broadway actor Jim Charles, 47, moved back home with his partner Tony Rivera, 35, a dancer with a background in management, the city of Cohoes has had not just a theater but also a professional theater company.

C-R Productions at the Cohoes Music Hall, as their nonprofit organization is known, has a paid staff of five, an annual lineup of a half dozen musicals and a hopping box office. Between the main productions and a variety of children's programs, last year's performances were attended by more than 20,000 people. The company has a base of 1,000 loyal subscribers. Its final production of the season, Stephen Sondheim's "A Funny Thing Happened on the Way to the Forum."

"Their performances have brought thousands of people to downtown, where we never had anybody coming to downtown previously," says Cohoes Mayor John T. McDonald III. "The shows bring people from a radius I never would have dreamed of, like people from the Berkshires. Five or six years ago, I never would have believed that would happen."

Although Charles and Rivera carry the respective titles (and ensuing duties) of artistic director and producing director, they occasionally appear on stage as well. Charles himself is leading the cast of "Forum." He plays Pseudolus, the high-strung singing and dancing slave who goes through madcap antics to gain his freedom.

Actually, the role isn't much of a stretch for Charles, since juggling myriad tasks and maintaining a generally good humor is how he and Rivera run the Music Hall on a daily basis.

"We've been here four years, but just now got the go-ahead (from the city's historic preservation watchdogs) to put some stuff on the walls," says Charles, standing in the lobby and rolling his eyes at the empty brown walls as only an actor could. "We're very lucky," he continues, "the community loves this place."

Charles and Rivera's first show in Cohoes was "Tonight, Tonight, Tonight!" a one-night-only revue in March 2002. It was born out of a post-9/11 desire to look beyond life in Manhattan, where the couple had been living.

"We called about 15 of our friends from off-Broadway and television and said we want to do a revue-type show," recalls Rivera. "We got a cellphone with a 518 area code, and that was our box office."

"Tonight" included local as well as out-of-town talent, as have all subsequent productions, and met with huge popular success. And it led to Charles and Rivera being courted by new fans in Cohoes.

"I used to call them every other day and say, 'Get up here,'" recalls Eunice Antonucci, owner of Smith's Restaurant. As one of the only dinner spots in Cohoes, Smith's has benefited from the traffic brought in by the theater, and Antonucci has joined the board of C-R Productions. But she appreciates more than the commerce.

"We like coming out of their shows singing and tapping our feet," she says. "We need that. This is a depressed area with a loss of the mills and business."

"We've cornered the market on the musical theater fix people need from September to May," says Rivera, who played Bernardo in the 2004 production of "West Side Story."

Every season at Cohoes includes a mix of classic Broadway musicals alongside newer staples from the '80s and '90s. For example, next year features "Carousel" and "42nd Street" as well as "Little Shop of Horrors" and "Miss Saigon" (but don't look for a helicopter on the small Cohoes stage).

Each show is rehearsed and mounted in a tight two-week production period and runs for three weekends. A typical cast numbers 12, with half that many more musicians in the pit. Last fall's "Ragtime" was the largest production to date, with an onstage company of 37.

What sets Cohoes apart from almost any other professional house in the country is the absence of amplification. In contrast to today's Broadway, where the sound is as powerful as at the movies, hearing the natural voices of the performers re-emphasizes the intimacy and immediacy of live theater.

"When Jim first told me it was an acoustic house, I said, 'You're kidding.' That's very rare and it means we have to get actors who can handle it," states music director Michael McAssey. A 20-year veteran of off-Broadway and regional theater, McAssey relocated from Aspen to join the Cohoes team this season. He continues, "In a lot of ways (singing without a mike) is a lost art."

That observation is borne out every time auditions are held.

"A lot (of young actors) don't get the concept," says Charles, "I say, 'We're an acoustic house,' and they say 'What?'"

"C-R Kids" is the umbrella name for a variety of educational activities at the theater. Coming up is a Circus Summer Camp. In December, 3,000 children saw school-day performances of "The Sound of Music." The January production of "Disney's High School Musical" featured a local cast of 32 kids, culled from 250 who auditioned.

"We treated them like professionals. We're not like the high school, where you rehearse for four months," says Charles, who recalls that his own teenage theatrical ambitions were met with a dearth of local opportunities for training and performance. He's gratified that one place where he did connect with like-minded souls is still around – the Spenwood School of Dance and Gymnastics.

"You knew from the beginning Jim would do something with the theater, one way or another. He was a showman, he came in that door and you knew," recalls Margie Pascale, who's run Spenwood for 45 years and gave Charles his lessons in tap dancing.

When Charles came in the door again, this time as a producer and director, Pascale had no trouble recognizing him. In fact, the two did more than renew acquaintances. Dancers from Spenwood were prominently featured in the revue "Tonight!" and the school's studios are frequently used for rehearsals of upcoming shows.

C-R Productions has received some of its most substantial funding for its education programs, including a $22,000 grant from the federal No Child Left Behind program to fund after-school enrichment activities for Cohoes middle schoolers. The largest grant to date has been $50,000 from New York state, secured by Ron Canestrari, the majority leader of the state Assembly and former Cohoes mayor. The funds are designated for capital improvements including lights, sound equipment and curtains.

The organizations' current operating budget stands at around $300,000, with approximately two-thirds of that figure covered by earned income from ticket sales and subscriptions.

The city of Cohoes provides gratis use of the theater and covers the utilities. But the company does pay rent in downtown Cohoes – on a 2,500-square-foot scene shop and seven apartments that house actors. "That's seven National Grid bills," says Rivera, who hopes to one day have all operations outside the theater consolidated into one building.

To date, Rivera and Charles have not given themselves salaries, functioning in essence as full-time volunteers. To cover their own living expenses Rivera teaches gymnastics at Spenwood and Charles gives voice lessons to 20 or more students a week.

Except when one of them is performing in a production. Then, something has to be cut from the busy routine. But as they look toward a fifth season and beyond, Rivera and Charles have reached a certain comfort level so that even during the peak of a production period, they'll take time to leave the theater and have dinner. Carving out personal time will become an even bigger priority, since the couple is taking steps toward adopting a child in the next year.

"We've grown into this. ... It's not as consuming at this stage," says Charles. "We're in this for the long haul, with our commitment to the city, the community and the building."

CHRIS GARRETSON-PERSANS

FEBRUARY 3, 2008   CULTURE CRITIC

Big on small wonders

Chris Garretson-Persans cried when her husband drove her over the Congress Street Bridge into Troy for the first time 21 years ago. He was about to become a physics professor at Rensselaer Polytechnic Institute, and they were leaving behind a farmhouse in a rural New Jersey that was an easy driving distance to the thriving environs of New York City and Philadelphia. "It was so depressed here," recalls Garretson-Persans.

Despite their dour first impressions, the couple became happily ensconced in a large old house in Watervliet, where they raised a daughter. But Garretson-Persans, 55, can still identify with folks who just don't connect to the Capital Region. As a part-time employee at the Albany Visitors Center for the last few years, she's encountered countless bewildered tourists who walk in from a sleepy downtown and ask, "Is there anything to do here?"

Garretson-Persans' answers can now be found in "The City Dwellers' Smalbanac: An opinionated guide to things in and around the Capital District." An eclectic and affectionate look at the quirks of our region and its many hidden treasures, "The Smalbanac" has just been released in its winter edition (the premiere issue came in the early fall). It's 68 pages long and has lots of recommendations for arts and cultural activities, restaurants, shopping and just hanging out.

A homemade feel comes from Garretson-Persans' unvarnished writing, simple design and cheerful drawings. That's Henry Hudson on the cover, standing atop The Egg. According to The Smalbanac, no known images of Hudson actually exist.

The guide's title is a smashup of two or three words, depending on how you look at it. First, there's almanac an appropriate, slightly old-world designation for such a compendium of sundry factoids and viewpoints. And then there's the contentious nickname Smallbany. While that term is typically used in a pejorative voice, Garretson-Persans thinks it's time for it to be reconsidered.

"Half the people laugh and say, 'I always call it that,' while the other half say, 'How dare you?' she says. "People should embrace it and make it their own. Just like how the early Americans were called 'Yankee Doodles' by the British. It was an insult, but it became embraced and worn with pride."

Still, Garretson-Persans is aware of the region's scars and its ongoing, fitful attempts to modernize.

"Albany is a small city, boxed in by the river," she says. "Rockefeller knocked down one vital neighborhood (to build the Empire State Plaza), but we don't have to start over from scratch, especially with the arts. There's a small corps that is interested in making it grow. The city needs to recognize that and stop worrying about a convention center or the next hotel."

In the pages of the "Smalbanac," such invective is rare and mostly reserved for city officials and urban planners, past and present. But Garretson-Persans does believe that it's "time for (a guide book) with a point of view." That's why she won't be taking advertising, claiming, "Once you get their ads, you can't be mean to them." But the emphasis, she says, is on "celebrating the good stuff."

Toward that end, the new edition contains an in-depth look at the revival efforts in Troy, a recap of the top attractions in Albany, extensive listings for galleries, bookstores, used clothing stores and more, and a calendar of events through April ("The Smalbanac" is published three times a year).

"I'm Bored" is a section that addresses head-on the notion that there's nothing to do. "I want people to know there's an open mic every night of the week," says Garretson-Persans. "I included volunteering because I think that's an essential part of being in the area. And there's a Sky Calendar because it's free to look up."

"I'm enjoying the area much more now that I'm discovering it again," says Garretson-Persans. "Every day I find something that cracks me up."

A favorite recent example is the case of Gen. Philip Sheridan, the fellow who sits on a horse outside the State Capitol and facing City

Hall. He's covered in "The Smalbanac" as one of the "Four Famous Phils of Albany" (the others being Livingston, Schuyler and Hooker).

According to Garretson-Persans' research, Sheridan was a fierce soldier who might or might not have been born in Albany. He burned large parts of Virginia during the Civil War and was accused of genocide in a later campaign against American Indians. His horse, Rienzi, was stuffed and is now at The Smithsonian Institution. And though the Capitol's statue depicts the soldier and his mount in impressive stature, Sheridan was known as "Little Phil" and stood only about 5-foot-5.

"The Smalbanac" entry concludes: "The statue of Sheridan and Rienzi was unveiled in front of the State Capitol Building in October of 1916. By the by, in a letter to Gov. Whitman a year earlier, Mrs. Sheridan protested that the planned memorial statue 'did not bear any resemblance to her husband.' She was overruled by committee."

Now an inveterate gatherer of Albany (and Capital Region) facts and lore, Garretson-Persans made a recent find at a flea market: an old tourist guide called "See Albany," dated Sept. 16, 1929 one month before the great stock market crash. Among other things, the booklet states that Albany has the largest factories in the world for toilet paper, potato chips, dominoes and checkers, as well as the largest garage in the world. "Oh, the glory days," concludes the reprint in "The Smalbanac."

Perhaps in the distant future "The Smalbanac," too, will become a kind of time capsule, revealing the facts and flavor of life after the turn of the millennium. Certainly for Garretson-Persans, the publication is more than just a pastime. "This is my midlife crisis," she says. "It lets me do something fun and lasting."

ISOM HERRON

MATHEMATICIAN/ARTS PATRON   DECEMBER 28, 2003

Listening for melodic differentials

Shostakovich cinched the deal.

It was early 1992, and Isom Herron was being wooed by Rensselaer Polytechnic Institute to leave Howard University in Washington, D.C., where he had taught for 18 years. When Herron and his wife, Myra, came to check out the Capital Region, they saw that a Shostakovich festival was happening at the Troy Savings Bank Music Hall.

Although the couple wasn't able to catch a performance during that visit, they figured that if a community could support such an undertaking, it must be OK.

"We could live in a place that could have a Shostakovich festival," says Herron, now in his 11th year as a professor of mathematics at RPI in Troy.

Music has led the way in many of Herron's life decisions, and it's made him a prominent member of the region's cultural community over the past decade.

Three years ago, he was elected president of the Friends of Chamber Music. The 55-year-old organization, which presents six concerts annually at the Emma Willard School in Troy, is run entirely by board members. Herron's leadership position has given him yet another perspective on music.

"There was music in the house," says Herron of his childhood home, recalling that his mother sang in choirs and his father was partial to jazz. But Herron, 57, could just as easily be speaking of his current home, an imposing, century-old house in the Albia section of Troy adjacent to Emma Willard. During the 1940s, it served as the RPI president's official residence.

The front parlor is the music room. It's where Myra Herron, a semi-professional cellist and retired classroom music teacher, rehearses daily.

150

Although the couple met at a Presbyterian church in Washington, D.C., music is what brought them together. Myra was a member of an all-black female string quartet that was working on Samuel Barber's Adagio for Strings. One Sunday she shared with a fellow member of the congregation her difficulty in finding a recording of the string quartet version of the popular piece.

"Isom would have that," the friend replied. Myra did a double-take, not yet aware of his avid interest in classical music and record collecting.

"My interest had been primarily in orchestral music," says Isom, who served as a DJ on the college station while earning a Ph.D. at Johns Hopkins University. He bought his first classical LP – Leonard Bernstein performing Gershwin – as a teen in Kingston, Jamaica, where his father served as an American diplomat.

He did have the recording Myra needed. Soon thereafter his tastes turned to chamber music, and he became a particular fan of one female cellist. The couple, who often vacation at music festivals, has been married for 22 years.

"Joining the Friends (of Chamber Music) was a natural thing," says Isom. After being subscribers for five years, he and his wife both were asked to join the board. The duties for each of them grew when he ascended to the president's post three years ago. "They realized they could get two for one," he says.

"Loose-ends coordinator" is how Susan Blandy, the organization's immediate past president, describes the post. "It's a matter of knowing the music, watching the budget, audience-building and relations with Emma Willard School," she says.

"Now I realize why people have full-time jobs with this," says Isom, referring to how larger organizations have paid staff.

Hard-working board members aren't unique in organizations with the longevity of the Friends of Chamber Music. But African-Americans in leadership positions in the classical arts are rare, at least in the Capital Region.

"Diversity of leadership reflects well on an organization," says James Jordon of the New York State Council on the Arts. As the agency's music program director, he monitors the activities of hundreds of organizations statewide.

"I don't think that there's a lack of appreciation," says Jordon, who is black, "just a lack of communication and lack of opportunities for African-Americans to serve."

"Coming from Washington, we don't feel exceptional in any way," says Myra, adding that in larger cities like Baltimore, Philadelphia and Atlanta, African-Americans are a regular part of the classical music scene.

"We take pride in seeing African-Americans being successful in the arts," says her husband, who keeps a picture of soprano Leontyne Price on the mantel in the music room. "The numbers may be small, but they're there."

Although Isom is not a trained musician, he's accustomed to the sometimes rarefied lingo of classical music. The terminology seems nothing compared to the language used at the advanced level of mathematics, in which he has excelled.

"I've been studying applications of differential equations to problems of fluid flow, using new techniques of mathematics," says Isom, who has published more than a dozen articles on his work. At RPI, he teaches math to engineering students and supervises a few Ph.D. students.

"Thinking logically and motivating students," says Blandy, "applies to knowing your (musical) material and motivating your board."

On the connection between math and music, the Herrons are rather philosophical.

"A lot of people say there's a connection, and point to the symbols and structures," says Myra. "But I think it's at a higher level."

"It just appeals to my aesthetic sense," says Isom, who can cite the opus numbers of Beethoven String Quartets like a professional and gets excited discussing Brahms.

"I find myself wondering, since he's not a musician, how he hears," she says. "Often after a concert it just embarrasses me that he's understood it better than I have. I'm listening analytically, and he's just enjoying the performance."

MICHAEL MacLEOD

IMPRESARIO

Riding opera's crest

When Michael MacLeod took over as the new general director of Glimmerglass Opera last fall, he bought a house on the lake just two miles from the company's Alice Busch Theater in Cooperstown. The short distance makes for an easy drive or perhaps even a leisurely walk during the off-season. But MacLeod's favorite means of commuting lately is his new boat.

A 22-foot C-Dory Cruiser, with a 90-horsepower Honda outboard motor, the gleaming white vessel is christened *The Flying Scotsman*, in reference both to opera (Wagner's "The Flying Dutchman") and to MacLeod's heritage.

"Paul Kellogg told me the Baseball Hall of Fame is important and the opera is important, but what dominates this community is the lake," says MacLeod. "This epitomizes my desire to be part of the local community, not some bloody foreigner." (Kellogg, Glimmerglass' artistic director, will retire at the end of August, when MacLeod will become general and artistic director.)

The Glimmerglass board gave MacLeod the option of living in Manhattan, where so many foundations and opera patrons are based, and spending time in Cooperstown or the other way around. So far, his choice to focus on Otsego County, as well as upstate New York in general, is going over well.

"He's certainly fallen in love with the lake and boating," says Robert B. Schlather, chairman of the Glimmerglass board. "He seems very at home in Cooperstown."

MacLeod, 54, may be putting down roots as an upstate impresario, but in a conversation a few days before opening night, he emphasized the importance of building Glimmerglass' international reputation. Given the man's personal history, a broad world view comes naturally.

The youngest child of an American mother and a Scottish father who was in the foreign diplomatic corps, MacLeod was born in Bogota,

Columbia. By his 6th birthday, his family had also lived in Turkey and Austria in addition to brief stints in Denver and Los Angeles. His early schooling was at their next posting in Africa and as a teen he attended a boarding school in Scotland, where on the rugby fields he became mates with future Prime Minister of Great Britain Tony Blair, who was one year his junior. A full scholarship to Amherst College in Massachusetts brought him back to the States.

"I was asked once in college, 'What would be the ideal job?'" recalls MacLeod. "My answer was to sweep the stage at La Scala ... nice place to work, meet the stars, hear the music."

MacLeod did eventually make it to the famed Italian opera house, through the course of his 12 years as manager for British conductor John Eliot Gardiner and his touring ensembles, the Monteverdi Choir, the English Baroque Soloists and the Orchestre Revolutionnaire et Romantique.

From 1996 to 2001, MacLeod was executive and artistic director of the City of London Festival and from 2001 until last year he was the chief administrator of the New Haven Symphony. A job in Connecticut was desirable because of MacLeod's relationship with Mary Miller, another Scot who was director of that city's annual Festival of Arts & Ideas. But last year, Miller took on the task of organizing yet another arts festival in Stavanger, Norway. Since the event takes place in 2007, she is currently living there.

"Before I even knew of the Glimmerglass situation, I applied for jobs in or near Norway," says MacLeod. "But when Glimmerglass got in touch and said this would be general *and* artistic director, even my Mary said, 'You've got to go for that.'"

Miller and MacLeod make a point of speaking twice a day by phone and take turns crossing the Atlantic for a monthly rendezvous. This Memorial Day weekend they met half way, in Reykjavik, Iceland.

Among MacLeod's travels, a favorite was a bike ride at age 28. "I had this wanderlust and thought, 'I'd kill three birds with one stone,'" he recalls. "I wanted to get fit, go to the outer Hebrides, the island in the top left corner of Scotland where my branch of the MacLeods come from, and being in the music business ... I thought I should get to know what the 'Ring of the Nibelung' sounded like."

Starting and ending in London, the 2,000-mile ride took three weeks. The continuous soundtrack came from cassettes of the Wagner's four-opera cycle.

"It was a fantastic holiday," says MacLeod.

MacLeod plays opera recordings throughout most of his waking hours, and admits, "I eat opera for breakfast." But he sees himself arriving at Glimmerglass as someone decidedly not from the operatic mainstream. In the same way that Peter Gelb, the new general manager of the Metropolitan Opera, comes from the realm of film and recordings, MacLeod has primarily been a festival producer and orchestra manager.

The first indication of his vision for the company's new direction is the 2007 season. It is a mix of baroque, romantic and contemporary works that have never previously been performed at Glimmerglass. Most importantly, they are all centered on the myth of Orpheus. It's the first time that a Glimmerglass season has had a theme.

The idea came from the 400th anniversary of Monteverdi's "L'Orfeo," typically regarded as the beginning of western opera. Filling out the season will be the Berlioz version of Gluck's "Orphee et Eurydice," Offenbach's "Orpheus in the Underworld," and Philip Glass' "Orphee," in honor of the composer's 70th birthday.

On top of it all, there will also be two concert performances of Haydn's "L'anima del filosofo" (another Orpheus-themed opera), plus a seminar weekend of scholarly commentary, and screenings of Jean Cocteau's 1950 film "Orphee," on which the Glass opera is based.

After being unanimously approved by the company's board, MacLeod's 2007 slate of operas was announced in January, a full six months earlier than usual. John Conklin, the stage designer who is also the company's associate artistic director, is among those who likes the new direction.

"The Orpheus season, that's completely his idea, and that's a festival idea, not an opera repertory company idea. ... I think that's great and I completely agree with that philosophy toward Glimmer-glass," says Conklin, who was a member of the search committee that hired MacLeod.

Another first is that tickets for next season went on sale opening night of this season. "You want people to encourage people while they are here to sort out their accommodations and tickets for next year and commit," explains MacLeod. A themed season, he adds, makes it more desirable for audiences to see all four shows.

MacLeod is already looking for audiences for 2008 and so far has committed to one work for the season, Wagner's "Das Liebesverbot," which has never been staged in America. Based on Shakespeare's "Measure for Measure," it is a rare, almost unimaginable operatic commodity – a Wagnerian comedy.

"The Wagnerian societies and aficionados around the world are the kind of people that plan a year or two in advance, so I want to be marketing to them soon," says MacLeod.

"It is my desire, to reach out to everyone, the local community, as well as people who go to Bayreuth," says MacLeod, referring to the German home of Wagnerian opera. Toward that end, he's been traveling around upstate, making appearances at community events in Syracuse, Oneonta and Albany, where he spoke at the Fort Orange Club. He's also become fast friends with a dozen or so Glimmerglass enthusiasts from Troy.

"He interacts smashingly," says Hannelore Wilfert, who with her husband Karl Moschner, have hosted two gatherings in MacLeod's honor at their home on Troy's Washington Park. "He definitely has the qualities of an impresario ... but is very approachable and open to suggestions and ideas."

Paul Kellogg also sees in MacLeod the right mix of talents for the demanding post. At an opening night reception, Kellogg made a slip of the tongue that indicated not only his admiration for MacLeod but also his own eagerness to relinquish the company: "(MacLeod) is wonderful at understanding the needs of artists, which is one of the chores – I mean joys – of the job."

Besides working with finicky singers, building audiences and leading a staff that swells to more than 300 during the main season, MacLeod is also addressing the long-term financial security of Glimmerglass Opera.

"I would say maybe 85 percent of my job is begging," says MacLeod, "(but) it all ultimately comes down to the artistic product."

BILL RICE

MUSIC CRITIC   APRIL 3, 2005

Gentleman with generous ears

For 35 years the local music scene has had a faithful and insightful observer in Bill Rice, critic for The Daily Gazette in Schenectady. He retired last Friday after 10 years as a staff writer, and a quarter-century prior to that spent as a freelancer.

"I'm pretty much going to sit on my porch until the summer, when I may do some reviewing. I have no plans yet," says Rice, 69, clearly holding out the possibility that he may not let the busiest part of the music season completely pass him by.

Over the years, few concerts by the Albany and Schenectady symphonies, the Union College Concert Series, the Saratoga Performing Arts Center or numerous other series and venues have passed without a notice from Rice. He's been thorough and articulate as a reporter, and patient and kind in giving critiques.

It's probably rare that a music critic is regarded as "beloved," but a sign of the community's good feelings toward Rice comes from two local conductors whose performances he's covered regularly. In recent conversations, both David Alan Miller of the Albany Symphony Orchestra and David Griggs-Janower of the Albany Pro Musica referred to Rice as "a gentleman."

"He's a real old-world critic (whose) writing on music stems mainly from his love for it and his pleasure in it," says Miller. "He may not be the most critical critic, but he's a potent and wonderful advocate for music."

"We've always appreciated his gentle but knowledgeable reviews," concurs Griggs-Janower.

After studying bass trombone at the Crane School in Pottsdam and playing in the U.S. Army Band from 1959 to 1962, Rice got his start in journalism at the Troy Record writing about skiing. He's continued writing about the winter sport in the Gazette as well. (Rice isn't the only long-lasting journalist at the Gazette; Arts editor Peg Churchill retired in 1999 after 41 years with the paper.)

Among the thousands of concerts and operas Rice has heard over the years, he quickly named a particularly memorable performance: Gil Shaham's "incredibly electrifying" rendition of Vivaldi's "Four Seasons," at the Saratoga Chamber Music Festival in August 2001.

"That's a piece that I didn't care to hear again, but he played it so spectacularly. He just seemed to inspire the other musicians," says Rice.

But there is one piece that Rice definitely hopes to never again endure: Pachelbel's Canon. "There was a time when everybody was playing it. It was everybody's encore," he says.

Rice also recalls being wowed by the pianst Lang Lang, who tore through Tchaikovsky's Piano Concerto No. 1 two years ago at SPAC. Although the young musician is often criticized for being too showy on stage, Rice stayed focused on the music.

"If somebody is flashy, be it a conductor or a soloist, if you can hear the flash in what the play it doesn't matter," he says. "If it's flashy and nothing happens (in the music), then it's all show."

Since the '70s, Rice has been filing his overnight reviews on a Radio Shack TRS-80 laptop computer. During a recent visit to Denver, where his son lives, he saw the same model in a museum. "They had it in a case with a bunch of old cameras," Rice recalls with a chuckle.

DEBORAH SEGEL

VIOLIN REPAIRER   FEBRUARY 6, 2005

Nursemaid to fiddles

Violins are people, too.

OK, Deborah Segel never actually said those words in my presence. But after spending a morning with the owner of Segel Violins in Troy, I almost expected her to make such a statement. Segel has a palpable attachment to the fiddle.

"I've loved the violin ever since I can remember," says Segel. "They're all different and have their own voices, just like people do. You hear people's voices and you can recognize them. Violins are like that, too."

Long before she opened her shop, four years ago, Segel was collecting violins the way others take in stray animals. She even calls old homeless violins "stray dogs."

"It's a cute nickname for some of these pathetic beater violins I pick up," she says. And she's picked up more than a few.

When her collection reached 60 to 70 instruments, it became time to go into the business of repairs, refurbishing and sales. Whether it's a "beater" for beginner students or a professional model, she treats each instrument with loving care.

"(From) the way she'll handle a fiddle when she's looking at it," says Terri Lukacko, a customer and friend, "you can tell she cares a lot about the instrument."

Segel, 51, came to music relatively late in life. An interest in the recorder led her to the local early music community. Soon came violin lessons. "It doesn't matter if you're thirty-something, you can do these things. So I did," she says, while conceding that she's no virtuoso.

Initial training and encouragement in violin repair came from Herb George, the proprietor of the now-shuttered George's Music shop on Central Avenue in Albany, who continues to fix up and sell string instruments out of his home in Delmar. "There's room for more repair people in this area," says George. "So many kids are taking string instruments in school today."

Further studies for Segel were with Horst L. Kloss, a master violin maker out of Needham, Mass. The repair field has no accreditation programs, according to Segel, so rather than having a certificate on the wall of her workshop, she's got a work apron that bears the logo of Kloss' school.

Since each instrument is unique, there's no typical job for Segel. But there are similarities to what people bring in.

"Most commonly it will be like this violin," says Segel, holding a instrument of burnished wood that to the naked eye looks like any other violin. But Segel points to a worn-out bridge and spots in the body that have come unglued. "Somebody brought it in. They want somebody in the family to play it. It's been in the family and has been neglected."

Hanging on the wall near Segel's workbench are more than a dozen instruments awaiting her care.

"I always have a backlog of work," she says, adding that her typical turn-around is a couple of weeks. "I try to turn around bows in a couple days because players really need those."

In December Segel relocated her business from a basement space on Second Street to a substantially larger street-level location at 44 Third Street. In addition to violins, bows and all the essentials for string players, she also carries other products of her handiwork: a range of beaded jewelry and lots of colorful monotype prints, which are framed and matted.

Segel takes pride in offering sheet music for a variety of instruments and levels. "You don't make a lot of money on sheet music, but it's almost a public service. No one around has any" for sale, says Segel.

Segel Violins has also become a community center for local folk musicians. Every Wednesday at noon, a handful of string players gather to jam in the store's sitting area. They are often joined by other instruments – a dulcimer player was leading the music during my visit – and listeners are always welcome.

A larger community feel comes from being nestled in the same downtown block as Aldrich Pianos and the recently relocated coffee bar The Daily Grind.

"It's becoming a nice little professional block," says Segel. "There's a lot of cool stuff happening."

JACK SHEEHAN

Listening and clapping like no other

He was known as Jack the Clapper.

A passionate and devoted follower of classical music, John J. "Jack" Sheehan – according to his own accounting – missed only two concerts in the Union College Concert Series in Schenectady during a period of about 25 years. He died on March 23 at age 64.

From his regular seat in Memorial Chapel's front left balcony, he could be seen clapping for every piece in a slow, broad motion with his hands above his head.

"It's easier," said Sheehan of his distinctive ovation style. "I guess some people think it's for extra approval and they're entitled to think that. But you keep doing this (he demonstrates clapping in a normal fashion) and you start tightening up. That's the secret. I hate to disabuse anybody. I discovered it in some dry hall. It makes a better sound as well."

By an odd turn of fate, I interviewed Sheehan at an Albany coffee bar on the afternoon of March 22, the same day he suffered a fatal heart attack. Clapping was the last topic in a long conversation about his lifetime of enjoying music and the company of musicians.

"I love it all. I'm not a fan of chamber music but music," he said. He proved that assertion every summer by driving an estimated 6,000 to 7,000 miles to performances at Tanglewood, the Saratoga Performing Arts Center, Glimmerglass and smaller venues like South Mountain and Aston Magna. "In July and August there aren't too many days I don't go to something," he said.

"Jack was one of the most avid concertgoers, and he was cherished by all of us performers," said Charles Dutoit, who conducts the Philadelphia Orchestra at SPAC, by phone from a tour in Asia. "He will be sorely missed."

"I had become accustomed to seeing him at every concert, clapping in his unusual way," said violinist and Saratoga Chamber Music Festival director Chantal Juillet via e-mail from Montreal. "He had this friendly way of going up to artists and discussing the music world – something we had been doing through e-mails as recently as a few weeks ago."

Many famed musicians also admired Sheehan's keen appreciation of their performances.

"Music must have meant an incredible amount to Jack. He was enjoying the kind of addiction that we wish more people could have," said cellist David Finckel of the Emerson String Quartet. "He was always (seated) in the same place, and when he was listening he was leaning forward as far as he could get. His yearning to experience music was so powerful, you could feel that throughout the hall."

While Sheehan took natural pride in friendships built over many years, he approached musicians as regular folks.

"We talk about any old thing, sometimes it's music, or 'How are the kids?'" he said. "Music is fascinating but to people doing it, it's still a job."

In addition to his presence at Union College, Sheehan also made contacts during the 1980s and early 1990s at the Apple Tree Inn in Lenox, Mass.

"Many of the artists and musicians who played Tanglewood would stay there for their term," said Sheehan. "That's how I met Dutoit. ... We gabbed by the swimming pool. That night, he noticed me and asked me to join them (after the concert)."

A native of Troy and graduate of Siena College, Sheehan retired in March 2003 from the state Department of Labor, where he had worked for 33 years. Also an avid sports fan, he was an umpire for a youth baseball league throughout the 1970s. More recently he took particular enjoyment in following hockey on cable TV.

At Union College, Sheehan was on the organizing committee and known for diligently counting audience members prior to each concert. "I count the darn folks one by one," he said. He was also a past member of the board for the Friends of Chamber Music.

Sheehan's love of serious music started as a teen, thanks to a fellow baseball player. "He kept pestering me to listen ... he had the patience of a saint."

One night after baseball practice, Sheehan relented and sat down to hear a recording. The vibrant rhythms and subtle colors of Ravel's

"Bolero" did the trick and started him on a life of listening, primarily at concerts. "I discovered Beethoven very quickly," he added.

Sheehan advised new listeners to regard the classics not as "some lofty human undertaking so far beyond your capacity," and to always read the program notes – but after the concert.

"Go with the thought that this enormous canvas of music is all there for you," he said, "if only you come to it with an open heart."

MICHAEL WEIDRICH

ARTIST/COMMUNITY ORGANIZER   JUNE 3, 2007

Streetwise artist takes charge

At last month's Champaign on the Park, the annual fundraiser for the Lark Street Business Improvement District, Michael Weidrich did something of a runway turn on the stage. First, he was presented with an award for his work as founder of First Fridays, the successful gallery night based primarily in the Center Square neighborhood. Moments later he returned to the stage having just been re-introduced as the new executive director of the BID.

Though duties in his new post are varied, from working with street cleaning crews to organizing restaurant nights, Weidrich's immediate attention has gone to Art on Lark, the annual day of exhibitions, demonstrations and sales on the sidewalks of the main thoroughfare in Albany's Center Square that takes place Saturday afternoon.

"Lark Street is the heart of the arts in Albany, and it's becoming the capital of the arts for the whole Capital Region," says Weidrich. Citing the recent start of gallery nights in Troy and Schenectady, he adds, "First Friday created a ripple effect that all comes back to Lark Street."

Much of it also comes back to Weidrich, 34, who's lived in Albany since 2003 and in Center Square since 2005. He's a native of Buffalo and holds a bachelor's of fine arts degree from Syracuse University. To join the BID, he left a position as director of technical services and office manager of the Albany law firm Green and Seifter.

Weidrich's hiring might be viewed as a new acknowledgment by the Lark Street BID that the arts can be a key to vitality in the region, especially since his two predecessors had backgrounds in real estate management and architecture. But working with the arts community actually dates to the organization's earliest days.

Art on Lark was the first activity that the Lark Street BID produced after its establishment in 1996. Initially, artists were invited to show art along the avenue every Sunday afternoon for most of the summer. In subsequent years, the plan was retrenched to one Saturday afternoon in early June, with exhibitors dispersed on Lark Street between Washington and Madison avenues.

Although weather is always an unknown factor, registrations have held steady in recent years at about 70 exhibitors, who pay $35 for a 10-foot-square space. Up to 5,000 people are expected to attend this year.

"Art on Lark is my favorite show," says potter Mary Sanza. "The (other) artists are fun to be with, and the crowds are usually an interesting mix of people. I have a couple of repeat customers, who I enjoy seeing year after year."

Weidrich says that in addition to the independent exhibitors, this year's fair will continue some traditions and also include some new offerings.

The People's Choice exhibit will return for a second year to the Upstate Artists Guild, where viewers of a special exhibit vote with ballots for their favorite pieces of art. Last year, more than 40 artists participated, paying $5 to show up to two pieces each.

New this year will be the closure of two side streets for special activities. On Lancaster Street there will be a chalk art contest. And Hudson Avenue will be the site of "Creative Chaos," in which artists will demonstrate their working methods, and folks can also try things out themselves, from painting to pottery.

Creative Chaos is presented by eba Inc., the dance and fitness studio that has been a fixture on Hudson just off Lark since 1977. Showing the public how art is made (and not just the finished pieces) was part of the original concept of Art on Lark, says eba founder Maude Baum, who's also a founding board member of the Lark Street BID. Says Baum, "Sharing in the creative experience of what the artist is doing makes people much more interested in the arts and in pursuing the arts themselves."

Baum successfully tried out the Creative Chaos idea at last year's Lark Fest – the annual September event when Lark Street is closed to auto traffic for a full day. It's the Lark Street BID's largest production. She says that participatory art-making and an additional stage with more family-friendly entertainers has helped move Lark Fest away from being "a college drinking fair."

Coordinating First Fridays for the past nine months has allowed Weidrich to arrive at the Lark Street BID with a built-in network of artists, business owners and neighbors. Add to that his other involvements – director of the Romaine Brooks Gallery in the Capital District Gay and Lesbian Community Council building, board member of the Albany Charity for Arts in Education, and contributing writer for Upstate Fashion and Art Magazine – and it doesn't seem like too much of an exaggeration when he says, "I feel like I know everybody and everybody knows me."

But thanks to Weidrich's revealing digital photographs, gallery goers sometimes also see a rather intimate side of him.

In April, a meeting of Lark Street restaurant owners was held in the UAG gallery. After Weidrich was introduced as the new Lark Street BID director, he rose to speak and quickly realized that a piece of his art – in which he poses nude – was displayed on a nearby wall.

"Everybody was looking back and forth at it and at me," he recalls with a laugh.

The particular piece, "Tsohanoai" (after the Navajo sun god), was created specifically for UAG's "Angels and Devils" show and depicts a golden-toned, winged Weidrich against a flaming background. It's part of an ongoing series of pieces in which original digital photos are fragmented and manipulated into circular patterns, like the effect of a kaleidoscope. Weidrich uses the Hindu term *mandala* to describe them, and has created about 200 such pieces since 2004.

"At my peak, I could produce a dozen pieces in a week. That's when I had nothing else to do," he says. Over the past year, new pieces have been created in the odd late-night hours and mostly for entry in particular shows.

Regarding the nudity, Weidrich says, "I started with some clothing and sort of lost it all along the way."

Coinciding with Weidrich's rising prominence in the community, a new and less self-referential direction began to evolve in his art last fall with three pieces created for the "Vacancy" show, a popular annual fundraiser for the Historic Albany Foundation showcasing artistic depictions of empty city buildings. The works maintain the mandala technique but focus on the Wellington Row buildings, across from the State Capitol.

"Michael is pragmatic but also a visionary," says Jeff Gritsavage, a Center Square resident who is the Lark Street BID's new president. "The combination of a business sense and artistic creativity is not always the easiest to find, and with Michael we think we have that."

Weidrich, however, plans to bone up on his fundraising and accounting skills by enrolling in a certificate program in nonprofit management at The College of Saint Rose. He's already completed a similar postgraduate program at Saint Rose in computer education. Also on his agenda is a greater outreach to the various neighborhood associations that have vested interests in the success of Lark Street.

"I feel a great responsibility to everyone in Center Square," Weidrich says. "There's no place like Lark Street. It's a universe unto itself."

CHAPTER THREE
Visiting Artists
IN FOR THE NIGHT

MARIN ALSOP

CONDUCTOR

From the lawn to the podium

Typical of a major conductor in our jet set age, Marin Alsop, who appears with the Philadelphia Orchestra at the Saratoga Performing Arts Center on Wednesday, has bases of operation located in a variety of far flung cities.

First is Baltimore, where in September she begins her second year as the music director of the Baltimore Symphony Orchestra. With her 2005 appointment to the post she became the first female leader of a major American orchestra. And there's Santa Cruz, California, where she's completing her 16th summer directing the Cabrillo Festival of Contemporary Music.

Alsop also recently ascended to the post of conductor emeritus with the Bournemouth Symphony Orchestra in England, after completing a six-year tenure and a series of acclaimed recordings there. And she maintains a home in Denver, where she's music director laureate of the Colorado Symphony Orchestra and where her companion teaches horn and plays in the orchestra.

Alsop, 51, says she got the conducting bug at around age 9 at a Young People's Concert with Leonard Bernstein, who later became her mentor. But she probably first developed a taste – or tolerance – for a conductor's peripatetic life even earlier because of annual July visits with her parents to Saratoga Springs. Her dad, violinist LaMar Alsop, was concertmaster of the New York City Ballet Orchestra for 30 years and her mom Ruth remains a member of its cello section.

"(Saratoga) was a very idyllic experience as a kid," Alsop said during an interview in the late spring. "I remember attending rehearsals, and lying on the SPAC lawn listening to music. There's nothing like that."

She's continued to visit over the years, staying at her folks place and enjoying some of the local sights. "My mom especially likes the horse racing and is friendly with the trainers. That's a nice contrast to the music part for all of us," she says.

But the Alsops never stray far from music.

"Growing up as the only child of professional musicians, there's not a lot of discussion about what you're going do," says Alsop, who began piano studies at age 2 and violin three years later. "I had a brief detour as an undergrad at Yale and was thinking about mathematics but ended up transferring to Juilliard for violin performance. My parents are very passionate and led wonderfully fulfilling lives and they wanted me to have the same kind of life experience."

Alsop and her family will spend the better part of this week in Saratoga. She and her partner of 18 years Kristin Jurkscheit have a five-year-old son, Auden Alsop, and this will be his second time to the area. "He remembers (the last visit) a bit because of pictures but this will be more poignant and memorable," she says.

Naturally, the boy is already studying music.

"I vowed I'd never do to my kid what mine did to me, but we're forcing him to play the violin," says Alsop, adding that he's recently gotten beyond variations on "Twinkle, Twinkle."

Although Alsop hasn't made a judgment yet on his musical promise, she says her son – who bears the same name as the British poet – shows remarkable gifts for language. "You'd know what I mean if you had a conversation with him," she says.

Alsop has a musical history with Saratoga that's more than just familial. Before turning to conducting, she was a freelance violinist who gigged with a variety of orchestras, great and small, including the New York Philharmonic and the American Composers Orchestra, as well as in the pit at some Broadway shows and alongside her folks in the New York City Ballet Orchestra. The latter included some summers in Spa City.

Her conducting debut at SPAC came on Sunday July 5, 1992, leading the Ballet Orchestra – sans dancers – in its first ever performance on the SPAC stage. The program included Tchaikovsky's "Romeo and Juliet" Overture-Fantasy, Stravinsky's "Firebird Suite," and an encore of "Stars and Stripes Forever."

Alsop's relationship with the Philadelphia Orchestra dates back even further. She made her debut on a subscription program at age 33. "I was pretty doggone scared," says Alsop. "They're one of the great orchestras of the world. They know that and they're proud."

But Alsop has returned to lead the Philly on a regular basis and watched its membership take on more musicians her age and younger.

"I feel that the orchestra's evolving and it has a little bit of a different perspective, though they're still very established and steeped in tradition," she says. "Now it's just fun with a lot of friends, a reunion in a way. I love guest conducting these great orchestras. It's a dream come true."

While racking up the frequent flyer miles, Alsop has also received important honors in recent years. In 2005, she was awarded a MacArthur Fellowship, sometimes called a genius award. And this spring she was elected to the American Academy of Arts and Sciences, in a "2008 class" that includes Supreme Court Justice John Paul Stevens, filmmakers the Coen Brothers and jazz musician B.B. King among others.

Then there's that ongoing thing about being "the first woman" to do this or that in the field of conducting.

"I am shocked by the fact that in the 21st century there can still be 'firsts' for women," she's said, ever keeping the focus on the music.

Yet the firsts keep happening. In Milan this past April, Alsop was the first woman to conduct in the 230-year history of La Scala. In the midst of the experience, she wrote the following for her on-line journal:

"The musicians seemed curious and slightly bemused for a few minutes at our first rehearsal and then we quickly got down to the business of making music together and the woman issue was a non starter!"

BANG ON A CAN

The future looks bright

The cutting edge is a difficult place to find. But it's almost impossible to live there, especially for musicians. What's hip changes so quickly that even the word "hip" isn't very hip anymore.

In the little niche of classical music known as the avant-garde, the term avant-garde is seldom used today. "New music" is the more common if less evocative term. It speaks of an era, began in the 1980s, when contemporary composition wasn't bad medicine anymore, but rather something that could actually provide pleasure and amusement.

Minimalist opera composer Philip Glass and the fashionably attired Kronos Quartet were new music's first break-out stars. Bang on a Can is their successor.

It started out in 1986 as a low-budget project of three young composers – David Lang, Michael Gordon and Julia Wolfe – who met while studying at Yale. Their first concert was approximately 12 hours long, and took place in a run-down auditorium in Manhattan's East Village. Music marathons became their trademark, and Lincoln Center and the Brooklyn Academy of Music eventually presented their annual events to large audiences. But concerts in New York City were just the beginning.

The Bang on a Can All-Stars, an international touring ensemble, was founded in 1993 and was soon recording for Sony and Polygram; a few years ago, Bang on a Can started its own record label, Cantelope Music. (Full disclosure: I worked with Bang on a Can during the early 1990s, producing three discs of live recordings from their festival as well as discs by Lang and Gordon.)

This week, the Bang on a Can Summer Institute – a kind of new music summer school – concludes its second year at MASS MoCA in North Adams, Mass., with a six-hour concert on Saturday afternoon.

Without a doubt, Bang on a Can is a terrific success story for new music. But can it go from being a few young composers with a hey-let's-put-on-a-show mindset to an organization with an annual budget of approximately $1 million and still be cutting-edge? In other words, can the avant-garde be institutionalized?

Staying fresh and lively is actually quite simple, according to Bang on a Can's founders and some of the institute's students, who spoke between rehearsals and concerts at MASS MoCA. It's about being true to one's self, having an open mind and keeping a positive attitude.

"When I heard a Bang on a Can recording for the first time, I thought it was a breath of fresh air," says Miriama Young, a 28-year-old composer from New Zealand who is participating in the institute.

Despite the sense of optimism that pervades the group's projects, it's not modern music wearing a smiley face. Bang on a Can's music often has a gritty texture, makes frequent use of new technologies, is driven by rhythm and underscored by an intellectual rigor.

The critics have fitted the group with adjectives like postmodernist and post-minimalist; neither have stuck, partly because the music concerns itself with the future, not the past.

"We're passionate idiots about what we do," says Lang.

The three founders have never made a salary: "Whenever it looks like we can pay ourselves, we say, 'Wouldn't it be better to hire a professional for this next project?'" As more staff keeps getting added – with four full-time and up to 10 during peak production periods – the demands on Lang, Wolfe and Gordon still never seem to let up. Gordon estimated that 25 percent of their time is devoted to the organization. No longer freewheeling young artists with nothing better to do, each of them now receives important commissions from orchestras and theaters around the world.

The group's musical adventurousness is matched by its creative approach to arts philanthropy. Its People's Commissioning Fund is an imaginative alternative to the standard practice of big foundations paying select composers to write new pieces. Instead, Bang on a Can pools hundreds of small donations and guarantees that every person who contributes gets his or her name on the newly written score. In five years, the fund has commissioned more than a dozen works that have been premiered by the All Stars.

Bang on a Can's renown and influence has grown to the point that it is practically a trademark. A budget of roughly $1 million provides a considerable measure of security, especially in the perpetually under-funded arena of new music.

"It makes you seem like you're more stable than you are," says Lang of the sizable budget. "But it's great to have a label to do what you want, a band to play your music and the music you want to be surrounded by."

"It just means we're doing more stuff," says Wolfe. "We couldn't have kept going without building certain infrastructures."

"A million dollars means you have six under-funded projects instead of one under-funded project," concludes Gordon.

It's probably impossible to teach young composers and musicians how to be part of the vanguard. Instead of focusing on technique or trade secrets, the Summer Institute aims to build a community and empower individuals.

"Part of what we're teaching is the love and care and concern for the experimental musical culture," says Lang. Recalling how his life changed in his 20s when he met Gordon at the Aspen Music Festival, Lang says, "It's important to learn that there are others around who are also dedicated to this music – and to put them together when they're young."

"We just let them be," says Wolfe, sounding like a proud parent. (She and Gordon are married with two small children.) "If they follow what is within them, they'll wind up in strange and unusual places."

During the institute, days are structured more like a retreat than a school. Mornings start with a stretching class followed by an hour of music played as a gamelan, the mellow Asian percussion orchestra. Afternoons are spent in rehearsals and informal concerts.

Faculty play alongside students in all of the ensembles. Composers, who receive no private classes, are encouraged to show up at the beginning of the institute with new pieces ready to be tried out and discussed.

"When I was at Tanglewood, I spent hours alone writing a piece," recalls Lang of his student days. "That was time I should have been out meeting people."

Rehearsals and discussions happen in MASS MoCA's vaulted galleries and smaller back rooms. A recent stroll through the rambling complex brought to mind a conservatory atmosphere: Music, far louder than what would be heard at Juilliard, leaked out of every doorway.

Although days may be full, students can't seem to get enough; they spend most evenings jamming.

"There's a feeling of fun," says Betsey Biggs, a 37-year-old composer from Fairfield Connecticut. "It's like a music camp, but everything is at a very professional level."

Whether it's widening one's network, learning new repertoire, or experimenting with unusual sounds, Bang on a Can is about expansion.

"No one ever (tells young musicians) their career in music should be optimistic," says Lang. "The future should be bright."

BETTY BUCKLEY

ACTRESS/SINGER   JUNE 29, 2003

Talking dads and Texas

Betty Buckley and I bonded over our late fathers. This was a significant improvement over a half-hour earlier, when she said I had insulted her and insisted, twice, that we restart the interview.

Our fathers were common and safer ground. Both engineers, they were colleagues in Texas many years ago. They both also withheld praise and were indifferent to the artistic accomplishments of their children.

At the beginning of our interview, I told Buckley that I, like she, grew up in Fort Worth, and that our folks knew one another. I also mentioned that when she was on Broadway starring in "Cats" in the 1980s and "Sunset Boulevard" in the '90s, I went backstage after the performances and introduced myself.

Then we turned to the reason for our chat, the Williamstown Theatre Festival's production of "The Threepenny Opera," in which she co-stars with an impressive cast that includes Jesse L. Martin, of TV's "Law & Order." As part of a question, I described her character, Jenny, as an "aging prostitute."

That was too much for her.

By referring that way to Jenny, a role created by the German chanteuse Lotte Lenya, she thought I was pointing out how she herself was getting on in years. I hadn't meant any such thing, but that was her interpretation.

Later, as we talked about the misunderstandings, she suggested I write that the interview got off to a "bumpy" start. Very well, then: The interview got off to a bumpy start.

A change of scenery helped. We walked together down the immaculate sidewalks of historic Williamstown in the early evening. I mentioned the one time I remember her parents being at my childhood home, for some engineers' function that my parents hosted. She was starring in the TV show "Eight is Enough," which featured kids who were about the same age I was at the time. I recalled her father not thinking much of the contemporary subject matter the show dealt with.

And that began our commiserating about fathers. Even when Buckley had reached the top level of American theater, her dad wouldn't attend the Tony Awards. Later, over finger food at a nearby restaurant, she talked about his death from lung cancer about 13 years ago, and how she, her mother and younger brothers kept a six-day vigil by his bed.

She tried to comfort him with the South Dakota folk songs he had once taught her. But even in his weakened state, she said, he tried to shush her famous voice.

Prior to his death, her father attempted a reconciliation with at least one child. "He did apologize to my brother" for their difficulties, she said.

Buckley continued, "Right after his death I went home and started looking for the letter that he had to have written to me." When she explained to her mother that she was searching for the documentation of her father's love and acceptance, her mom replied, "There's no letter, Betty Lynn."

Texas and horses are what Buckley most wants to talk about these days. Last year, she bought a 6-year-old gray cutting horse named Purple Badger. She's started competing with him ("cutting" refers to how the horse separates a calf from its herd) and has already won some prize money, $850 at one event in April.

"That's about what I got for a night of 'Elegies' at Lincoln Center Theatre," she said, referring to a revue by composer William Finn, which played in the spring and was recently released on CD.

She also performed at Lincoln Center in the weeks after Sept. 11, 2001, and a poignant collection of songs from those concerts, "The Doorway," is also newly available on CD.

Jolted by the terrorist attacks into reprioritizing her life, Buckley has listed her Upper West Side Manhattan apartment for sale and started shopping for a ranch north of Fort Worth, where her mom still lives. "I always wanted to be successful enough to own a ranch and work with horses," she said.

A former head cheerleader at Texas Christian University and first runner-up in the 1966 Miss Texas Competition, Buckley remains extremely popular in Texas. In Fort Worth, there's a new series of annual awards for high school drama named in her honor.

Most Texans are not prone to easily sharing deep feelings, certainly not with strangers. Buckley agreed that while sunny smiles may be the norm in our home state, anger and hostility often exist just below the surface.

So how did Buckley come to have such a broad and deep well of emotions so readily accessed in life as well as in art?

She has been in therapy since her 20s, she said, and in "serious analysis for the past 10 years." She added that she regularly brings scripts to her therapist for insight into the characters she's to play.

Her broad emotional range is precisely what makes her such a compelling performer. And it translates across genres, allowing her to excel in theater, television and film.

Buckley now teaches her craft at the Terry Schreiber Studio in Manhattan. Once a week during rehearsals in Williamstown, she traveled back to New York for weekly interpretation classes for actors and singers.

"You make yourself a vessel ... to be part of the flow," she said. "I also teach meditation, and I meditate as I perform."

That must explain how she cries seemingly every time she sings her signature ballad, "Memory," from "Cats" – a feat, I said, that I've seen repeatedly.

Oops.

"Well, I don't just *make* myself cry," she said, a bit distressed and defensive.

Time to switch topics.

On the HBO prison drama "Oz," she played an inmate's mother who works in the prison as a music therapist. She conceived the character and storyline on the spur of the moment over dinner with "Oz" producer and writer Tom Fontana, who is an old friend.

But neither of us could recall the name of the inmate whom she taught to sing during the last season. After she remembered that it was Omar, she referred to her memory slip as a "senior moment." She'll turn 56 on Thursday.

The bumpy start had led to a mostly pleasant 90 minutes together. Thinking back, she said, "I don't know what happened."

I don't either.

As we bid goodbye, she drew me into a big, warm embrace. She said, "I've always pictured myself as one day being this extreme, eccentric, weird older woman and I think I'm becoming that now."

JENNIFER HIGDON

COMPOSER   JULY 13, 2003

Getting better all the time

Composer Jennifer Higdon has been looking backward lately. It's not that she's studying Renaissance part-writing or analyzing the genius of some Romantic master. She's simply been listening to the music that captivated her as a youth, and it has given her some insights into why she composes the way she does.

"I listened to 'Sgt. Pepper's ...' every day for a year," the 40-year-old composer says, referring to the classic 1967 Beatles album. Also on her adolescent playlist were the Kingston Trio, Simon and Garfunkel, and Peter Paul and Mary.

Higdon's trip down memory lane ended with a realization: "Oh, that's why I write like that."

Although the source had been a mystery, Higdon's musical priorities have been obvious to her for some time: "The enjoyment of melody and the need for clear rhythm."

It's a simple combination, but one that's not so easy to master, as any pop songwriter will agree. Yet Higdon's distinctive music including works for orchestras, chamber ensembles and choruses is a long way from the clattering and pounding that typify some of today's pop-influenced contemporary music.

"Her music has a terrific sense of forward motion and drama," says Robert Maggio, a composer who, like Higdon, lives near Philadelphia. "There's also a distinctive sense of American lyricism which is very spiritual."

Local audiences will have several opportunities to hear Higdon's music at this year's Tanglewood Festival of Contemporary Music.

Higdon is a child of the '60s in more than just her early musical taste. "My parents were hippies," she says. "And they took me to so many experimental film festivals where I heard 'be in the moment' again and again."

Although born in Brooklyn, she was raised in Atlanta and Seymore, Tenn. Her father was a graphic artist who liked to dabble in film and who, today in retirement, fashions bamboo flutes.

The standard flute was Higdon's gateway to music. "My mom had a flute lying around," she recalls. "I picked it up and taught myself to play."

Higdon was in middle school at the time, which, she points out, made for a relatively late start for music. But things progressed steadily after that: first-chair flutist in high school marching band – again, prominent melody and a strong beat – and flute study at Bowling Green State University in Ohio soon followed.

Her graduate work in composition was at the University of Pennsylvania with composer George Crumb, himself something of a '60s rebel, known for unusual musical notation and unorthodox use of instruments.

"I think her strong performance abilities fed right into her compositions," says Crumb, from his home in West Virginia. "There was something about her music early on. The notes on the page leaped out and made music."

"I've never written in an established form before," says Higdon, who avoids using any musical jargon in discussing her compositions. "I just write instinctively. I'm following my ear completely."

Higdon is now a teacher herself, at the prestigious Curtis Institute in Philadelphia, where she is a colleague with Ned Rorem, another former teacher of hers. She encourages her students to find their own musical voice, not to mimic hers or anyone else's.

Higdon's ability to look past stylistic camps, combined with her instinctive knowledge of what makes instruments sound good, has brought her music to prominence across the country. She'll have more than 100 performances this year, a remarkably high number for a relatively young composer.

Most remarkable of all is the success of Higdon's recent Concerto for Orchestra. Commissioned by the Philadelphia Orchestra, the piece was premiered last June during the annual convention of the American Symphony Orchestra League. It garnered a standing ovation from the audience of orchestra executives.

"It was as big a debut as you can get in the orchestra world," says Higdon. "I'm still amazed they took the chance."

Now, a year later, the 35-minute showpiece is making the rounds of some of America's top orchestras. Earlier this month, Andrew Litton and the Dallas Symphony Orchestra performed it in Vail, Colo., as part of the Vail Valley Music Festival, where Higdon held a brief residency. In the early fall, the piece will be taken up by the Milwaukee, Atlanta and National symphony orchestras.

Conductor Robert Spano, director of this year's Festival of Contemporary Music at Tanglewood, is Higdon's most important advocate in the orchestra world, and he has taken a special interest in the piece. In the festival's final concert he will lead a performance with the Tanglewood Music Center Orchestra in Ozawa Hall. And, as music director of the Atlanta Symphony Orchestra, he will record the piece for an all-Higdon orchestra disc slated for release next year.

"I'm so busy I don't have time for anything else," says Higdon, when asked about personal pastimes apart from music. Although she likes to keep up on independent films and enjoys reading fantasy novels, she is consumed with commissions. She's booked for the next two years and was unable to accept a commission from Tanglewood for the coming festival.

"It broke my heart," she said, adding that this week will be her first time on the grounds in Lenox, Mass.

In addition writing music, Higdon is also running her own publishing house.

"Philip Glass once told me that if you want to make a living as a composer," she says, "keep the copyrights to your music."

Retaining ownership of the rights to her works has meant that Higdon must also take on the preparation and delivery of her scores, tasks traditionally handled by publishing houses. Such is not uncommon for young composers, aided by computer engraving programs and neighborhood copy shops. But with the amount of performances and inquiries that Higdon receives, the work is formidable.

"I don't know how she does it," says Maggio, the Philadelphia composer.

Higdon does her best to also make time to be with her partner, Cheryl Lawson, who works as a convention planner. The two met in the flute section of high school band and have been a couple ever since.

While being an out lesbian in classical music circles may be unusual, a more common difficulty facing Higdon in professional gatherings is that she stands about 5 feet, 4 inches tall.

"Composers will talk over my head and not pay attention to my presence in the room," she says. "But the minute they find out who I am, they come over to talk."

SHARON ISBIN

Born to strum

Sharon Isbin first picked up the guitar out of obligation. She was 9 years old at the time, and her family was living in Italy. "My older brother had requested the guitar," she says, "but his fantasy, unbeknownst to my parents, was to be the next Elvis Presley."

After considerable effort, their parents had lined up a distinguished teacher who had studied with guitar master Andres Segovia. But Isbin's brother quickly withdrew.

"My parents said someone in the family has to study with this guy it's too good an opportunity," says Isbin. "So I raised my hand out of family duty. I took to it right away."

Isbin went on to study with Segovia, too, and to become today's most prominent classical guitarist. And although she may have come to the guitar out of a sense of responsibility, Isbin's talent – to communicate, to break down barriers, to console – has given her a remarkable sense of freedom. Her ample gifts and wide-ranging musical tastes will be on display in a recital at the Troy Savings Bank Music Hall on Saturday.

"I'm in a very comfortable place right now, where I can just do my thing," Isbin says, on the phone from her home in Manhattan. "I don't have to convince people that you should take guitar with orchestra or bring me into your series. It just happens. That frees me to spearhead a lot of interesting projects."

Among her varied activities over the last 20 or so years, Isbin founded the guitar department at The Juilliard School in Manhattan, in 1989. From that position and her monthly advice column in Acoustic Guitar magazine – she calls herself "the Dear Abby of acoustic guitars" – she's been an advocate for female guitarists. But they remain rare.

"I've had students from 15 different countries, but very few women," she says. "It takes time."

Something that makes Isbin even rarer is that she's an "out" lesbian in the highest ranks of classical music performers. In the 10 years since she disclosed her sexual orientation to the gay press, she's found it remarkable how seldom she's asked about it and disappointing that few female colleagues have followed suit.

"When an artist in the classical world comes out, no one gives a damn," she says. "But if artists are still turning down the gay press, then we have a long way to go. Even if that fear is only internalized, it's not healthy."

New works for guitar are regularly on Isbin's agenda. She has dramatically expanded and diversified the repertoire by commissioning and premiering more new concertos than any other guitarist.

A new Joan Baez Suite harkens back to Isbin's early love of folk music, which was another reason she agreed to try the guitar as a kid. "I've always loved folk music," Isbin says. "Now later in life, I've come full circle, and a lot of the music I'm doing is folk-inspired."

When Isbin won a Grammy Award in 2001 – making her the first guitarist to win as a classical soloist in 28 years – it was for a collection of folk-inspired music, "Dreams of a World" (Teldec). A centerpiece of that record was "Appalachian Dreams" by the British composer John Duarte. It was written for Isbin and uses traditional tunes like "Black is the Color of My True Love's Hair," which Isbin suggested to the composer.

"It's because I so adored that work," she says, "that I decided to approach (Duarte) with the idea of the Joan Baez Suite."

The result is a seven-movement piece that uses 11 famous songs, including the traditional "House of the Rising Sun" and Pete Seeger's "Where Have All the Flowers Gone?" Isbin premiered the piece in San Francisco in October, with the singer's blessing.

"Joan couldn't come that night because she had already started her East Coast tour," recalls Isbin, "but she sent her 90-year-old mother, who turned out to be a fabulous person, and we hung out for three hours afterward."

With an international touring schedule of about 100 concerts each season and a discography of 20 recordings, Isbin knows how to bring music to audiences. But a year and a half ago, she felt the power of her art like never before. It was at ground zero in New York City, exactly one year after the 9/11 attacks.

Part of a group of elite musicians that included cellist Yo-Yo Ma, violinist Gil Shaham and the Juilliard String Quartet, Isbin played during the reading of names.

"People were descending into the pit all afternoon, and for the first time were allowed to touch the ground," she says. "I remember having eye contact with many of them and to this day, some of their expressions remain with me."

Prior to the event, Isbin considered withdrawing, nervous about her ability to maintain composure. But a sense of duty again came to the fore. "I remember looking out to this sea of 24,000 family members and survivors. Many of them were holding up photos of their lost loved ones," she recalls. "It just was such a powerful experience to know that at this very moment music filled a healing role that could not be equaled by any other medium, and I realized that this is what it is all about. This is why music is here."

CHRISTIAN MARCLAY

NOVEMBER 2, 2003   SCULPTOR

Seeing the sound

Music is slipping free of its containers these days. Teenagers consider songs and albums less as physical objects and more as electronic files passed freely through the Internet, stored on computers and heard through portable players.

It is the slow end of a 100-year era in which the recording industry tied music to a succession of tangible media such as 78s, LPs and CDs, not to mention eight-tracks and cassettes. An inherently ephemeral art form became a commercial commodity that could be collected and even treasured.

This stuff around music – the look, the weight, the texture – is what Christian Marclay makes into original works of art. His creations, mostly sculptures and wall pieces, are about music, but they seldom make any noise. Like the reverse of music with no container, it's media that only suggests sound.

In a retrospective exhibit on view at the Center for Curatorial Studies at Bard College in Annandale-on-Hudson, 80 Marclay works from the past 20 years explore the connections between the ear and the eye.

All around are remnants of records, tapes and instruments, as well as microphones, telephones and loudspeakers. But the pristine white galleries are filled mostly with an eerie quiet.

"Silence is an easier way to get people to think," says Marclay, 48, during an interview at his loft in lower Manhattan.

A trim and soft-spoken man, he avoided sound in his early visual works out of consideration for other artists whose works were shown alongside his own.

"It takes over," he says of sound. "And in group shows, one has to be considerate."

No longer relegated to multiple-artist exhibits in offbeat galleries, Marclay now commands the attention of major institutions. The retrospective now at Bard started at UCLA's Hammer Gallery and later will be shown at the Seattle Art Museum and the Kunstmuseum Thun in Switzerland. Marclay is represented by the prestigious Paula Cooper Gallery in SoHo in Manhattan.

Although Marclay's prominence has allowed him a larger megaphone for his ideas, his works have remained mostly in the realm of silence.

"Chorus II," from 1988, consists of 29 framed photos of mouths opened in song. There's dental work, lips and mustaches to look at. But what are they all singing? "Secret," from the same year, is a shiny metal disc, the size of a 45, with a large padlock intersecting its center hole.

"From Head to Ear" is a more traditional sculpture from 1994 that touches on the tactile nature of music. Made of beeswax, it connects a life-size ear to an arm and hand. It is modeled directly after a Bruce Nauman's 1967 piece, "From Hand to Mouth."

In a series of oversize instruments from the last few years, Marclay evokes the larger-than-life nature of musical superstars. "Drumkit" has the standard mix of snare drums and cymbals, a part of any rock band, but they stand about 20 feet tall. "Accordion" extends the instrument's bellows to a 14-foot reach.

"His altered instruments have a morbid curiosity, like a freak show," says Thaddeus S. Squire, a conductor who leads the Relache Ensemble in Philadelphia, for which Marclay recently created a performance piece tied to an exhibit. "All his work has very immediate aesthetic and sensory impact that's really cool or funny."

LPs always have provided fertile ground for Marclay's work, but he denies being a true record collector.

"I have lots of recordings, but I don't obsess," he says. "If I finding something interesting for a few dollars in a thrift shop, I get it. I have tons I use for my sculptures and sound work as well."

Some of his most colorful and provocative visual works combine photos from several album jackets to make new images. It's something like his work as an avant garde DJ making a new music out of many samples.

"I like that you can't look at covers without remembering what the sound is like," Marclay says.

In the "Body Mix" series, famous and anonymous heads, torsos, arms and legs are joined. "Magnetic Fields" assembles a face from seven covers in an almost cubist construction. "Footstompin" takes Michael Jackson's reclined upper body from "Thriller" and attaches female legs.

"Christian is always finding interest in what might appear to be banal," says Marina Rosenfled, a New York-based composer and "turntablist" who has collaborated with Marclay in performance.

Classical recordings are particularly rich fodder. A patchwork quilt of 25 covers that each depicted a black-clad, stern-looking conductor is titled "Dictators."

Another LP series, "Abstract Music," uses classical and jazz covers that reprint famous or anonymous modern-style paintings. Marclay paints over the type announcing the performers and repertoire.

"With classical music," Marclay says, "they put a Poussin (painting) or something classical on a piece of junk to make the plastic more precious."

In contrast to the quiet of the exhibit, there are two adjacent rooms filled with sound —screening rooms with continuous showings of Marclay's latest work in video.

His "Guitar Drag" is a 14-minute film of a red electric guitar being dragged behind a pickup truck across dirt roads and other rough terrain. The soundtrack blares.

Another 14 minutes of sound and image is "Video Quartet," completed in 2002. It may be Marclay's most subtle and refined work to date. Showing on four screens placed side by side are brief musical clips from a multiplicity of Hollywood films. There's Dick Van Dyke in "Mary Poppins," Ella Fitzgerald scatting, the Jets and Sharks from "West Side Story," and dozens more famous and obscure moments.

Through quick edits, simultaneous screening and precise synchronization, Marclay creates duets, trios and choruses. Pianos are tuned, fingers snap, toes tap. As if following a musical score, the video sweeps through a wide dynamic terrain.

"I wanted to create a visual narrative because it's a cinematic composition as well," says Marclay, who spent a year at the project, editing it himself on a computer. "I come up with a vague idea and build as I go, and spent hours at a time for months completely obsessed with it."

Marclay "runs from musical room to musical room, slamming and opening doors, running down historical hallways and souping up the past, present and future," says DJ Olive, another denizen of the downtown experimental scene.

Amid the mute visual works in the Bard galleries is "Tape Fall," the only sculptural piece that emits sound. At the top of a tall metal ladder is a reel-to-reel tape deck that plays recordings of gently trickling water. As the tape rolls off of one reel, it drops onto the floor below. New reels are added throughout the nearly three-month-long exhibit, and the loose tape accumulates into a large random pile. It takes on a dark, liquid character, evoking the tape's origins in petroleum.

As the tape on each reel keeps running out, it also suggests how time is running out on most recording mediums – something Marclay has long been aware of.

"Music is becoming more and more intangible," he says. "The poor record companies are figuring out they don't have an object to sell, only ideas."

AWADAGIN PRATT

PIANIST

Nothing to dread

Sometimes it doesn't take much to shake up the classical music world
– or at least to make audiences do a double take. When Awadagin Pratt,
41, was beginning his career as a piano soloist, all he had to do was show
up and things were different.

Pratt is African-American and wears dreadlocks. "I've had them
since before my career started," says the pianist, who will perform
Saturday night with the Daedalus String Quartet for the Friends of
Chamber Music in Troy.

Yet once audiences hear Pratt's playing, they can be at ease. Unlike
Daniel Bernard Roumain, the dreadlocked hip-hop/jazz/classical com-
poser-performer, Pratt isn't charting new musical territory. The classics
still suit him just fine.

Take his 1994 debut recording, "A Long Way From Normal" (EMI).
The title is a play on the fact that Pratt grew up in Normal, Ill.,
although the program features straight-ahead works by Liszt, Franck
and Brahms.

Pratt's career strides are also eminently mainstream. He won the
Naumburg International Piano Competition in 1992 and two years
later was awarded an Avery Fisher Career Grant. Since 2004, he's been
on the faculty of the College Conservatory of Music at the University
of Cincinnati.

But the popular mind-set of what a black musician should be doing
is slow to change.

"People still can't meet me at a piano without asking what kind of
music it is that I play," says Pratt. "They'll say, 'Well, do you play jazz?
What else do you play?' The associations are still very strong with what
I don't do. I don't think most white musicians will get asked, 'Do you
also play jazz?' "

Nonetheless, Pratt sees progress. He has observed more young musicians of color making it into conservatories, and points to the existence
of Detroit's Sphinx Competition, which encourages young black and

Latino musicians, and the success of new groups made up of black musicians, including Imani Winds, a 10-year-old quintet out of New York City, and the Ritz Chamber Players based out of Jacksonville, Fla.

Pratt's own notoriety might even have something to do with the trend.

"The sight of someone who looks like you doing what you want to do is powerful and compelling," says Pratt. He speculates that the fame of Yo-Yo Ma may be a factor in the rise of an entire generation of Asian musicians, and says that when he was young, "Andre Watts was the man."

Another hero was Glenn Gould, the late Canadian pianist and eccentric.

"If anything came out, I read it and I listened to everything (he recorded) for quite a long period of time, not to the exclusion of other artists, but he was essential," says the pianist.

Like Gould, Pratt has been known for using an unusually low piano bench – only 12 to 15 inches off the ground. Although he first experimented with playing close to the ground because of Gould, Pratt committed to it around 1984 when the low bench brought relief to his wrists, which had developed cysts.

Throughout the '90s, Pratt traveled with his own bench, which he collapsed and reassembled with an Allen wrench. But in the post-9/11 world, lugging it on and off airplanes became impossible ("I never check bags") and shipping it ahead to different gigs was workable for only so long. When it didn't arrive in time for an orchestral date a few years ago, Pratt began re-examining the issue.

"The nature of my body has changed quite a bit," he says. "Now I sit fairly normal."

As did Gould, Pratt also enjoys being in control of more than just what's going on at the keyboard. Trained in violin and conducting as well as in piano, he's able to use those skills through his own programming and leadership of the Next Generation Festival, a 10-year-old summer series in Harrisburg, Pa.

But the ultimate musical experiences for Pratt are performances of concertos – usually classical-era works by Mozart or Hadyn – in which he is both pianist and conductor.

"If I'm playing and a conductor wants to mimic my phrasing, he can, but it's not quite the same," explains Pratt. "It's very satisfying doing both (playing piano and conducting). Then, if I have a problem with the conductor, I consult my psychologist."

NED ROREM

COMPOSER   AUGUST 24, 2003

Wise sage or playful child, take your pick

The increasing longevity of humans has advantages for composers. Because the music world gets obsessed with birthdays and anniversaries, composers who make it to age 70 and beyond can expect tribute concerts at least every five years, and heightened attention to their music in general. Performers and audiences are led to think, "There's a living master in our midst we best pay attention."

Two who fit that bill are Elliott Carter, 95, and Milton Babbitt, 87, both of whom still compose and attend concerts of their music. But before either Carter or Babbitt became senior citizens, they were already old men in a certain sense: Their complex music epitomized the intellectual rigor and ivory-tower mentality that gave contemporary music its bad name.

Their foil has been the eternally nimble and youthful presence of Ned Rorem. Long before the return of Romanticism, Rorem steadfastly wrote in a tonal and accessible style. He's best known for success with the humble medium of the art song, and along the way has been a dry and insightful commentator on music and life.

It seems impossible, but Rorem is on the verge of also becoming a grand old man. He turns 80 on Oct. 23.

"He's supposed to be old," says David Alan Miller, music director of the Albany Symphony Orchestra, who conducted Rorem's Double Concerto for violin and cello in February. "But whenever I talk to him he seems fresh, vigorous and full of new ideas."

In residence for the month of August at Yaddo, the artist colony in Saratoga Springs, Rorem continues to focus on what is in front of him, which is always music. He's at work on a percussion concerto and looking ahead to new projects that will carry him well into his next decade, including his first full-length opera.

In a late-afternoon discussion, Rorem is relaxed and typically witty.

"To become 80 is what your grandparents do, and I really can't believe it," he says. "If I died right now, I'm not ashamed of what I'd leave in the way of books and music."

Fifteen books, some 300 art songs and dozens of orchestral, chamber and choral works is indeed an accomplishment, maybe even enough to allow the creator to take a break. But Rorem remains productive. And rather than drift off toward unknown realms, he continues to write what will bring in income.

"I haven't written anything not on commission for 40 years," he says. "I'd rather get paid than not get paid. It wouldn't occur to me to sit down and right a song cycle. If I wanted to write a song cycle, I'd get someone to commission it."

Rorem's current project, a Percussion Concerto commissioned by the British soloist Evelyn Glennie, is a stark example his workman-like approach to composition. He is writing the piece despite a marked indifference to percussion.

"I'm morally opposed to percussion," he says. It's one of a repertoire of phrases that Rorem likes to throw about as much for shock value as anything else.

"In contemporary music, there's almost no music that doesn't sound better if you just leave (percussion) out," he says. "It's always doubling. At the climax you don't need the cymbal crash."

Rorem's solution is a piece in seven movements, each focusing on a pitched percussion instrument, including marimba, glockenspiel and chimes. "In other words I'm writing music," he says, "instead of noise."

All this begs the question, why is he writing it at all?

"Money, and it seemed like a good thing to do," he says. "There's no such thing as an illegitimate format. Percussion is perfectly legitimate format, though I don't happen to dig it."

"All my friends are dead," says Rorem. It may be another of his provocative overstatements, but his confession to loneliness is understandable.

In 1999, Rorem's companion of 32 years, James Holmes, died after a long battle with AIDS-related illnesses. Rorem chronicled Holmes' long decline and his own wrestling with mortality, as well as more day to day foibles, in "Lies: A Diary 1986-1999." Released in 2000, it is Rorem's sixth published diary and probably his most poignant.

"In many practical ways he held my life together," says Rorem of Holmes, whom he referred to as "JH" through his decades of recording their lives together in diaries. "He did the taxes, he ran the show."

A niece has taken up the logistical chores of Rorem's life, including managing finances and the like. And a year ago this month, during another residency at Yaddo, Rorem began a relationship with a man nearly 40 years his junior. His new companion still maintains his work and residence in the Capital Region but regularly visits Rorem at his homes on the Upper West Side of Manhattan and in Nantucket, Mass.

"I told him I may be older," says Rorem, "but I think of myself as about 11 years old, and I expect to be treated that way."

When Rorem says, "The older I get, the simpler I get," the line seems supported by the economy and clarity of his current music and the general simplicity of his life. But it is betrayed by Rorem's embarking on the largest work of his career, a new opera based on Thorton Wilder's classic play "Our Town."

"We got the rights to it, which people have been trying to do for 50 years," says Rorem.

His librettist and creative partner is the poet and editor J.T. McClatchy, who was instrumental in securing permission for the adaptation. The piece is being commissioned by a group of companies, led by Indiana University and also including the Lake George Opera.

McClatchy, an old friend of Rorem's and an executor of the Wilder estate, is editor of The Yale Review. He has previously written librettos for operas by Tobias Picker, Bruce Saylor and Francis Thorne.

"The time has sort of come" for the opera version of "Our Town," Rorem says. "It's too good to turn down. Most people think it's a good idea. Those who don't, think it's dangerous because it's famous." The pair's work on "Our Town" will take three years.

In the meantime, Rorem and his music are being celebrated in concerts across the country. During the last weeks of October, there will be veritable Rorem festivals in New York and Philadelphia, where he is on the faculty of the Curtis Institute. Among the highlights, the Philadelphia Orchestra will premiere his new Flute Concerto, and the New York Festival of Song will reprise his magnum song cycle, "Evidence of Things Not Seen."

"Everyone wants me to go to everything," says Rorem. "I can't, and I just hate the word 'hotel.'"

He remains focused on new works and has a few other commissions on his list before embarking on "Our Town." Rorem doesn't admit that work keeps him young, although that seems to be the case.

Four years ago, when he was elected president of the American Academy of Arts and Letters an elite group of leading artists, composers, writers and architects he posited a theory of the artist that is his response to growing old: "If an artist stops being a child, he stops being an artist."

DANIEL BERNARD ROUMAIN

COMPOSER/VIOLINIST   FEBRUARY 22, 2007

Composing a business

It has become nearly impossible to miss Daniel Bernard Roumain's name in the world of contemporary performing arts. Actually, he often chooses to be billed with nothing more than his initials, DBR – standard practice for hip-hop artists, but less so in the realm of Itzhak Perlman and Yo-Yo Ma.

Then again, Roumain is a classically trained musician who boldly blends the style and sound of hip-hop and J.S. Bach. In the process, this composer and violinist, who sports dreadlocks to his waist, has become a powerhouse – a 35-year-old with top-level management, his own production company and a touring ensemble.

Local audiences will get a chance to check him out Saturday night at The Egg, when DBR & The Mission perform "24 Bits: Hip-Hop Studies and Etudes."

"He does seem to be the composer of the moment – a wonderful, interesting guy," says David Alan Miller, music director of the Albany Symphony Orchestra, which commissioned Roumain twice in the late 1990s for the Dogs of Desire Ensemble, and most recently for 2004's Spirituals Project.

Roumain has also written for or appeared with the orchestras of Dallas, Memphis, San Antonio, St. Louis and Brooklyn, among others. In addition, he holds a residency with the Orchestra of St. Luke's in New York, and is music director of the Bill T. Jones/Arnie Zane Dance Company. Roumain just completed a guitar concerto for virtuoso Eliot Fisk, and last month gave the keynote address at the annual convention of the International Society for the Performing Arts held in Manhattan.

Amid this remarkable level of activity, Roumain came off in a recent conversation as an omnivorous artist and highly focused professional.

"I'm of the iPod generation," he said. "I want to hear everything and know it all and do everything, too, and play everything. The question is, how do you do that responsibly and in a sophisticated manner?"

As if answering his own question, Roumain spoke a great deal about business models. No surprise, then, that he was recently named by Crain's New York Business to its annual list of "40 Under 40 Business Stars."

"If I sell myself only as a composer, it's going to be very limited (in terms of) where my music is played and how much I can take in from those performances," he said. "But as a band leader, performer and collaborator, it allows me to have serious collaborations with very serious artists, and my interest can be supported (financially)."

Roumain drops lots of names in conversation, constantly mentioning those who have influenced and inspired him. Musically, he links the seemingly unlinkable: Nine Inch Nails and Korn with the composers William Bolcom and William Albright – the latter two among his teachers at the University of Michigan, where Roumain earned a doctorate in composition in 2001.

But he's at least as enthusiastic about musicians who are also successful entrepreneurs, including Philip Glass, Ani DiFranco, Prince, Madonna and even the middle-aged New Age pinup boy Yanni ("a multimillionaire composer!" gushes Roumain).

Whether the map is a musical score or a financial ledger, the realms of classical and popular music have always been one continuous landscape for Roumain, who began playing in garage rock bands just a few years after picking up the violin.

Borrowing from the vernacular is nothing new for composers. The signature musical styles of 20th-century greats such as Bartok, Bernstein and Gershwin relied heavily on folk and popular sources. But for today's composers looking to infuse their music with the sound of today, Roumain says that immersion is even more crucial.

"You have to go to clubs. You have to be in a rock band," Roumain said. "You can't assimilate and try to translate what happens in rock music to a string quartet unless you've done these things." His recent String Quartet No. 5 "Rosa Parks," for example, includes a percussionist who gets the audience to clap along in the final movement.

Perhaps Roumain takes his greatest inspiration from hip-hop disc jockeys, who literally blend music with their hands. "(They) have a wonderful way of instantly translating things that seem disconnected," he said.

Roumain even compares his instrumental technique to that of a turntable artist: "My sound is a result of the techniques of not only Paganini but Prince and Grandmaster Flash," he said. "The scratching, the beating of the instrument – those are things I got from non-violin players."

Roumain looks even farther afield for guidance in managing his business and life. Best-selling novelist Stephen King has been one model. "I was reading some of his (auto)biographical writing, and he says he writes four hours a day," Roumain said. "That had a big impact on me – I started doing that immediately."

Roumain's current level of collaboration and management support allow for more than just greater penetration into the cultural marketplace. It also helps him maintain a certain level of sanity.

"There was a time in my life I could work from 8 a.m. to 2 in the morning, but that's unhealthy," Roumain said. When he's not on the road, he knocks off at 8 p.m., spends time with his girlfriend and tunes in to political pundits on cable TV at his Harlem home.

But no matter what he's busy at, Roumain holds himself accountable.

"If you want to be successful, account for every hour of every day," he says. "That's a very clear practice – coupled with ambition, goals and dreaming. Don't forget the dreaming."

JENNIFER TIPTON

Finally alone, in the spotlight

With an ever-increasing schedule of events leading up to its grand opening in October, Rensselaer Polytechnic Institute's Experimental Media and Performing Arts Center is becoming reliably unpredictable. EMPAC's latest happening is a grand spectacle of outdoor lighting, but comes more than a fortnight after the season of holiday lights has gone dark.

In "Light Above the Hudson," which began on Friday evening at sunset, the acclaimed theatrical lighting designer Jennifer Tipton casts colorful, changing light upon the EMPAC construction site.

With the EMPAC has commissioned one of the foremost theatrical lighting designers of the past 30 years. Tipton received a Tony Award in 1989 for lighting "Jerome Robbin's Broadway," and has collaborated extensively with Paul Taylor, Twyla Tharp and Mikhail Baryshnikov, among many others.

Although Tipton has been credited in countless playbills and programs around the world, her name typically appears a few lines below her more famous colleagues. At RPI, she gets top billing for perhaps the first time in her career. During an interview prior to the holidays, she discussed this and other unique aspects of the project in Troy.

"This is unusual in that it's all ... all me," said Tipton, 70, her deep and confident voice faltering briefly. "I don't know how I'll feel about it until it's over, until I've done it."

Tipton's objective, as she sees it, is "to broadcast the building to the community." To do this, she has shone bright changing colors onto the reflective skin of EMAPC's southern and western facades and placed subtly flickering lights inside the small windows that face south. For the dramatic northern bank of windows, nearly 300 feet long and several stories tall, the light comes entirely from within.

Tipton hopes her treatment will evoke "some kind of mystery and hopefully a desire to see what's going on in there."

Given the changing nature of a construction site, the technical challenges have been considerable. But Tipton has plenty of experience at being part of the birthing process of artworks and has generally taken the difficulties in stride. "It's like the playwright is writing new things," she said.

Most of her own artistic choices were to be made on site last week prior to the opening. "It's like when I'm working in the theater, I do a plot (or diagram) and I call the plot the 'light language' of the play or production," explains Tipton. "So I have given myself a light language for the EMPAC construction installation and will use that language in the way that I find best when I get there."

The invitation from EMPAC was unexpected, but welcome. "I work in pieces that are downtown-theater small to grand-opera large, but this was larger than anything that I've ever done," said Tipton.

Stepping into the role of principal artist actually hasn't been that much of a leap for Tipton, who said, "I've taken this on cold and used my own imagination." And though she normally consults extensively with choreographers and directors, she admits to never even giving a thought to calling up EMPAC's architect.

Still, Tipton swore that she enjoys the collaborative process, calling it "the dirty art." A recent production of Balanchine's "Jewels" for the Royal Ballet in London is an example of how it can go. "There were about five bosses that all had things to say to me – make it brighter, make it dimmer, make it quicker, make it slower," said Tipton. "So maybe given that experience, I'm going to enjoy just having the voice from my own head in my own ear."

BASIL TWIST

Wings, webs and strings

"Striking frogs and getting fairies ready!"

It's the first rehearsal for act one, scene one of "Sleeping Beauty," and Basil Twist is telling the frogs how high to hop (and when to "strike," or leave the stage) and the winged fairies how to glide through the air with grace. A crew of 12 young puppeteers does its best to make the creatures respond.

Twist and his company have come to MASS MoCA in North Adams, Mass., for two weeks of work to stage Ottorino Respighi's 80-minute, three-act puppet opera "La bella dormente nel bosco (Sleeping Beauty in the Woods)."

By late May, when the production premieres in Charleston, S.C., at the Spoleto Festival USA, the stage will be filled with a seemingly effortless beauty. But building a world of fantasy requires dealing with numerous hard realities.

For the preview at MASS MoCA, the piece will still be a work-very-much-in-progress. Not all of the puppets are built yet, let alone costumed. Large chunks of Styrofoam suspended on strings have been filling in as substitutes. And the music will come from a recording. Eventually, the Gotham Chamber Opera will become part of the production, adding seven vocalists, a chorus of 20 and a 34-piece orchestra.

With a budget of nearly half a million dollars, "Sleeping Beauty" is the most ambitious undertaking thus far in the rapid rise of Basil Twist. Five years ago, at age 30, Twist created an underwater abstract treat-ment – "puppet show" seems hardly the right description – to Berlioz's "Symphony Fantastique." It was produced on a budget of $40,000 for a four-week run at Here, a small performance space in New York City's SoHo district. The piece caused a sensation and played for 18 months. After a national tour, it returned to New York last year for an off-Broadway run of six months.

"Since I did that, the music world opened up to me," says Twist. "People were excited about how I treated the music." Since then it's been one high-profile production after another for Twist, all involving puppets.

His "Petroushka" premiered at Lincoln Center in 2001 and also played at Jacob's Pillow, as well as five other venues across the country. It caught the attention of conductor Neil Goran, director of the 4-year-old Gotham Chamber Opera.

"I thought it was one of the greatest evenings I've ever had in the theater," says Goran. "It was unbelievably inventive in every possible way, one unexpected moment of genius after another."

The biography of Basil Twist III says that he's a third-generation puppeteer. But that implies something a little grander than reality.

"There's many puppeteers who belong to dynasties. I don't come from that kind of lineage," says Twist, who grew up in the San Francisco Bay area.

His mom was a part-time puppeteer who mostly entertained children "very kind of 'Sesame Street'-style," says Twist while his grandfather was a professional musician. "Puppets were a hobby of his and were part of his act sometimes," Twist says.

Even if Twist doesn't have the finest of puppetry pedigrees, the art form is certainly in his blood. His affinity for it showed up early on.

"I made all these 'Star Wars' puppets," he says with a bit of hesitation and a shy toothy grin. Recalling his childhood in the 1970s, Twist says, "I made R2D2 out of L'eggs pantyhose containers."

Twist arrived in New York City in the late 1980s but soon departed for France, where he spent three years at the International Institute of Puppetry in the rural town of Charleville.

"Charleville ends up being like North Adams," says Twist, quietly laughing again as he sits in the cafe at MASS MoCA. "(It's) out in the middle of nowhere, but there is this incredible thing happening there ... this mecca for puppetry. People come from all over the world."

The school's broad curriculum gave Twist a fluency in the range of international puppetry styles and techniques. Today, when he mixes traditions within one piece, such as putting string puppets and hand puppets on stage at the same time, he's called avant-garde. But Twist thinks of himself as something of a traditionalist.

"I'm real old-fashioned in that I like the puppeteer to be hidden," he says. "When I was in France, and in most contemporary puppetry these days, like say 'Avenue Q' (a puppet musical that's been playing on Broadway for 18 months) the puppeteer is visible on stage. It's almost the definition of a modern puppet performance. I got so sick of that."

Although Twist is clearly ready for the challenges of major productions, he still has the most fun making a new puppet in a few hours for an impromptu show. Most often over the years such productions have been in the company of New York City drag queens.

"There are not many puppeteers hanging out in that world," says Twist, who has performed at many of Manhattan's gay nightclubs as well as at the famous drag festival Wigstock. He even has immortalized as a puppet the Lady Bunny, Wigstock's founder and host.

"We would do duets. The real Bunny and the puppet Bunny ... the stupidest stuff, but when a puppet does it, people just die," says Twist.

Becoming an opera director allows for less spontaneity.

"I used to do everything myself," says Twist, "but once a show gets so big, I can't possibly build everything myself. It is a struggle for me to let go and have others do the work."

With "Sleeping Beauty," Twist is getting plenty of practice at delegating.

"He's very easy and very silly," says Jessica Scott, a puppeteer in the current production. She also assists Twist at his studio in Manhattan's West Village, where work on the current production will continue after the MASS MoCA residency.

"Something that characterizes Basil (is) the way he gets you to commit," says Scott. "He's consciously cultivated a community."

Twist has been building his team ever since "Symphony Fantastique." As an administrator at Here, Barbara Busackino commissioned that piece and has produced each of his subsequent projects.

"He is extremely controlling, extremely decisive, and he is wonderful because of that," says Busackino. "If he says there will be a dance of 12 rose nymphs, there will be a dance of 12 rose nymphs in the end. ... You can get a team behind that and realize it. Of course there's tons of experimentation and failures along the way."

It's not just other puppeteers who are getting behind Twist's vision. Prestigious institutions also continue to seek him out. Lincoln Center has recently come on board for "Sleeping Beauty" and will present the production at its annual summer festival this year.

In the meantime, Twist is keeping busy creating more stage magic.

"I'm into spiders. That's part of what sold me on this show," he says. "I saw spiders (in the story) and was like, 'Great!'"

CHRISTOPHER WHEELDON

Inspiration from the corps

Ballet is a lot more than tutus and arabesques these days, and that's due in large part to Christopher Wheeldon, New York City Ballet's 32-year-old resident choreographer.

Some of the most memorable images of the last two seasons at the Saratoga Performing Arts Center were in Wheeldon pieces: A lifeless ballerina was dragged off a darkening stage in last year's "Shambards," a theatrical exploration of Scottish dance and culture; and in 2003, there was "Carnival of the Animals," a colorful crowd-pleaser that featured actor John Lithgow swaying about in drag while surrounded by dancers in animal costumes.

Next on the boards is "An American in Paris," Wheeldon's newest piece for the company, which opens Saturday night at the SPAC Gala and continues into the following week. The piece, set to Gershwin's beloved score and additionally inspired by the 1951 Gene Kelly film, debuted in New York in late April.

In it, pedestrians in the opening scene make way for a man wearing a yellow racing shirt and whizzing by on a 10-speed bike. "It's the winner of the Tour de France," said Wheeldon, with a smile. "It so happens that Lance Armstrong is the most famous bicyclist in the world today, but the Tour de France is a big part of the (summer) in Paris."

The real focus of "An American in Paris" is principal dancer Damian Woetzel's wide-eyed experience of a colorful foreign city.

"It's a great ballet for someone who hasn't been (to the ballet) before very easy popular music, colorful, uncomplicated," said Wheeldon during an early-May conversation.

Audience development was on Wheeldon's mind that morning in New York City. He had just stepped out of a meeting on the topic with City Ballet board members. Reports had shown subscriptions have been dropping, but audiences for new ballet have increased by a healthy 25 percent.

209

Whether that increase can be attributed to pieces like "Carnival of the Animals" is hard to say. But Wheeldon knows part of his job is to create appealing new works, not just fascinating new steps.

"Working for a big company like New York City Ballet, there are certain responsibilities. It can't always be about your inner creative journey," said Wheeldon. "You have to look and see what it is you're contributing to the repertoire. Because I enjoy stretching myself in new directions, it works well."

Wheeldon has been making dances for City Ballet almost since he arrived as a member of the corps in 1993. While learning the company's great works by George Balanchine, choreographer Jerome Robbins and Ballet Master-in-Chief Peter Martins (he attained the rank of soloist in 1998), Wheeldon also participated in choreography workshops. He was named artist-in-residence prior to his current post and retired from dancing in 2000 to focus exclusively on choreography.

"When he came to audition as a dancer and he was a brilliant dancer he said, 'I'm interested in choreography as well,'" said Sean Lavery, assistant to the ballet master-in-chief. "They don't usually say that (at auditions)."

Before Wheeldon arrived in New York, Lavery and Martins had already heard good things from colleagues in London, where the British-born Wheeldon studied at the Royal Ballet School.

Lately Wheeldon's reputation has grown so dramatically that a less secure talent might freeze up under the pressure.

Some of the most lavish praise came in 2001 from Joan Acocella, dance critic for The New Yorker, who is an unrelenting critic of the post-Balanchine City Ballet. "Wheeldon makes lively ballets that seem to have some heart beating in them," wrote Acocella. "Like Balanchine, he is superlatively musical and works in easy intimacy with his scores." (One has to wonder, however, if Acocella's final statement, that Wheeldon is "the best thing to have happened to New York City Ballet in almost 20 years," wasn't partly intended as a swipe at Martins, her favorite whipping boy.)

"I have nothing but gratitude toward how my career has been supported in this country," said Wheeldon, whose contract with City Ballet calls for two new works a year and runs for another five years.

While also taking commissions from companies like the San Francisco Ballet, the Pennsylvania Ballet and the Royal Ballet, Wheeldon has already created a dozen works for City Ballet. His other new piece from this year, an introspective pas de deux titled "After the Rain," opens Tuesday night.

Wheeldon said he's had a smooth progression in the company from being just another boy in the chorus to being the choreographer who tells the dancers what to do. "A lot of the younger (members) in the company don't remember me as a dancer," he said, adding that turnover has been fairly fast in the corps. During the past five years, Wheeldon estimates, roughly a third of its members have departed.

"It's not really acceptable to get results from a dancer by intimidating them. I don't even think young people these days would accept that," said Wheeldon. But he adds, "My teachers were *incredibly* intimidating."

Wheeldon said the politically correct trends in dance are worse in England than in the United States.

"In many ways, it's creating just a general deterioration of society, because I think there's a lot to be said for healthy competition. I'm not for pitting people against each other, but that's how through history people have improved by being challenged."

Wheeldon's nostalgia for a bygone era of dance might surprise some of his critics – he said he does have them – who saw the dead ballerina in "Shambards" as an attack on romanticism in dance.

"So many people seem to think that I'm trying to instigate the end of the idealization of the ballerina, the woman on point," Wheeldon said dismissively. "It's just a statement, really a response to the music."

Music is central to Wheeldon's creativity, and his choices have been diverse. Contemporary Scottish composer James MacMillan wrote a new score for "Shambards," while other Wheeldon works have used Saint-Saens (for "Carnival of the Animals"), Arvo Part ("Liturgy" and "After the Rain"), and Richard Rodgers ("Carousel: A Dance").

"I usually like music that frightens me at first, that I find slightly intimidating," he said. "There's always the fear ... 'Can I really choreograph to this?'"

FRANCESCA ZAMBELLO

Standing up to armies, singers, waiters

Picture the multitude of soldiers, horses and weapons that populated the recent blockbuster film "Troy." Add in myriad satyrs, nymphs and fauns plus a score of ego-driven opera singers. Then squeeze them all onto a stage for four hours and you'll begin to grasp the job of Francesca Zambello, who directed "Les Troyens" last year at the Metropolitan Opera in New York City.

Zambello is an opera director. In other words, she's fearless.

Dealing with powerful impresarios, delicate singers and bossy conductors comes with the territory. But Zambello puts it simply, saying, "I'm a storyteller."

Sometimes her challenge isn't who she's working with but what she's given to dramatize. Take her latest piece, Shostakovich's rarely performed 1928 opera "The Nose," which opens at Richard B. Fisher Center at Bard College in Annandale-on-Hudson on Friday.

In the opera, a man's proboscis is accidentally cut off at the barbershop. It runs out the door and takes on a grand new life of its own. And a cast of 27 principals and 24 chorus members sing about it in Russian for about two hours.

"It's a rather bizarre, quirky, zany wonderful story," says Zambello. "The nose looks like a big nose a 5-foot nose. And as he grows in self-importance, he grows from being a regular-size nose to a supernose."

If anyone is up to the task of the supernose, it's Francesca Zambello.

"She's at the top of her form and the top of her field," says Leon Botstein, Bard's president, who will conduct the American Symphony Orchestra in "The Nose."

Botstein engaged Zambello for the production about a year ago, which is relatively short lead time in the world of opera, especially with a director as in demand as Zambello, who regularly works in the major opera houses of Europe, including the Paris Opera and London's Covent Garden.

Zambello's renown has come, at least in part, for her faithfulness to operatic tradition. This stands in sharp contrast to directors like Robert Wilson and Peter Sellars, who find fame by making themselves and their vision such an obvious, sometimes intrusive, part of what's on stage.

"I'm a populist," says Zambello when asked to describe her style, during a recent discussion between rehearsals at Bard. "I'm interested in getting opera out there to the widest number of people through means that make it as accessible as possible."

Staging a piece in the 3,800-seat Met certainly means reaching audiences. But Zambello also points to a production early this year of "La Boheme" at the 5,000-seat Royal Albert Hall in London. "Seventy-five thousand people saw that," she says.

Zambello approached "The Nose" as she does every opera – with months of historical research, long discussions with the production team and a gut instinct about what works on stage and can speak to contemporary audiences. "It's a satire from the 1920s, based on (the short story) by Gogol, which was written in the 1830s," she says. "It's about class climbing, and that's something that's endemic all the time. (It's also) about everyman versus bureaucracy, and anybody could relate to that."

Composed when Shostakovich was 21 years old, the music has an optimism that became increasingly rare in his music, as he struggled to be an artist under Soviet rule. "It shows brilliant virtuosity and tremendous influence of Stravinsky," Botstein says of the score. Zambello sees in the opera's quick pacing Shostakovich's interest in film. "It moves forward in real time, almost a cinematic time," she says.

Along with a multinational cast that includes six Russians, Bard's "Nose" team features as set designer the Latin American, New York City-based architect Rafael Vinoly. Follows in the footsteps of Frank Gehry, who designed the Fisher Center as well as the sets for last year's production of Janacek's opera "Osud," Vinoly is planning a new science building for the Bard campus and in the meantime takes a stab at opera.

Says Zambello, "When you collaborate with someone from outside the theatrical realm ... it's always stimulating intellectual dialogue, and eventually you have to find a way to get it on the stage, and we're getting there."

After recent summers spent in France, Austria, Japan and Seattle, Zambello is enjoying the summer at Bard since she has a home less than an hour away in Gardner, near New Paltz.

"It's wonderful to be able to work and sleep in your own bed. It boils down to something so simple," she says. Zambello shares her country home and a Manhattan apartment with her companion of 15 years, the Pulitzer Prize-winning writer Manuela Hoelterhoff, and their three beagles.

Hoelterhoff has written on opera and music for the Wall Street Journal and has an upcoming book on Hitler and Wagner. Recently she was named to a new post overseeing cultural reporting for Bloomberg Media. The new job will make it even harder for Hoelterhoff to travel with Zambello, who says, "It's not good to have your partner with you when there's so much work."

The couple did collaborate on one opera, "Modern Painters," based on the life of John Ruskin. Zambello's production premiered at the Sante Fe Opera in 1995. The libretto was by Hoelterhoff and music by David Lang. "I'm sure we'll end up collaborating on something else," says Zambello. "We both have our thoughts on each other's work. It's great to have artistic discussions with her. She's a keen thinker."

As a leading American figure in opera, Zambello is often approached by composers eager to write for the stage. "I try to be as helpful, positive and nurturing as possible, because that's a very isolated world," she says.

Though it's not often Zambello does direct a new piece, her track record with them is good. An operatic take on the classic French book "The Little Prince" premiered last year at the Houston Grand Opera with music by the Academy Award-winning composer Rachel Portman ("The Piano"). Six other companies have since lined up to remount the piece, including the New York City Opera.

Also in the 2005-06 season, the Metropolitan Opera will present Zambello's staging of the premiere of Tobias Picker's "An American

Tragedy," based on the novel by Theodore Dreiser. It's her third collaboration with the composer, who lives near Rhinebeck. "It's truly an upstate (New York) opera. Most of it takes place in the Adirondacks," Zambello says. Picker admires Zambello's abilities as a director, having seen her in operation both in and out of the opera house.

"She's a real director," he says. "You go to her house and two people are sitting near each other and she tells them to talk to each other or look out the window. She's always directing. ... I love going out to eat with her. You get good service."

CHAPTER FOUR
Unveiling a New Gallery Scene

One Night Stands

FEBRUARY 22, 2004

The coolest art shows in Albany recently are modeled on concerts rather than traditional visual art exhibitions. By staging one-night-only art events in unexpected spaces, groups of young artists are short-circuiting the art world convention of gallery or museum displays that stay for weeks or months.

Their efforts not only bring out viewers, they also build community, engender fresh collaborations and even generate income.

"All the good things that go on here are underground," says Chip Fasciana, an Albany artist and musician. His assertion is not so much a revolutionary declaration as a statement of reality. The cold gray ambience of William Kennedy's novel "Ironweed," Fasciana says, is an apt depiction for his own experience of Albany. As in the novel, the warmth and the magic lie beneath the exterior.

"If you just experience Albany from a surface level, you're going to be bored," says Fasciana, who moved here from Syracuse about a decade ago on a corporate transfer but abandoned company life a year later. "If you find the undercurrent, you're going to have a much better time."

Fasciana is something of a leader in the community of young artists, less because of his age — he's 35 — than for his industriousness. Over the last three years, he's staged five "one-off" gallery nights in various alternative spaces, mostly shuttered storefronts in the Center Square neighborhood.

"The Cheesecake Show," for example, was in a space on Hamilton Street where a dessert shop is scheduled to open. For one night in early January it was filled with photographs and paintings, all by local artists.

"We have an absolute sea of artists who don't have an opportunity to show," says Fasciana.

Also last month was a Thursday night show at Ego, the menswear shop on Lark Street, organized by Tommy Watkins, 26. There were works by a dozen or so of his friends and acquaintances, including Fasciana. Nearly 400 people attended.

"I wanted to revive the local artists' spirits," says Watkins. He cites Changing Spaces Gallery, the 3-year-old Center Square Gallery that is closing, as "one of the last strongholds." The response to his event encouraged him to continue.

"Chip has been putting up shows for a while. He's a veteran," says Watkins. "I said, 'Why don't we combine our efforts ... so we can keep going?'"

Their first collaboration, under the new moniker Albany Underground Artists, is Friday's "Bakery Show." In addition to each preparing new pieces for exhibition, Watkins and Fasciana have been putting in long, hard hours cleaning and painting the former Carosello Bakery, which is being loaned by its new owner, Hollis Milark. She says the fresh paint and general buzz about the space should help her find a new commercial tenant while she's busy fixing up the upstairs apartments.

By the time the show opens, Watkins, Fasciana and friends will have put in an estimated 200 hours of combined time. "The place was pretty hammered," says Watkins. If the turnout equals or exceeds that of the Ego show, they say, all their effort will have been worth it.

"Until Chip asked me to be in one of his shows, there were probably six artists who live in a three-block radius of me who I'd never met," says Shaina Marron, who lives in Center Square. The 24-year-old photographer now feels part of an artists' community.

Marron also sold a number of her color photographs through Fasciana's shows. She describes the events as an "almost punk-rock way of putting up a show and trading resources ... like creating a party and art show all in one night."

"When you go to a show and you can afford to buy," says Marron, "you do it. ... It helps artists and helps your community." Adds Fasciana, "we've got things from $2 to $2,000."

Although nobody's earning enough to quit a day job, Albany's young artists are finding a model that works. Art lovers just have to stay attentive for the next showing – it'll be gone in a flash.

"It's going to come together when it comes together," Watkins says of his and Fasciana's plans. "When we find a place, we strike and pop it up."

Underground Artists
at the Institute

SEPTEMBER 9, 2005

When Albany Underground Artists stages its latest contemporary art happening in the Albany Institute of History & Art next week, it will be as if the stepchildren of the local arts scene have been invited to the grand ball.

The dramatic debut in one of the region's premiere art museums follows two years of struggling to show contemporary homegrown paintings, photographs, sculptures and installations in alternative spaces. Previous Albany Underground Artists events have been held in a defunct bakery, a cavernous downtown bank lobby and a prominent old mansion on the edge of Washington Park, among other locales. Audiences numbering in the thousands turned out for the one-night-only events and the local arts establishment began to take note.

"It's a total experience to go to their openings," said Christine M. Miles, the director of the Albany Institute. The exhibits "have a density of individuals in the arts probably higher than any other activity you could go to on one night."

Miles first made contact with painter Chip Fasciana, a founder of Albany Underground Artists, three years ago at Art on Lark when she purchased one of his works for her personal collection. Thereafter, she kept an eye on Fasciana's work as both painter and arts entrepreneur.

"I'd been talking to him very casually, and we realized we had a gap between shows at the Institute, and this would be a great time," said Miles. "I've been telling a lot of people who are into conventional art to come and experience (an Albany Underground Artists show). It's a scene. It has a great flavor to it, and says a lot about how dynamic and useful our artists community really is."

A couple of blocks from the marble halls of the Albany Institute, the Underground Artists have set up shop in the dingy gray space that was once the Carosello Bakery on Lark Street. In the waning days of summer, Fasciana and fellow painters Tommy Watkins and Mark Gregory spoke about the upcoming event as a bittersweet mix of achievement and drudgery. But that's the way it always has been.

"People think because we're having success, we're doing well financially. That's not true at all," said Fasciana. "After the Bank Show (in May 2004), everyone in the world wanted us to go do a show at their place. They didn't want to give us anything, but they wanted to be part of the hype."

But Albany Institute's offer would have the added benefit of lending a certain above-ground imprimatur to the work on display and the organization itself. And in a departure from the one-night-only model, the exhibit will remain on view for four days after the free opening-night party.

"We're getting no financial support," said Fasciana with a sigh. "We're experiencing the exact same thing as the past, it's just now at the Institute."

While operations may be on the proverbial shoestring, the Albany Underground Artists collected $20 application fees from artists seeking to be part of the show, and will receive a 40 percent commission on sales. Still, making something happen from nothing is part of the allure.

"They're a group of artists who say, 'We're not going to wait for a gallery show,'" said Miles. "They took matters into their own hands and had a positive, constructive approach to having their work and others' exhibited. It's responsible and self-reliant, which is really refreshing."

In terms of the sheer quantity of art, "The Institute Show" is the Albany Underground Artists' most ambitious undertaking to date, with work from approximately 70 artists on display. That figure, according to Gregory, represents half the number of submissions the group received, but is twice as big as any previous show. For the first time, the lineup includes artists from throughout the Hudson Valley and New York City.

Among the participants is Shawn Lawson, a 28-year-old media artist and faculty member of Rensselaer Polytechnic Institute in Troy. He has exhibited work in venues like the Chelsea Art Museum, but never locally. On view at the Institute will be an interactive "Mona Lisa" that Lawson created in collaboration with Iraqi artist Wafaa Bilal.

"I heard about it from a friend," said Lawson, referring to Albany Underground Artists' call for submissions. The show "looks like it's going to be big."

Painter Luke Williams, a veteran of past Underground shows, lives in Albany's Center Square neighborhood. "There's a particular quality of having work on display," said Williams, who became a full-time artist about a year ago. "You acquire a more objective eye for your work when you see hundreds of people viewing it."

Besides being a behind-the-scenes organizer, Mark Gregory said he has benefited from having work in the shows. "The Bank Show gave me a sense (that) if you want to do it, you can do it," said Gregory, who recently left a full-time job to devote more time to painting. "It gave me the courage to make the leap."

Perhaps it's the thrill of the openings or the opportunity to meet the artists, but the organizers believe they're witnessing the emergence of a new group of local art collectors.

Christine Miles should be among the potential buyers and this time, perhaps for Albany Institute's permanent collection. Miles says that over the past 10 years, the Institute has acquired works by 60 or 70 new artists, most of them local.

"We have to make sure that what we're buying is part of the artistic fabric of the region," Miles said. She sees the upcoming show as a way to get to know "the next generation of artists in our area."

Beyond giving good parties and moving the occasional piece, Watkins says the Albany Underground Artists have a bigger goal: building a strong local arts scene.

"Two years ago, the art scene was dry. Now it's out of control," said Watkins. "What we set out to do, we've done. If one can't get into a gallery or an institute, you do it your own way."

Upstate Artists Guild:
A collective is born

APRIL 2, 2006

Clothing and accessories never seemed to make it at Albany's 247 Lark St., the storefront across from Bombers Burrito Bar. Over the years, Goth fashions were available at Web of Threads, later known as Unchained. Then came hip-hop attire with the short-lived Hot City. Youthful color and style are available yet again, but this time in the form of art works.

The collective of young artists known as Upstate Artists Guild announced themselves at last year's Lark Fest, with a rather impromptu show in the beleaguered space. The landlord had agreed to lend its use for one day in exchange for cleaning it up and making some general repairs. The UAG has been there ever since.

"What we want to do is be a guild, where people learn how to create and make things and have a variety of tools and skills and equipment ... a place where we can make art, show art and hopefully sell art," says painter Nina Stanley.

So far, there are more than two dozen members of the UAG who pay dues of $120 a year. A core committee of 10 artists oversees the ongoing operations, including managing the space, organizing exhibits, and offering classes in drawing and painting. Committee members also contribute financially each month as needed when membership dues, entry fees for shows and even the occasional commission on a sale of art don't add up to make the rent. UAG is conceived as a not-for-profit, but is awaiting government approval.

Currently, the guild is exhibiting its second official show, "Illumination," with most of the contributing artists in their 20s and 30s. It's a good sign for UAG's outreach that there is very little overlap of "Illumination" participants with the 15 artists in the collective's first show, "Dead of Winter," which opened in February.

Colin Wilkinson, a member of the UAG organizing team, says, "We find through our theme shows that people don't ask, 'Can I do something for that?' but, 'Does that fit my work?'" Wilkinson himself is represented in "Illumination" with a succession of backlit abstract paintings on plexiglass titled, "I Carried My Cat Through a Dead Field (A Dream in Three Layers)."

For veteran gallery goers, "Illumination" will be an imaginative introduction to some new talents. But one name on the roster will ring familiar – Charles Steckler. The 60-year-old artist has a show of his stage designs currently on view at the Nott Memorial at Union College in Schenectady. In "Illumination," he's represented with "Pete & Repeat," a whimsical collage of found elements (including a working light bulb) mounted on a roller skate.

Steckler was drawn in by the idea of "Illumination" and the spirit of the UAG. "I liked their energy and their space and the ideas they're putting forth," he says.

The individuals behind UAG have found, however, that running a gallery takes more than energy and ideas. "I don't know what it is, but it's unbelievable the amount of time and effort we put into keeping it running," says Curtis Canham, who works primarily in digital art. But Canham may point to the key to the gallery's success thus far when he adds, "We're based in community."

"We're an army of artists trying to rally for the same cause," says painter Tommy Watkins. Well known as an organizer of the Albany Underground Artists, Watkins contrasts the UAG with the more free-form Albany Underground Artists: "We're trying to be more permanent, not so loose."

Troy Night Out: Waking up downtown

FEBRUARY 18, 2007

There's a trend that keeps climbing up the Hudson Valley: coordinated art openings on a single night. It's a simple idea that concentrates the public's attention and turns out crowds. Back in 2004, the arts communities of four cities launched Art Along the Hudson, with openings in a different locale every Saturday. Each month the cycle begins with events in Kingston on the first Saturday, followed by Beacon, Poughkeepsie and Newburgh on successive Saturdays.

Last fall, Albany caught on to the idea and launched First Fridays, primarily in the Center Square neighborhood. In just six months it has become a genuine phenomenon: 20 venues participated on Feb. 2, drawing more than 800 people.

And now the Collar City is getting into the act with Troy Night Out, a citywide happening running from 5 to 9 p.m. Friday and continuing on the last Friday of every month. Expectations are high for the event to spotlight the city's arts scene, as well as its range of shopping, dining and entertainment options.

"There's a critical mass that's finally accumulated here," says Karen Schlesinger, who conceived the idea for the event, pointing to myriad new galleries and retail establishments, primarily in downtown Troy. "There's also a nice sense of community and that's what's going to make this event a success," she says.

Schlesinger, 30, is herself the proprietor of one of Troy's latest art venues, Digital Artist's Space, a service bureau and art gallery that opened last April. She moved to Troy a little more than a year ago with her husband, Chris Jordan, a faculty member at the Sage Colleges. Both are photographers. "I loved the feel of Troy, the walkability, the architecture and the artsy feel," she says.

As she got to know both the arts and business communities, Schlesinger noticed a familiar refrain: "Wouldn't it be great if ... ?"

"After hearing that for a couple of months, I was like, 'Why doesn't somebody do something?'" recalls Schlesinger. Early last fall, she

226

decided to take action by calling a series of open meetings that got the momentum going.

Sharing the bulk of organizing duties with Schlesinger is another Troy newcomer, Elizabeth Young, 29, owner of Living Room, a six-month-old shop at 274 River St. A third-generation antiques dealer and descendant of Philip Schuyler, Young was raised in the Capital Region and resettled here in the past year with her fiance, Steven Scarlata, a French horn player. They previously lived in New York City and Tokyo, but found Troy to be "a Victorian jewel."

Other event sponsors include the Arts Center of the Capital Region, which has provided meeting space and financial coordination, and ID29, a Troy-based communications firm that has come through with graphic design and marketing support.

So far, Troy Night Out will feature 15 galleries, 20 retail shops, and about a dozen restaurants and cafes.

"Look around at the new people and business of the last six months," says Schlesinger. "It's finally enough to counter the resistance and apathy that's kept anything from happening."

Seasoned Troy-watchers know what she's talking about, as past renaissance efforts have come and gone.

"We joke that we've been here for nine of the last 12 revitalizations," says Kathy Bloom, of J.K. Bloom Jewelers, formerly known as Hummingbird Designs, located at 29 Third St. "But this is a good one, with new people and energy," says John Bloom. The couple will not only be keeping their shop open late on Friday, but also using the occasion to celebrate their 25th anniversary of doing business in Troy.

"Recently, there have been little happenings all over, and everybody (in the arts) knows everybody else, so the timing is really good," says Colleen Skiff, founder and director of the 10-year-old Fulton Street Gallery. When Skiff was new to Troy, she organized some quarterly "Art Happenings," but found it hard to maintain momentum. She sees strong potential in the monthly aspect of Troy Night Out and the organizational team that has come together. "Everyone knows their strengths," she says.

Joe Mancino, general manager of the two-year-old Flavour Cafe and Lounge at 228 Fourth St., welcomes Troy Night Out as a sign that "everyone is banding together for one purpose, which is to promote Troy and downtown business."

Art Night Schenectady: Turn on the lights

MAY 17, 2007

For art lovers of the Capital Region, three out of every four Friday nights are now booked. Surrender your cynicism. We now have a scene.

In the beginning there was First Fridays, the Albany gallery night that started in September. The Collar City was next, claiming the last Friday of the month for Troy Night Out, which has been going since February. Organizers of those two events report crowds of up to 1,000 people hoofing it around the participating galleries, museums and alternative venues.

Starting this Friday – that's the third Friday of the month – the Electric City is turning on to the trend with Art Night Schenectady. Up to 4,000 people are expected to pour into downtown Schenectady for the evening, since Art Night coincides with the opening of the long awaited Bow Tie Cinemas' Movieland, at State Street and Broadway, as well as a concert (anticipated to sell out) by Frankie Valli and The Four Seasons at Proctor's Theatre.

With the ongoing renovations of Proctor's and the various projects of the Metroplex Development Authority, which has been behind the movie theater and the recently opened Hampton Inn (also on State Street), millions of dollars have been pumped into the revitalization of downtown Schenectady. But like the events in Albany and Troy, Art Night Schenectady has come about not from corporate planning meetings and budgets with lots of zeros, but from the inspiration and sweat of an artist.

Mitch Messmore, 35, is a photographer who works as a project manager for Active Host, an Internet service company and is plugged into the network of young artists in the region. Although born and raised in Schenectady, Messmore lives in Albany, because his European-born wife says her husband's hometown is "a provincial little village."

Obviously, Messmore has an impetus to change perceptions.

"I remember as a kid in the '70s, there were *people* in downtown Schenectady. I'd skip school to hang out on Jay Street and take pictures," he says. "I got my art background here; I want to give back."

By bringing together the cause of downtown Schenectady with artists looking for audiences, Messmore's instincts are on target and on time.

"The idea took off instantly," says Bob Buccieri, executive director of the Downtown Schenectady Improvement Corp., which is helping out with printing, promotion and other in-kind support. According to Buccieri, planning for Art Night began less than three months ago. He adds, "Mitch is a fabulous resource with contacts and experience to create these kinds of events with minimal effort."

It's no surprise that businesses like Open Door Bookstore on the Jay Street pedestrian mall have responded with enthusiasm for anything that might bring new customers. But it was galleries that first came together to make things happen in Albany and Troy – it's "art night" after all. Yet in terms of spots for visual art, Schenectady is actually rather lacking.

Granted, there's the Two Spruce Pottery Studio on Jay Street and Five Star Frame and Art Shop around the corner on Clinton Street. Plus, Proctor's shows art in its Delack Guild Room but that's up on the second floor of its atrium. While all these are participating in Art Night, that's about it in terms of existing venues in downtown.

On the other hand, according to Messmore, the Mandeville Gallery at Union College and the Schenectady Museum were quick to commit to Art Night. Union College is also lending use of its trolley to shuttle folks around to more far-flung venues. Contrast this to Albany, where First Friday had been going for months before the Albany Institute of History & Art and the State Museum joined in.

Schenectady has also got a secret weapon: working artists. More than a dozen painters, weavers and musicians lease studio space in the Working Gallery/Studio in the 440 Arts Building and the Jay Street Studios, both of which are in the heart of downtown and administered by Proctor's.

Painter Catherine Minnery drives daily from Saratoga Springs to her workspace in the 440 Arts Building. Since she's in the front of the building, just the other side of the windows that serve as the de facto gallery, she's accustomed to drop-in visitors.

"It's amazing: I would say every week I speak to a new person who says, 'Oh, I didn't know you were here,'" Minnery says. "It's a great studio space, and nice being on the street. Many wonderful things have happened because of me being here."

Robin Rosenthal rents space at the Jay Street Studios and will be on hand to show her oil paintings, but she's pleased that Art Night is also including a special show for the Schenectady Arts Society, a 40-year-old collective of which she's a member. "There are a lot of talented people in Schenectady, and this showcases them," she says.

Another old-line collective, the Oakroom Artists, will also have a show. Both groups are getting space in vacant storefronts, as are some student artists from Schenectady High School.

Messmore sees these and other shows placed in alternative venues as twofers: "They're going to highlight art and the available real estate," he says.

General Electric's systematic retreat from Schenectady was a blow that has left the city reeling for decades, said Richard Genest, who opened Moon and River Cafe on Ferry Street in the Stockade district three years ago. "Now we've found another growth industry – entertainment and art," he says. Genest describes his business as throwing parties with live music seven nights a week; he'll be happy if Art Night brings some more guests.

Another recent arrival who's bullish on the arts is Geraldine Puente. Less than two years ago, she and her husband left Manhattan and chose downtown Schenectady for their retirement. "I have all the amenities I would expect from a city – a bookstore, library, a theater and movie theater, and several wonderful restaurants all within walking distance," says Puente. "It also has an intimate feel. I know more people on a first-name basis in a year here than in 20 years in Manhattan."

The Puentes purchased and have just finished renovating two large buildings on Jay Street directly across from City Hall. They hope to entice artists to live and work in the 40 available units.

"Any city really is a reflection of its artists' community. It reflects the hopes for the future," says Puente. "(Artists) are visionaries, the core group of people that give us the spark of hope and energy, because we can see they're willing to take risks. And you have to take risks in Schenectady. It's a changing city."

Saratoga's
Beekman Street

Artists & realtors jockey for space

The horses are running this month in Saratoga Springs, and not just at the racetrack. Equine art is on display all over downtown, from the paintings and posters in the windows of shops and galleries to the 34 artfully decorated and near-life-size horses that populate the sidewalks.

Horses are also trotting through the city's Beekman Street arts district, especially in the Flores Studio, the gallery and workspace of painter Frankie Flores. When Flores was based in New Orleans during the 1990s, his canvases – bright with color and thick with paint – focused on jazz musicians. But since he arrived in the Spa City four years ago, horses have come to represent about 40 percent of his work. "I painted a few, and people started liking them," he says.

Flores has found such success that he's just opened a second gallery at 468 Broadway, as a further showcase for his work. Yet he remains committed to Beekman Street.

"It's where artists can have studios and house their work and have galleries," says Flores. "Beekman is home."

Maintaining Beekman Street as a haven for artists where they can be inspired by horses, ballet dancers, or whatever else strikes their fancy, and have space shielded from the stampede of real estate development has become a challenge for the district's founder Amejo Amyot.

"We are constantly fighting developers trying to turn this into downtown. We didn't think because five of us bought buildings it would happen. We thought we were safe," says Amyot, who is a sculptor and teacher. "I feel like a mother bear, protecting the street and its original vision."

It was just four years ago that then-Mayor Ken Klotz cut a red ribbon to open the newly designated arts district – three blocks of historic two-story homes and storefronts in the West Side neighborhood.

After being priced out of downtown proper, Amyot and a handful of fellow artists bought properties to serve as working studios.

233

They opened modest galleries to show their work and help bring in some income. Other commerce in the area, they hoped, would be of limited scale.

"We wanted something up close and personal, with little shops and little restaurants, the sense that (downtown) Saratoga had 10 years ago, before the Gap," says Amyot.

Prior to the arrival of the artists, the West Side neighborhood had a rough reputation. Amyot recalls finding broken bottles on the streets nearly every morning in 2004. But in just a few years, property values in the city of Saratoga Springs have risen exponentially. This allowed some elderly longtime residents to afford to move away, but it also invited speculators and even new construction.

At the corner of Beekman and Grand Avenue, the Phinney Design Group, a local architectural firm specializing in green projects, has erected a new three-story headquarters. A restaurant is planned for the first floor of the building, which is in final stages of construction.

Amyot's feelings about such economic growth are mixed at best. She's witnessed small galleries come and go, and no artists have purchased property since the arts district designation was made.

"Eventually there could be no artists in the arts district. That's happened in city after city across the country," she says.

A five-minute walk from downtown Saratoga Springs, Beekman Street still has a feeling of retreat. An intimate scale and personal touch certainly come through inside 79 Beekman Artists Studios & Gallery, which Amyot runs. The feel of the whole place is relaxed and funky – unlike most anywhere else in Saratoga Springs.

Currently 20 artists lease out space from Amyot. They work in a wide range of mediums, including pottery, fiber art and painting. Among them is Kevin McKrell, better known as a Celtic musician, who paints portraits of the Irish working class that he photographs when traveling. Each artist tenant pays $75 a month for approximately 6-by-6 feet of space.

"These aren't lofts, they're cubbies," says Amyot.

A selection of finished pieces by many of the tenants are available for purchase on the first floor. Outside, there's a sculpture garden with a dozen or so pieces, mostly goddess-type figures.

Construction work is a common presence on Beekman Street, not just at the new building on the corner of Grand but also at 79 Beekman, where the facade is being restored. That work is being financed in part by New York Main Street, a state program dedicated to the revitalization of historic neighborhoods.

Two years ago the Saratoga Springs Preservation Foundation was awarded a grant of $190,000 through the Main Street program for the restoration of properties on Beekman Street. Seven properties will benefit from facade restorations as well as more extensive rehabbing of certain buildings.

Beyond the satisfaction of seeing Saratoga's historic West Side in increasingly good condition, Carrie Woerner, executive director of the Preservation Foundation, believes good buildings lead to good art. "Artists really value authentic spaces," she says. "People say they create better in an authentic, well-cared-for space."

During the arts district's short history, some galleries have had short lives. But recently one has expanded and another opened.

"Art for Home and Wear" is the motto for Mimosa, a two-year-old enterprise at the corner of Beekman and Oak streets. Mimosa recently expanded into a second, adjacent storefront that's being used exclusively for the display of fine art and handcrafted furniture.

A few doors down, there's Artworx Fine Art Gallery, which opened in February. In the modestly sized exhibition area, owner Thomas Alexander is currently showing two local artists, Deirdre Turner, who makes colorful sketches of Saratoga pedestrian life, and Tony Shortway, a young chef at Yaddo, who creates large duotone paintings on glass.

The featured artist currently on view is Erica Nordean from Washington state. The focus of her oils and pastels is horses. Acknowledging that an equine show is not unusual for Saratoga Springs in August, Alexander says, "I wanted to call this the No Horses Gallery, but I thought I'd get kicked out of town."

CHAPTER FIVE
Albany Symphony Orchestra
TRADITION AND INNOVATION

A visit behind the scenes

SEPTEMBER 12, 2002

The administrative offices of the Albany Symphony Orchestra are located in a streetfront portion of the Palace Theatre. It's a space that was probably never intended to be an office, and it's outfitted with mismatched furnishings, aging equipment and posters from past seasons hung randomly on the walls. The overworked and underpaid staff has a high turnover rate.

All this is rather typical for a small nonprofit arts organization. But amid the clutter are some things unique to the ASO, including stacks of scores from hopeful composers seeking the attention of music director David Allan Miller, and a pile of plaques that the orchestra has received from the music industry over the years for outstanding and adventuresome programming. From this drab setting, there emerges each year some of the most vibrant and forward-looking orchestra concerts offered in the nation.

This air of success amid tumult befits the season ahead, as the ASO struggles with recent upheaval on its board and financial challenges endemic to arts groups in a sagging economy. Whether the outlook is partly sunny or partly cloudy depends on your perspective.

The ASO launches its new season tonight at the Canfield Casino in Saratoga and Friday night at the Troy Savings Bank Music Hall. The weekend's program blends the novel (a concerto for harmonica and orchestra), the current (a newly commissioned work by American composer Richard Einhorn in memory of 9/11), and the timeless (Mozart's Symphony No. 25).

The mixture typifies the rest of the season, which includes three more world premieres by American composers, a half-dozen other American works from the last century and a healthy portion of blue-chip works by Beethoven, Tchaikovsky, Mendelssohn and others. This year's nine subscription concerts also feature an impressive array of internationally known soloists, including violinist Cho-Liang Lin, pianist Yefim Bronfman and cellist Sharon Robinson.

If the heart of the ASO is the music and the performances, the backbone of the orchestra is its administration, specifically the staff and the board.

In April, three prominent ASO board members – with a combined tenure of more than half a century – resigned over a dispute about the organization's leadership and future direction. The resulting story was the kind of publicity that such institutions strive to avoid: When arts groups appear to have internal problems, the external impact can be far-reaching, affecting the minds of donors or even the decision-making of legislators.

Talking recently with Miller and executive director Sharon Walsh at their office, the conversation flowed easily on matters of music, programming and audiences. (Both are in their 10th year with the institution.) But when it came to questions of relations with the board and business matters beyond cursory facts and figures, Walsh was especially reticent.

"Things are stable," they said, almost in unison.

Given the 71-year history of the organization, its faithful core of more than 800 annual subscribers and approximately 1,000 individual donors, and its recent track record of balanced budgets (about $1.2 million annually now), there is no apparent reason to doubt the diagnosis of moderately good health.

But Alan Goldberg, in his second year as chairman of the board, spoke with slightly more candor: "My goal is to continue to provide for this community the quality presentations the symphony has historically made," he said in a separate interview, "and to do that in this environment – post-Sept. 11 – is significantly more difficult for nonprofits who have tight budgets."

Goldberg discussed the importance of increasing the number of subscribers and donors, strengthening the endowment (currently less than $300,000), revising the bylaws, and ensuring greater involvement from board members – all in the context of a long-term planning process recently begun by the board. His message seemed to be that everyone is working in tune these days.

The end result should be a five-year plan designed, in Goldberg's words, "to build up enough financial stability that no one event, no one difficult season, affects the long-term survival of the orchestra."

As a businessman and philanthropist, Goldberg is almost without peer in the Capital Region. The president of the investment firm First Albany, he's also a former chairman of the Albany Institute of History & Art, to which he made a $1 million gift two years ago.

Goldberg's broad view and calm demeanor stand in sharp contrast to the approach of former chairman emeritus Peter Kermani, one of the three directors to quit the board last spring. Apart from its music directors, there is no one more associated with the history and profile of the Albany Symphony than Kermani. Also a former chairman of the nonprofit record label CRI and of the American Symphony Orchestra League, he is an entrepreneur who runs a retail business in Niskayuna and owns the Albany Music group, which has a record label and national distribution network.

Despite an outspoken nature, he refuses to address his departure from the board, but took pride in the orchestra's premieres and revivals of numerous American works. "My most sincere hope is that as the planning process goes forward the mission the symphony has had for many years is not forgotten or distorted," he said.

Over the last 10 years, 14 CDs of the ASO have been released on Kermani's Albany Records, all of 20th-century music, mostly by midcentury American composers. That a half-dozen more recording projects remain in various stages of completion seems to guarantee that Kermani's vision for the ASO will continue in future seasons. In addition, there's the ongoing leadership of another new-music advocate whom Kermani was influential in hiring a decade ago: David Alan Miller.

Miller "is a wonderfully engaging, enthusiastic champion of the work that the orchestra does," remarks Jesse Rosen, who leads the American Symphony Orchestra League in Manhattan and attended several orchestra events last spring.

The 41-year-old conductor has put down roots in the region and expanded the symphony's offerings with an annual festival of American music, more educational programming, new composer residencies and the establishment of The Dogs of Desire, a chamber ensemble dedicated to cutting-edge repertoire.

"David is the only music director to ask me for suggestions about young, unknown composers," says composer Randall Woolf, who has written for the Dogs of Desire.

Miller's current three-year contract is up for renewel at the end of this season. In addition to the formulation of a five-year plan, holding on to Miller could serve as another cause for the newly constituted board to rally around.

Gangster Legs Diamond inspires mean-guy music

NOVEMBER 14, 2004

He was a bootlegger, womanizer, murderer and all around thug who reigned from Manhattan to Montreal. And long before he was shot to death in a rooming house on Albany's Dove Street in 1931, Jack "Legs" Diamond attained the status of celebrity.

Today, across the Capital Region, there are seemingly countless roadhouses, diners and hotels bearing the proud designation of once being a hangout for Legs Diamond and his cronies.

More than a folk legend, Diamond also has become the subject of a variety of artistic works. Along with a 1969 noir film and a 1988 Broadway musical flop, there is "Legs," the acclaimed 1975 novel by William Kennedy, the Pulitzer Prize-winning local author.

And on Friday night, the newest Diamond-inspired artistic work "Eyeball High" by Kevin Beavers will be given its premiere by the Albany Symphony Orchestra in a concert at the Troy Savings Bank Music Hall.

For his ASO commission, Beavers, 33, drew inspiration from Kennedy's novel as much as from Legs Diamond, the man. Both author and composer found him a potent topic for artistic exploration.

"Why was a son of a bitch like this so popular? He was on the order of a movie star," says Kennedy.

Although the author may still like to ponder the reasons for Diamond's renown, he went a long way toward illustrating them in "Legs." Seen through the eyes and ears of a fictitious attorney named Marcus Gorman, Diamond is mesmerizing.

"This man was alive in a way I was not ... He hit you, slapped you with his palm, punched you with a light fist, clapped you on the shoulder, ridding himself of electricity to avoid exploding. He was conveying it to you, generating himself into yourself whether you wanted to receive him or not."

So states Gorman of his first gander at the 5-foot-7 gangster. A magnetic attraction and repulsion toward Diamond carries the character through the rest of the novel.

243

Kennedy first came upon Diamond's legend in the 1960s, when beginning work on a novel. But that project, "Roscoe," finally released in 2002, was put aside so Kennedy could give full chase to Diamond.

"I discovered Legs Diamond in the morgues of the newspaper. The files on him were extraordinary. He was in the paper every day in 1931 and very often (in) 1930 and 1929," says Kennedy, 76, who estimates that he interviewed between 300 and 400 people who knew Diamond. His novel is a balance of biographical fact and imaginary dialogue and relationships.

Kennedy's open-ended "Albany Cycle" of novels now numbers seven titles, and he's currently at work on a play. But his fascination with Diamond continues.

For more than a decade he has owned the Dove Street townhouse where Diamond finally met his maker at age 36. Although Kennedy lives in Averill Park, the former rooming house makes for a handy inner-city office.

"I work there, I socialize there. ... We like to think we can get a little closer to the era when we're in there," the author says.

When ASO conductor David Alan Miller asked Beavers for a new work that somehow related to the city of Albany, the composer thought of his fondness for Kennedy's "Legs."

"Some artists could write pieces about Al Capone based on newspaper articles. I was responding to a literary work," says Beavers.

Rather than attempting musical depictions of events or characters from the book, Beavers' 12-minute orchestral work focuses on Diamond's dark, powerful character. Portions of his piece draw on the sound of ragtime, but Beavers describes the writing as mostly "turgid, tough, mean-guy music."

"I was just fascinated with the tension of trying to create something that was attractively violent ... almost a ridiculous task in music," says Beavers, who since April has lived in Germany, where his fiance is studying at the Freiberg Conservatory.

"Eyeball High," the piece's title, comes from a moment early in the book when Diamond teaches Gorman to use a machine-gun.

I press the trigger. Bullets exploded in my ears, my hands, my shoulders, my blood, my brain. The spew of death was a personal tremor that even jogged my scrotum.

"Close, off the right ear," Jack said. [referring to the target, a man's face] "Try again."

I let go with another burst, feeling confident. No pain. It's easy. I leveled the weapon, squeezed off another.

"Got him. Eyeball high."

According to Beavers, his piece could be considered a tone poem – a single-movement orchestral work that evokes a particular scene or narrative. Historical examples of the form include Mendelssohn's "Fingal's Cave" and Vaughan William's "The Lark Ascending."

Beavers is surely adding something new to the genre – "Eyeball High" depicts the sound of gunfire.

"You can easily hear that it's murder. It's something that's built toward ... the Tommy gun firing, a typical gangster machine gun," Beavers says.

Beavers and Kennedy agree that there is a quality to Diamond that sets him above the level of other famous crooks.

"Diamond had a quality that was different from most of the other gangsters ... a mix of an evil figure who was capable of the worst kind of torture and killing and at the same time a very social animal. Many people remember his great sense of humor, his intelligence and his literary dimension," says Kennedy.

As an example of Diamond's wide-range, Kennedy points to the crook's fondness for the 16th-century French author Francois Rabelais. According to Kennedy, Diamond was known to give away copies of the writer's classic satire "Gargantua and Pantagruel."

"The fact he was able to do that confused people. They were nonplussed by getting a copy of this literary masterwork from a high school level-educated hoodlum," says Kennedy.

Beyond literature, Kennedy says Diamond was known to also enjoy popular music though he wasn't a dancer. "That's one of the myths about him," says Kennedy.

A singing and dancing gangster is just too sellable an idea for some to pass up. Consider the success of "Guys and Dolls," the classical musical comedy from 1950 that depicts a bunch of gangsters and their lovable molls.

Perhaps that enduring hit was in the mind of the creators and producers of the 1988 Broadway show "Legs Diamond." The $4.5 million extravaganza was based on the 1960 film by Budd Boetticher, "The Rise and Fall of Legs Diamond," and featured music and lyrics by Peter Allen, who was also its star.

After an extended period of 72 previews, during which time Harvey Fierstein was brought in to help fix the problematic book, the show opened to poor notices and played for only 64 performances. Many critics expressed disappointment that the show was merely mediocre rather than genuinely awful. In his review for The New York Times, Frank Rich called it "a sobering interlude of minimum-security imprisonment."

A cast album released on BMG features 19 bright, buoyant and rather cliched numbers. But two of the songs recently came back to life on Broadway in the Tony Award-winning musical "The Boy From Oz." The show closed in September after a successful run of nearly a year. Hugh Jackman played Allen, the songster and showman who died of AIDS.

Given that authors, composers and Broadway producers have found fertile material in Legs Diamond, his legend will probably continue in future artistic works. But for Beavers, his musical foray into a world of violence and crime will probably be a one-shot deal.

"I've been a visual artist," he says, "and I've noticed that when you make a portrait of somebody frowning, you have to make a frown when you're doing it. And there's something about making works that are violent that's disturbing on the psyche."

Drums along the Hudson

MAY 13, 2004

Albany Symphony Orchestra 2004 Budget
Category: drums and assorted percussion instruments.
Item: 5 timpani. Cost: $38,000. Lifespan: 40 years.
Item: 7,000 shakers and rattles. Cost: $800. Lifespan: one night.

Where's the ASO putting its money lately? To the beat, baby.

Last month, using funds ponied up by its volunteer league, called Vanguard, the symphony invested nearly $40,000 into five new timpani. (The price did include travel cases.)

And for the season finale on Saturday night at the Palace Theatre, conductor David Alan Miller has concocted an evening of percussion and participation – everyone who shows up can pick up the beat.

The concert's centerpiece is "Night in the Tropics," a symphony by the 19th-century American composer Louis Moreau Gottschalk full of Latin rhythms and drums galore. More than 600 Cuban drummers are said to have participated at its premiere in 1859.

On Saturday, the ASO will easily beat that figure, so to speak. In addition to six ASO percussionists and 12 players from the percussion ensembles of the Empire State Youth Orchestra, the piece includes passages for participation of every member of the audience. That means 2,800 percussionists, if the ASO's trend of sell-outs continues.

If you're planning to attend, there's no need to bring your drums – "Please don't," urges the ASO management. All ticket holders will receive a small percussion instrument and will be coached in their parts by the maestro prior to the actual performance.

When it comes to percussion in the Capital Region, Richard Albagli is the man. The ASO's principal percussionist, he has performed with the orchestra since 1968 and was the snare drum soloist in last fall's "Bolero." He also teaches at the University at Albany and Rensselaer Polytechnic Institute in Troy, and has been a mentor to several generations of ESYO players, including the young jazz sensation Stefan

Harris. ("He's the type that taught himself," recalls Albagli. "You just throw stuff at him.")

Although Albagli won't be prominent on stage Saturday night, he's been essential to the concert coming together. More than a year ago, Miller came to him, explaining his idea for performing Gottschalk's "Night in the Tropics" in a new version that allowed for many, many participants.

"David just wanted to have people with instruments everywhere," says Albagli, "to make it a real street festival. And that's exciting."

But a distinguished symphony can't have a drum free-for-all. In fact, Miller says that Gottschalk's second performance of the piece "got away from him," and went on for five hours. (What would *that* do to the ASO's budget?)

This is where a composer and an arranger comes in, and Albagli is both. Miller asked him to add a percussion interlude between Gottschalk's two existing movements, and to expand the percussion parts in the second movement.

Note to musical purists: Calm down. There's no definitive score that shows how Gottschalk could have integrated a horde of percussionists into the piece. Even a musical mind as formidable as composer Gunther Schuller has taken stab at adapting the piece.

Albagli describes the new material as drawing on themes from the first movement and leading seamlessly into the second, but with "my own grand theme" added in between. He also refers to a "vaudeville-like climax."

The arrangement already has been tested twice during the past month with an audience of student participants. Leading those performances was Miller in the persona of "Cowboy Dave."

While ASO subscribers might require some encouragement to join in the music making, the concern with the student audiences was to keep them from incessantly rattling their little instruments.

"Cowboy Dave got them to take an oath, 'I promise ...'" says Albagli. "They followed along and stopped when they were to stop. We hope the adults will be as intelligent as the kids."

Author William Kennedy sings the song of Albany

APRIL 15, 2007

When he was 12 years old, William Kennedy ushered at the Palace Theater for a performance of "Aida." As a kid, he also performed in choirs and glee clubs and learned to play the banjo, an instrument he still picks up now and then. These days, the Pulitzer Prize-winning Albany author says that an evening with friends isn't complete without some communal singing, mostly of standards like "Happy Days and Lonely Nights," a favorite song of the late gangster Jack "Legs" Diamond.

Known for realistic depictions of the rough-and-tumble life of Albany in the first half of the 20th century, Kennedy's novels are enlivened by the vernacular voices of political bosses and Depression-era bums. But most of his books also share a lyric soundtrack, with the author referencing songs of the swing era that filter in and out of the characters' lives.

Music plays in Kennedy's nonfiction as well. The collection "Riding the Yellow Trolley Car" includes pieces on Frank Sinatra, Louis Armstrong and Pablo Casals. Also an avid record collector, Kennedy even co-wrote a song with Tom Waits, "Poor Little Lamb," for the 1987 movie "Ironweed," based on Kennedy's Pulitzer Prize-winning novel of the same name.

But for all his musical chops, there's one piece that leaves the author almost at a loss for words: "Eyeball High," a turbulent, almost violent tone poem by Kevin Beavers, based on Kennedy's novel "Legs." The piece was premiered by the Albany Symphony Orchestra in November 2004 at the Troy Savings Bank Music Hall.

"I couldn't tell you what was in the actual music," says Kennedy, still a bit taken back that a grand orchestral work was inspired by his writing. After starting and restarting a sentence several times, he finally concludes, "I just know that he understood, and his reflection of what he read seemed to me to be exciting and authentic."

ASO music director David Alan Miller agrees, and he was so pleased with the piece that he commissioned a sequel from Beavers. "Roscoe: Concerto for Violin and Orchestra," premieres Friday night at the

Palace Theatre. And this time, Kennedy won't be speechless. He'll be on stage reading selections from his 2002 novel "Roscoe," which serve as preludes to sections of the piece. The violin soloist will be Colin Jacobsen.

Referring to the 79-year-old Kennedy as "our leading literary celebrity," Miller and the ASO have organized nearly two months of ancillary events around the premiere celebrating the author and his writing. The activities have included readings, discussions and even trolley tours of "William Kennedy's Albany."

"There is this wonderful hard-boiled, Old World romance to Albany that he captures in such a poetic way," Miller says. "And there's some gritty element in Kevin Beaver's musical world view that I think is very good company to Kennedy's."

Where "Eyeball High" was a portrait of Jack "Legs" Diamond based on impressions from the first novel in Kennedy's Albany cycle, the new concerto will focus on specific scenes from "Roscoe," the cycle's seventh and latest installment.

Beaver's new score will surely retain a certain raw power, but some of the grisly edge of the previous work will be softened, since this time the central character isn't a murderer, just a treacherous politician. In Kennedy's fictionalized account of the Democratic machine that controlled Albany for nearly 50 years, Roscoe Owen Conway is a corpulent, behind-the-scenes politico.

"A corrupt politician is a wonderful topic," says Beavers, 35, who was raised in West Virginia and currently lives in Berlin, Germany. "Roscoe is a much more endearing character than Diamond, somebody you smile at more than anything else," he says.

It was five years ago that Miller urged Beavers to examine Kennedy's novels, a suggestion that has led him into new musical terrain. "When you have a subject matter that's not so obvious, it pushes you in new directions," says Beavers.

Beyond its literary inspiration, "Roscoe" will be an atypical concerto in other ways as well. According to the composer, the piece is cast in four movements, rather than the traditional three. And there will be a soloist other than the violinist, that being Kennedy as the narrator.

"I can't get over the way he writes dialogue and the wit of the characters," says Beavers. "I was just chuckling at so many lines, though it's a serious book."

"Roscoe" may be one of Kennedy's most explicitly musical books. Again the author fills the air with songs of World War II and music of the swing era, but he also makes frequent use of musical terminologies. For example, the pivotal account of Democrats recapturing power is titled "Opus One: Overture, 1919," with subsequent sections called movements.

"I guess there's a feeling that there's a symphony being created by Roscoe and Patsy McCall and the other people who are instrumental in taking over City Hall ... music as a metaphor for plot," explains Kennedy.

In his own perusal of the book, Beavers was drawn to short passages of fantasy that precede certain chapters. "There are these one-page dream-like texts, you could call soliloquies or meditations," explains Beavers.

The concerto's first movement is inspired by one of those passages, titled "Roscoe and the Silent Music." In it, Roscoe is having an imaginary, late-night conversation with Diamond, who warns that trouble is ahead and asks how he'll cope.

"I'll cope through virtue, and virtue I'll achieve through harmony. The musical scale, always a favorite of mine, is expressed in harmonious numbers: the octave, the fifth, and other fixed intervals, all reflecting an order inherited by this earth..."

Roscoe continues on for a bit about a theory of heavenly order and "the music of the spheres." To that Diamond replies:

"Virtue was always one hell of an idea."

Beavers' response is a quiet, harmonically unsettled music with high lyrical lines for the violin.

For a fast movement, Beavers went with Kennedy's suggestion of the section titled "Felix Declares his Principals to Roscoe." There, the aspiring political boss recalls his father's rapid-fire enumeration of every way to acquire money and power. One dictum goes: *Pave every street with a church on it.*

Another movement arises out of "Roscoe and the Flying Heads," a trippy fantasy set in a night club, where a chorus line is performing to the song "Somebody Else is Taking My Place." Kennedy explains that the song alludes to Roscoe and his friend Elisha being in love with the same woman. Beavers describes his musical interpretation as having "a dance element and a macabre element."

The concerto's finale is based on the closing pages of the novel, titled "On The Night Boat." Roscoe has died and his spirit is being invited into a casino onboard a ship. He hears strains of Wagner.

"There's no direct quote of Wagner (in the score). That's stuff you don't want to touch," says Beavers. But the composer points with amazement to the very last phrase of the novel: *I could use a little music.*

"It was almost like (Kennedy) knew what was coming. He calls for it," says Beavers. "How could he set up a last movement better than that?"

"Whatever I'm working with, there's an element of music and an element of timing and rhythmic pacing," says Kennedy. "It's just in my literary equipment."

But the creation of a musical line – strong enough to inspire a composer – out of the smoke-filled rooms of political wheeling and dealing is the sign of a master. And because it is Kennedy, it is also Albany.

"He's taken what he knows best ... a city of thugs, and has elevated it into high art," says Miller. "He sings the song of Albany."

It Takes More Than a Music Director

MAY 25, 2008

Perhaps in the days of yore when the king paid the way, musicians were free to learn and perform whatever new or old compositions happened to strike their fancy. But today's orchestras don't have such freedom; they must satisfy a variety of musical tastes and also balance the books. For the Albany Symphony Orchestra, which concluded its spring season earlier this month, the details of 2008-09 season have already been in place for months. The major decisions – what's to be performed, when, where and with which guest artists – came as the result of extensive artistic discussion and fiscal analysis on the part of both the staff and the board of directors.

Just as the days of royal beneficence are long gone, the supreme reign of a maestro is also largely a thing of the past. "You can't plan a season in a vacuum," concedes ASO music director David Alan Miller. "The process is driven by me, but it's not just about what the conductor wants to play."

Following is a chronological sketch of the ASO's process in arriving at a new season.

In the early fall of last year, Miller brought his initial ideas for concerts running September 2008 through May 2009 to the program committee, a group that consists of board members highly knowledgeable in the classical repertoire as well as some less conversant.

"I encourage them to challenge me and ask why does this (program) have so much French music, or this one not have a premiere, or why so many pianists," says Miller. "The less expert people often bring to my mind things I've not fully vetted."

"We're a sounding board," says committee chairman Edward M. Jennings. "There's a community awareness that goes into our discussions. We're conscious of offering pieces that people will recognize and also perpetually challenging the audience."

More than just responding to Miller's plans, committee members are also encouraged to offer their own ideas, and even lobby for their favorite composers. It was Jennings, for example, who a few years ago urged Miller to delve into the history of great explorers. That's turned out to be the theme for the '08-09 season, dovetailing with the impending celebrations for the 400th anniversary of Henry Hudson's voyage.

ASO general manager Sharon Walsh estimates that the programming committee met eight times last fall. "Everybody gets to dream and feel part of it," she says.

But dreams only go so far. Once the program committee has come together on a season, it's scrutinized by the budget committee and then sent back and forth a few times between committees.

At the ASO, this committee-based planning process has only been in place for a few years. "It's gone from absolute seat-of-the-pants-throwing-it-together-faster-than-you-can-believe," says Miller, "to an intelligent procedure of realizing our objectives and goals."

The ASO's time frame for deciding a season has also gotten progressively earlier, but Miller says it is not as far in advance as at major orchestras, which plan two or more years out. Still, the ASO's schedule does allow for greater flexibility in booking guest soloists.

"One has to be nimble and flexible," explains Miller. "When we got Yo-Yo Ma (in January 2006), his manager wanted him and these young artists to have a few chances to play together before New York and happened to think of us. If we'd been totally locked into a season already, we couldn't have accepted."

Miller says that he's contacted on an almost weekly basis about new works by American composers in need of performances. He has to turn down most, but sometimes the availability of a new piece can result in another programming coup.

Such a case comes in February next year, when virtuoso guitarist Elliot Fisk will premiere a new concerto by Robert Beaser. According to Miller, those artists have long wanted to work together, yet never found the right opportunity. When Miller was recently in New York conducting the American Composers Orchestra, where Beaser is an adviser, he learned about the project and soon a co-commission with that orchestra was in place. The piece also will be performed by an orchestra in Europe. "They're graciously giving us the premiere," says Miller.

In late fall, the slate of concerts is subjected to a cost and feasibility analysis by the operations manager, personnel manager and librarian. "It takes a month to dissect a season," says Walsh. Each piece is examined for the number of musicians, the doublings (one musician playing more than one instrument within a piece), and the need for extra percussion or nonstandard instruments. While these details affect the budget, it's also vital to know if a particular piece will fit on the stage.

For much of this information, the first place to turn is David Daniels' "Orchestral Music: A Handbook," a definitive 600-page reference book that gives the instrumentation, running time and publisher for most orchestral works. A typical listing uses numerical shorthand to communicate the number of woodwinds and brass. For example, the season's opening work, Beethoven's "Egmont" Overture, requires strings and tympani plus "2-2-2-2, 4-2-0-0," which translates as two flutes, two oboes, two clarinets, two bassoons and four horns, two trumpets, no trombone, no tuba.

"Some things you don't know until you actually have the score," adds Walsh. A case in point is John Corigliano's "Pied Piper Fantasy," a theatrical flute concerto written for James Galway in 1982 that's scheduled for next April with soloist Alexa Still.

"I intercepted the score before it went to the maestro," says ASO operations manager Susie Alderson, "and flags went off." Among her discoveries: the piece requires special lighting, as well as an ensemble of student musicians who follow the soloist down the aisle of the theater. Already Alderson has secured more lights for the music stands. But having been with the ASO for 14 years now, she's accustomed to waiting for certain details to fall into place, like who the young musicians will be.

There are still other committees of the board that have input in shaping the season. The development committee is represented from the beginning since its chairman, Barry Richman, is also a member of Miller's "kitchen cabinet" for preliminary brainstorming on programs.

The marketing committee, led by Steve Lobel, has discussions with Miller about the overarching theme of a season and how to effectively promote each individual concert.

"I like to get involved from the beginning to a get a feel for the direction we're going and the thematic feeling, so that we can creatively put the right spin on it," says Lobel. That process culminates with a subscription renewal brochure in the spring and a campaign for new subscribers in the summer but also continues throughout the season itself.

"We've become very integrated so that everyone will have had their input," says Walsh. "I would say it's a working board. People like that ownership."

The kind of collaborative relationship between music director, board and staff at the ASO is not uncommon among other American orchestras. But add in the extensive work with living composers plus the extra events at the annual American Music Festival, and you've got a uniquely energetic and productive orchestra that has earned a national reputation.

Alderson, the operations manager, says she's reminded of the orchestra's renown when attending the annual conventions of the League of American Orchestras. "When we wear our badges at conferences, people stop us and want to know how we do it."

Making Music
With a Sense of Place

SYMPHONY MAGAZINE, MAY-JUNE 2008

First settled by the Dutch in 1624, the New York State Capital of Albany and its surrounding environs were traversed by some of America's earliest explorers. A series of battles in the area marked a turning point in the Revolutionary War. In the 19th century it functioned as a vital commercial trade zone, thanks to the adjacent meeting point of the Eric Canal and the Hudson River. More recently, the workings of state government have set a national standard for rough and tumble politics.

By building a body of music that celebrates this rich and varied history, conductor David Alan Miller and the Albany Symphony Orchestra are making classical music a more integral part of local life. While still performing plenty of masterpieces from the European canon, they're also building engaged audiences for new compositions.

"I come from Los Angeles, a wonderful city. But other than a few pueblo remnants, there's not much historic back story there," says Miller. Currently in his 15th year as music director of the ASO, Miller has become fascinated with the lore of what is know as the Capital District, which also encompasses the cities of Troy, Schenectady and Saratoga Springs, and he's applying that ever deepening knowledge to his programming decisions.

"An orchestra needs to be about its time and place and in a close dialogue with the public. It gives the institution a stronger reason to exist and flower than if you're doing what the next orchestra is doing," says Miller. "I get the sense that there are many orchestras you could just pick up and put in another town."

Founded in 1930, the Albany Symphony has a tradition of playing new and unusual music that long pre-dates Miller. The late conductor Julius Hegyi, who reigned as music director from 1965 to 1988, had a solid reputation for performing the American symphonists such as Piston, Schumann and Gould as well as for premiering works by living composers like Druckman, Wuorinen and Laderman. Partnering with Hegyi in those years was ASO chairman emeritus Peter Kermani (also a former chairman of the League of American Orchestras), who hired

Miller to carry on that legacy. "Most orchestras have not invited the living composer back into their world the way we have. And so they're constrained to a body of fixed, existing music," says Miller, who has premiered more than 100 works with the ASO. "The beauty of working with a panoply of composers is they're usually willing to write on a specific subject."

Under Miller's tenure, most of the ASO's nine annual subscription concerts feature one new or recent work by a living American composer. Often it's an overture or tone poem of some sort, but the pieces that linger in the memory usually relate to a particular aspect of local history. Recent examples include Peter Child's "Washington Park," a tribute to Albany's 200-year-old park designed by Frederick Law Olmsted, and Kevin Beavers' two works inspired by novels of eminent local author William Kennedy.

Ten years ago the ASO launched its annual American Music Festival, an ambitious month-long series of events highlighted by a subscription concert of all-American works – usually a balance of something classic, by Copland or Bernstein perhaps, with more current fare. To encourage attendance, it's called Casual Night at the Symphony ("Really, it's okay to wear jeans," say the promotions.) In addition, the festival has a concert of the Dogs of Desire, a 16-instrument refiguring of the orchestra that's dedicated to new, pop-infused works and usually plays in alternative venues like a nightclub or even a television studio. Smaller events such as open rehearsals and a cabaret evening round out the offerings

Six of the American Music Festivals have also featured Capital Heritage Concerts, which are the ASO's most boldly original way of getting new music into the community and putting local culture into new works. Each event happens at an historic site and consists of three new chamber orchestra works composed specifically about the location. The afternoon format includes background from a local historian or guide, plus thoughts from the commissioned composers on how they set music to something visual, architectural or historical.

The inaugural events in 2000 and 2002 had audience members bused to a series of different churches in Troy that have prominent Tiffany windows. In the mid-19th century, Troy was the fourth richest city in America, and its lavish architecture still reflects that prosperous era. Beneath each window the ASO premiered new works. "They were modern pieces and I didn't hear a single grumble about not liking the music," recalls Miller. "The link of the music and the visual was so strong, people were completely open. It was historic art enhanced by new art."

The buses were dispensed with in 2003, when the sites – a government building, a temple and a museum – were all within walking distance of each other in downtown Albany. For 2004, the entire event happened inside the grand New York State Capitol, considered the most expensive building in American when completed in 1899. And in 2006 it was at the Saratoga National Park, site of the Battle of Saratoga, where American forces drove back the British army and changed the course of the Revolution.

At each of these outings Miller was a likeable and approached host with a contagious sense of enthusiasm and adventure. And as the audiences, usually numbering around 100, took in the history lessons and the three world premieres, a sense of community also came through.

It was back to government buildings for 2007, but with a different take on the series. Adjacent to the State Capitol is a gargantuan modern office complex conceived by the late Governor Nelson Rockefeller and known as the Empire State Plaza. With four skyscrapers, a theater, library and museum, it was completed in the 1970s at a cost of approximately $1 billion. The underground concourse that links all the buildings is pristine white, perhaps a quarter mile in length, and filled with significant and large-scale works of abstract art by artists such as Mark Rothko, Robert Motherwell and Louise Nevelson.

But ultimately it's still a government building, and Miller was concerned, if not aghast, to witness how desensitized the state workers have become to the eye-popping art that surrounds them. In response, the ASO commissioned 16 composers to write three-minute solos inspired by works from the collection. They were debuted by principal players of the orchestra in a four-hour marathon of art and music that also included a light supper. Among the many highlights, an effervescent piece for harp by Neil Rolnick was played beneath the heavy weight of a George Segal wall sculpture, and a free-form, devil-may-care percussion solo by Michael Woods was performed in front of an oversized Jackson Pollock painting.

These events appeal to museum goers and historic preservation buffs as much as to music fans, so each audience is as unique as the event. And that's the point, says Miller. "An arts institution needs to have as big a footprint in its community as possible, reaching people in lots of ways. The ideal orchestra is so much bigger than a subscription series."

While contemporary music is a prominent part of the ASO's local and national reputation, commissions to composers actually represent a modest amount of the annual budget. According to general manager Sharon Walsh, in the 2007-08 season $59,000 went toward fees to composers out of a total budget of $2.2 million. The figure decreases for 08-09 to around $30,000. Grants for commissions and other contemporary music activities are regularly received from Meet the Composer, the Aaron Copland Fund for Music and the Virgil Thomson Foundation among others. In recent years Key Bank has underwritten the American Music Festival.

Yet to maintain a consistent level of new music activity, projects sometimes proceed even without special grant funding. "We've been bold and courageous enough to pay for some of this through our general budget," says Miller.

There's also a certain musical slight of hand at work when the orchestra, for example, boosts of the 26 different world premieres that occurred during its 75th anniversary in 2005. To get to that total, the season included eight world premieres offered during subscription concerts, among them new works by John Harbison and Michael Torke. That series, "American Dreams, American Memories," was underwritten by board member Paul Underwood. But the larger season also included ancillary events like the Capital Heritage Concerts, when the orchestra is reduced to 13 players, and the annual outing of the Dogs of Desire, which is comprised of 18 players.

Miller also works primarily with younger composers who rarely get the opportunity to write for orchestra and therefore are willing to take rather modest fees. Most ASO commissions are in the range of $2,000 to $5,000.

This strategy sometimes pays off nicely. For example, Paul Moravec wrote a piece for the 2004 concert in the State Capitol and three weeks later made headlines for winning the Pulitzer Prize for an earlier composition. A homerun like that usually only happens by working with composers in an on-going and consistent basis. But such a success certainly helps justify the struggles to finance new works and to win over audiences for new sounds.

ASO board member Edward M. Jennings, a retired college professor who's lived in Albany for 40 years, would never describe himself as an avid fan of contemporary music. But like a lot of ASO patrons, he's been on hand for enough premieres to be long past shaking his head in disgust or shrugging his shoulders in confusion upon hearing something new. "Even if one of these new pieces is not exactly the kind of things we relish and want to hear again, there's always something interesting to talk about," says Jennings. "In our conversations outside the board room, that's how everybody feels... 'Gee, I didn't like that one,' and someone else said, 'Oh I liked that one, but not that one.'"

Such engaged discourse about new orchestral music is common among ASO audiences. That's because an ASO season is comparable to a tour in an art gallery. If you don't like this new piece, well, there's going to be another one right around the corner that might be better.

CHAPTER SIX
Remembering the Masters

AARON COPLAND

Restive patriot

The Dixie Chicks should take heart. Although they have had their songs dropped from radio stations and been booed at awards shows because of their statements against President Bush, a fellow Texan, they are not alone in the annals of American music for being shunned because of their politics. In his day, the great American composer Aaron Copland (1900-1990) also faced the difficulties of being a politically engaged artist.

In January 1953, Copland's orchestral work "Lincoln Portrait" was pulled from a Washington concert celebrating the Eisenhower inauguration. Later that year, he was compelled by subpoena to testify before Sen. Joseph McCarthy, all because of his alleged ties to communist organizations.

Last month, a lengthy FBI file on Copland was released in response to a 1997 request under the Freedom of Information Act by the Associated Press. The documents traced Copland's travels, associations and allegiances for 25 years, and reveal that he was deeply involved in socialist causes, primarily during the 1930s and 1940s. This is in sharp contrast to the image fostered by Copland and others that he was a musician who lived apart from the currents of international politics.

But Copland's progressive politics always have been clear in his music, which spotlights and ennobles the common man – "the great masses of the proletariat," as he himself once put it. The full extent of Copland's political activism, as idealistic and perhaps naive as it may have been, only adds to his remarkable legacy.

There's always been a certain irony in the fact that the signature sound of America was created by a left-leaning Jewish homosexual who was born in Brooklyn of Russian immigrant parents. But Copland's music has not only entered the mainstream concert repertoire. His "Fanfare for the Common Man" has become the soundtrack for presidential inaugurations and Olympic competitions.

Copland found his popular voice as a composer through a canny use of American folk melodies. His hat trick of ballet scores – "Billy the Kid" (1938), "Rodeo" (1942) and "Appalachian Spring" (1943-44) – were the result of great skill and thoughtful collaboration, not simple inspiration from the heartland.

The search for a distinctly American sound was an effort Copland shared with many other composers of his era, including Virgil Thomson, Roy Harris and Douglas Moore. Their emphasis on folk song was a means already employed by nationalistic composers from Europe for generations. But for Copland it also was of a piece with his politics.

The communist movement in America during the mid-1930s allied itself with nationalistic themes and promoted the integration of folk material into serious art. According to Howard Pollack's biography "Aaron Copland: The Life and Work of an Uncommon Man," from which many of the biographical details in this story were taken, Copland was no stranger to such discussions but, rather, was a supporter of the larger socialist ideals.

In 1934, the left-wing journal "New Masses" announced a competition for music for a new workers song with lyrics from a poem titled "Into the Streets May First." Copland's setting won. Late in life he downplayed the piece, calling it the "silliest thing I did." But in a 1935 letter to the Mexican composer Carlos Chavez he referred to it as "my communist song" and boasted that it had been published in Soviet Russia. "I should very much like to make a trip there," he added.

Copland got caught up with a band of communist-leaning farmers during the summer of 1934, which he spent in rural Minnesota with his companion Victor Kraft. He even made a couple of speeches, and wrote in a letter that farmers would come up to him in town "as one red to another."

The last hurrah for Copland and other prominent leftist artist was the Cultural and Scientific Conference for World Peace, held at the Waldorf-Astoria in New York City in 1949. Other participants were playwrights Lillian Hellman and Arthur Miller and Soviet composer Dmitry Shostakovich. It must have been obvious that the tide began to turn when Life magazine's coverage of the gathering began, "Red Visitors Cause Rumpus."

Copland's reputation first was attacked on the floor of the U.S. House on Jan. 3, 1953, by Illinois Rep. Fred Busbey, who, in light of the composer's suspected political affiliations, questioned the presence of Copland's music on the upcoming inaugural concert. The congressman subsequently placed into the Congressional Record a list of some 20 communist organizations, or "fronts," with which the composer allegedly had ties.

Five months later, McCarthy and his chief counsel, Roy Cohn, hammered away at Copland during two hours of closed-door testimony on the extent of his involvement with these same organizations. Copland kept his cool and often pleaded memory lapses and lack of preparation (he was given three days' notice of the hearing). He gave away little and often cited his involvements as purely artistically related.

The ammunition for Busbey and McCarthy's fusillades is contained in the recently released FBI file, which log Copland's associations, often in great detail. If some citations seem trivial ("According to the Daily Worker ... Aaron Copland was one of the sponsors of the American Youth Orchestra"), the bulk of them is convincing, if not damning.

While Copland was never called back by McCarthy for public testimony, the FBI documents show that the government continued to monitor his activities and considered indicting him for committing perjury and fraud in his Senate testimony.

"We all hung out with the left-wing intellectuals," says composer Ned Rorem, 79, who was a student of Copland's in the 1940s at Tanglewood, in Lenox, Mass., and remembers seeing him in Paris in 1953 shortly after the congressional testimony. Says Rorem, on the phone from his home in New York City, "Aaron was not a card-carrying communist, but he was a fellow traveler."

Another composer colleague, David Del Tredici, 65, recalls Copland describing the encounter with McCarthy, and that it included a distinct taste of homophobia.

"Aaron told me that one of the people on the panel was this gorgeous young man who said not a word," says Del Tredici, during a phone interview from New York. "He always thought that he was there to rattle him."

Perhaps because Copland did not otherwise discuss his youthful political activities, Del Tredici, like others, downplays the extent of his involvement.

"He might have gone to some kind of meeting," says Del Tredici. "A friend probably said 'Come on, it will be fun.'" One pictures the young Christopher Isherwood in the "Berlin Stories" discovering himself amid radicals.

But Del Tredici also allows for the sincerity and idealism that may have driven Copland. "There was the romance of socialism that interested him and others," he says. "It's so different now that we wouldn't have any idea of how it was once appealing."

"Today, there isn't anything you can call left wing," declares Rorem.

Perhaps that's all the more reason that Copland's courage of conviction can be almost as inspiring as his music. A line from his speech to the 1949 Cultural and Scientific Conference is especially apt today when slogans on T-shirts can raise the risk of arrest.

"I am here this morning," Copland said, "because I wish to protest an attitude that has turned the very word peace into a dirty word."

GEORGE GERSHWIN

More than a songsmith

"It comes drifting through the elevators," says soprano Elizabeth Graham, of the omnipresence of George Gershwin's music. "You can't get away from it." But Graham, for one, has never actually tried to escape Gershwin's melodic charms. As the female lead in "Porgy and Bess," she has been singing "Summertime," perhaps his most famous song, for nearly 20 years and will do so again Saturday, at Proctor's Theatre.

"Every time I hear the overture to 'Porgy and Bess,' she says, "I get excited."

The upcoming performances of Gershwin's only opera will launch a mini-Gershwin festival in the Capital Region over the next two weeks. On Friday pianist Jeffrey Siegel offers Gershwin's solo version of "Rhapsody in Blue" in a program at the Troy Savings Bank Music Hall and the next night at the Palace Theatre in Albany, the Albany Symphony Orchestra and pianist Kevin Cole perform both "Rhapsody in Blue" and the Second Rhapsody.

In separate conversations, all of these performers offered more than mere enthusiasm and appreciation for Gershwin; they gave emphatic validation of him as a serious composer, not just the songsmith of over-played standards or a composer for outdoor pops concerts.

"He's our American Mozart," says Cole, who lists the similarities: "a short life, a burst of genius, clear understanding of form, never dry of melody ... "

Gershwin's achievements started with songs "Swanee" was his first hit, although it's still more associated with Al Jolsen and continued with Broadway shows. In such popular works as "Strike Up the Band," "Girl Crazy" and "Of Thee I Sing," his memorable tunes brought to life the clever lyrics by his brother Ira.

"The songs are beloved like Schubert," says author Joan Peyser, whose Gershwin biography, "The Memory of All That," was issued in 1993. "They're great, great songs."

Melody also pervades Gershwin's handful of concert works, which include "Rhapsody in Blue" (1922), the tone poem "An American in Paris" (1928) and the Second Rhapsody (1932), sometimes called "New York Rhapsody."

At the premiere of "Rhapsody in Blue," with the Paul Whitman Orchestra, Gershwin played the solo piano part himself. Cole points to Gershwin's prowess at the keyboard as key to his writing, and the success of the "Rhapsodies"

"He was a superb pianist ... like Rachmaninoff and Listz," says Cole, whose rhythmically incisive playing has been compared with Gershwin's.

But during Gershwin's own life, nobody compared him to Mozart, Schubert or Rachmaninoff. Among the reasons for this is the great divide between classical and popular music, which was already well established.

Picture a pop star of today stepping into the classical world and then imagine the response from the cultural elite. Actually, no imagination is necessary: Paul McCartney and Billy Joel have done just that, and their classical works have not had legs, despite the best efforts of their record labels. Perhaps time will offer a kinder verdict. In the case of Gershwin, it's taken years for critics and scholars to fully come around on his side. But the music has never gone away.

America's cultural inferiority complex is another factor in the struggle for serious recognition of Gershwin. There's the persistent notion that if the art comes from Europe or if the artist studied in Europe it's better.

"America tends to underappreciate its own," says Cole. "It's hard still to get Gershwin played for (a symphony orchestra's) regular subscription programs."

The irony here is that it's the deeply American nature of Gershwin's music that makes his works so vivid and clear.

"I don't think there's a single composer so easily recognizable as an American voice," says pianist Jeffrey Siegel. "In this country we tend to think of Gershwin as the pops-concert composer. But on standard programs in Amsterdam and London he's not thought of as pop music but great American music."

In contrast to the Americana of Copland and others who depicted the Great Plains of the West, Gershwin's America is the city. Art-deco style, the rise of skyscrapers and new urban noise of car horns – hallmarks of the roaring '20s – are all there in the concert works. And in "Porgy and Bess," the Southern life of African-Americans is brought to life.

"It's amazing how this man could write music that identifies with the American experience so closely," says Graham, who has performed across North American, Europe, Asia and the Middle East in the production of "Porgy and Bess" that is coming to Proctor's.

"It's sad," she says, "that Gershwin never realized that he wrote the great American opera."

Closely tied to any discussion of Gershwin's greatness, including the common but long-debated assertion about "Porgy" that Graham offers, is the often-melancholy conjecture about what might have been had he not died of a brain tumor at age 38. Would he have continued to compose great opera? Perhaps full-scale symphonic writing was ahead.

Such ambitions might well have been on Gershwin's mind. Throughout his short life, he made deliberate efforts to deepen his craft to so-called classical standards.

Gershwin sought the tutelage of Ravel when the French composer visited America but was rebuffed, as he was during a tour of Europe, by the great French pedagogue Nadia Boulanger. Both claimed that the young man's gifts were already abundant and his voice well formed.

But in Gershwin's final years, spent mostly in California, another "serious European" composer, Arnold Schoenberg, did take him on as a student. An Austrian who immigrated during the World War II and settled on the West Coast, Schoenberg created a system of atonal writing, known as 12-tone composition. The method gave birth to the extremes of rational modernism, which drove audiences away from contemporary music for much of the 20th century.

"Melody and harmony were his incredible gifts, (but) were irreconcilable with the Schoenberg method," says author Peyser. "Perhaps he died at the right time, because not that much more could have come from him. He was already drawn into the vortex of the Schoenberg method."

To support such a surprising theory, Peyser compares Gershwin to Leonard Bernstein, who was also the subject of one of her popular-yet-controversial biographies.

"Gershwin was 36 when 'Porgy' was first mounted," she says. "Bernstein was 39 when 'West Side Story' appeared, and did he ever write anything as good? There's nothing (afterward) of that power and intensity."

LOU HARRISON

Generous queer spirit

Composer Lou Harrison, who died in February at age 85, was sometimes called the Santa Claus of contemporary music. He certainly looked the part, with a big belly and a white mustache and beard. The nickname was apt for other reasons as well: He was a joyous and generous man, and all his life he carried a big bag of toys.

That's what he called his many interests and pursuits. "From the start," he often said, "I spread my toys out on a large acreage." Indeed, in addition to musical composition, he excelled at painting, poetry and calligraphy, as well as instrument construction and typographical design.

Harrison's "toys" also included the remarkable breadth of styles in which he composed. Following in the footsteps of his mentor and friend Henry Cowell, he integrated the sounds of Asia and the Middle East into his compositions.

A former student of the great rationalist Arnold Schoenberg, Harrison borrowed from the 12-tone system at will. With the late John Cage, a lifelong friend, he established percussion music as a genre unto itself. His music foreshadowed minimalism in its use of repetitive rhythmic and melodic patterns. Above all, Harrison's music is characterized by beauty, which was often a radical notion during the 20th century.

Harrison's death continues to be mourned throughout the music world, especially by the many people who considered him a close friend, myself included. And his music is becoming ever more a part of the repertoire, as witnessed by a new disc just released on Mode.

The new recording, "Lou Harrison Works 1939-2000," was largely completed under the composer's supervision before his death and features a delightful sampling of instrumental and vocal works from throughout his career.

Most welcome on the disc are three excerpts from Harrison's second opera, "Young Caesar." The piece dates from 1971, but its history is complicated by the composer's penchant for revising and re-envisioning his pieces. The recorded arias and a duet were part of an expansion of the work completed in 2000 for a production by the Lincoln Center Festival that was never realized. The opera focuses on a young homosexual love affair between Caesar and Nicomedes. "I want to leave behind an explicitly gay opera," Lou once told me.

Lou himself was openly gay throughout his long life and maintained a 33-year relationship with William Colvig, who died in March 2000. The pair lived in Aptos, Calif., a few hours south of San Francisco, in a house that overlooked the ocean, which they built in the 1970s when the region was sparsely populated. By the time I visited them, in the mid-1990s, it looked more like suburbia.

The center of the household was the large music studio, known as the Ives Room, named after the great iconoclast composer Charles Ives, whose music Lou did so much to champion and who, in turn, helped support Lou in his early years.

The spacious but crowded Ives Room had a full gamelan (an elaborate set of Asian percussion instruments) plus a harpsichord, an aging stereo system and a large library on many subjects. There was also the grand piano, where Lou composed.

One night, after the old gentlemen had gone to bed, I slipped into the Ives Room, pulled out a score, and sat at Lou's piano. I quietly picked my way through the easiest Harrison piano piece I could find, "New York Waltzes."

Lou had lived in New York City for 10 years as a young man, working as a stringer for Virgil Thomson at the Herald Tribune. It had been a difficult time because the noise and frenetic pace disagreed with him. But in his piece named for the big city there were genial tunes and playful rhythms. Lou just wasn't the type to hold grudges.

LEONARD BERNSTEIN

Still on the rise

It would be easy to say that 14 years after the death of Leonard Bernstein, the legendary American composer, conductor and educator casts a long shadow. But sunsets, darkness and shadows are just not the right metaphors. Bernstein is still a star, and his glowing light seems stronger than ever.

Some evidence: Almost 50 years after its premiere, "West Side Story" receives an average of 300 productions a year in the United States and Canada, while the Tony Award-winning Broadway revival of "Wonderful Town" closes on Jan. 30, after having played more than 500 performances. In concert halls, Bernstein was the most-performed American orchestral composer during the 2003-04 season, according to the American Symphony Orchestra League.

Even the more thoughtful and less sunny aspects of Bernstein's work seem to be shining lately. A collection of his famed "Young People's Concerts" has just been reissued as a nine-DVD set, and his most daunting compositions of religious argument and political commentary including the cursing-the-heavens Symphony No. 3 "Kaddish" and the apocalyptic cry for peace "Mass" have been re-recorded and are getting performances on a surprisingly regular basis.

From the dancing to the preaching, virtually all facets of the Bernstein legacy can be seen and heard locally as part of The Egg's jam-packed festival "Leonard Bernstein's Living Legacy," which starts tonight. For two weeks, Albany will be the center of the Bernstein universe.

The lineup includes two orchestral programs, new takes on his music by jazz artists and a modern dance troupe, a theatrical exploration of his writings and ideas ("Score"), a visit from the composer's daughter Jamie Bernstein Thomas, and more.

"He was a natural choice," says series producer Peter Lesser of The Egg, explaining that the Bernstein fest is the first in the venue's new series of "Living Legacy" tributes to great artists from the state. Lesser adds that it was easy to program a wide-ranging series of events, drawing on both local and national talent, because Bernstein's influence stretches far beyond music and encompasses theater, dance and film.

"He managed to do a lot of different things well, (and) he didn't have a lot of snobbery," says Don Byron, a clarinetist and composer from New York City. "He always just showed that kind of openness to stuff, and then gave it all the same quality of effort."

Byron will bring his jazz ensemble to Albany for a performance with the Ellen Sinopoli Dance Company. Drawing on his deep knowledge of the Bernstein catalog, Byron selected mostly lesser-known songs and musical passages from shows like "Candide," "West Side Story" and "Mass." They will be performed in new arrangements with original choreography by Sinopoli.

Beyond his admiration of the music, Byron identifies with how Bernstein flourished in so many realms: Bernstein was an orchestra conductor who wrote successful Broadway shows; Byron is a black jazz musician who's recorded klezmer material and writes chamber music.

"It's about whether a person should be allowed to do this *or* that, or do this *and* that," says Byron. Too often, "people feel betrayed by artists who go from one genre or style to another."

The master was known to struggle with the kinds of conflicts Byron identifies. Besides his effort to break down the walls between the worlds of high art and popular entertainment, there was his desire to be both a conductor and public figure, and the need to write and compose in solitude. The constraints of time only added to the pressure.

All this plus the profusion of ideas that filled Bernstein's head will be brought to the stage Friday night in "Score." The 90-minute one-man show, drawn entirely from Bernstein's own writings, was conceived by director Anne Bogart of the New York theater group Siti Company, and adapted by playwright Jocelyn Clarke.

"It's one thing to hear the work of an inspiring giant, it's another to meet him," says Tom Nelis, who plays Bernstein. "This is an opportunity to be in the room with him speaking about his ideas." Portraying the legendary man, Nelis says, "is an amazing, caffeinated experience."

The inclusion of the Albany Symphony Orchestra in the Bernstein festival was a happy accident: Its program, a "Romeo and Juliet" evening, was scheduled long before The Egg announced its plans. "It just fell into place for us," says Lesser.

Along with "West Side Story" and Tchaikovsky's "Romeo and Juliet," the ASO will true to form also present the world premiere of a new work by Daron Hagen. The piece is a double concerto for Jeffrey Khaner, principal flutist of the Philadelphia Orchestra, and Sara Sant'Ambrogio, cellist of the Eroica Trio. It draws thematic inspiration from Shakespeare, and musical inspiration from Bernstein.

Sing the first two notes of that tune in your head ("Ma-ri"). The distance or interval between those notes is known as a tritone, something that standard musical instruction commands composers to avoid at all costs. Thus, Bernstein's profligate use of tritones throughout the song ("Maria, Maria, Maria") is quite audacious.

Hagen goes a step further by basing his entire concerto on the tritone. "The entire score of 'West Side Story' evolves from a tritone, and that little nuclear reactor fires my whole piece," says the composer, who received informal composition and conducting lessons with Bernstein in the late 1980s.

"In my life, he just represented the musical equivalent of very, very pure air ... a level of excellence and dedication and commitment to which one can aspire as a musician," says Hagen.

Yet another fresh perspective on Bernstein is in store with "The Bernstein Beat," a family program featuring excerpts from numerous works. It will be performed by the Empire State Youth Orchestra with narration by Jamie Bernstein Thomas, who is the co-author of the script. (She's also a songwriter, but keeps her works tightly under wraps.)

"The way we went about writing this concert was to use the subject of rhythm as our theme. That automatically steers you to all the jumpiest Bernstein music," she says. "I give (the kids) permission at the top of the concert to jump around and squirm in their seats to the music. I am personally incapable of sitting still while my dad's music is playing."

Bernstein Thomas regularly narrates "The Bernstein Beat" in concerts across the country, and keeps apprised of the myriad Bernstein recordings, performances and tributes. But his continued ascension into the pantheon of artistic greats has almost made her do a double take.

"I guess I just didn't see it coming that he was going to be viewed in retrospect as one of the big personas of the 20th century ... (but) that's how they talk about him," says Bernstein Thomas. "I knew he was terrific, but it seems to be going to the other level of reverence, and that's a surprise."

JEROME ROBBINS

Reviving his Saratoga steps

His ballet dancers called him brutal or worse, at least once they wiped away their tears. But if Jerome Robbins was tough in the studio, he created beautiful dance for the stage. Among his beloved ballets are "The Concert," often considered the funniest ballet ever, "I'm Old Fashioned," a lyric tribute to Fred Astaire, and "West Side Story Suite," featuring searing moments from the immortal musical.

These and nine other Robbins pieces will form the core of the New York City Ballet's 43rd season at the Saratoga Performing Arts Center. They represent a continuation of the company's Jerome Robbins Celebration that began in the spring at Lincoln Center to mark the 10th anniversary of Robbins' death.

Coming in the third week of the season for just two performances will be "Goldberg Variations," a monumental Robbins ballet that bears a unique attachment to SPAC. Set to J.S. Bach's keyboard work of the same name, it is tour de force of abstract choreography (there's no story or characters) that runs one hour and 20 minutes in length and took Robbins almost two years to create. Although the piece's official premiere was May 27, 1971, at Lincoln Center's New York State Theatre, it was first given a single "work in process" performance at SPAC on July 4, 1970.

When the cast of 39 dancers took to the stage that night, Robbins was still in the midst of making numerous decisions about the piece, including casting, costuming and even how the music was to be performed.

"By the time we got to Saratoga, we'd already worked on it for almost a year," recalls retired principal dancer Robert Weiss in a recent interview from Raleigh, N.C., where he is artistic director of Carolina Ballet. "He made you learn many many different sections, and some girls learned men's part and some men learned girls' parts, because he couldn't decide. In the end, everybody learned like nine parts and then you got to perform one part. It was a painstaking process."

Weiss also recalls wearing practice clothes on stage, because no costumes had been decided. In its final form, the piece begins with most of the dancers wearing simple unitards in coordinated colors, while the soloists appear in Baroque outfits, such as doublets for men and lace skirts for women. By the end of the ballet, the entire company appears in such finery.

Issues of Baroque style also had to be addressed in the music. Bach's "Goldberg Variations" begins with a statement of the main theme that's followed by 30 variations. Modern performance practice for this and other Baroque works typically ignores the repeat signs at the end of each variation. But Robbins chose to have each variation played twice, which made for an unusually long ballet.

Length seems to have been a Robbins obsession at the time. He began work on "Goldberg" in 1970, the year following the debut of his acclaimed "Dances at a Gathering," an hourlong essay to piano music of Chopin, which was his first ballet after returning to City Ballet from a string of successes on Broadway.

Robbins may have been committed to the full breadth of Bach's score, but he was ambivalent about whether it should be performed on harpsichord, as the composer would have heard it, or on a modern piano. For the Saratoga performance, he went with harpsichord.

"He wanted to see how the harpsichord would sound on stage in a big auditorium, and it didn't work," recalls Robert Maiorano, a "Goldberg" cast member and retired City Ballet soloist who has lived in Saratoga for the past five years. "The harpsichord didn't have the weight for all that space. It was little tinkly background music as opposed to music that draws us to dance. (Afterward) he reverted back to the piano."

Also in the original cast of "Dances at a Gathering," Maiorano recalls receiving an important lesson from Robbins during that work's creation.

"I remember him telling me, 'Don't dance to the music,' and I looked at him like he was crazy," says Maiorano. "With Balanchine it was boom-boom-boom. Sharp, clear on the beat. But Jerry said 'No, no, no. Let the music take you – dance the space between the notes,' which makes for a whole different quality of dancing that's essential to Jerry's work."

Maiorano adds that he was one of the few who largely escaped Robbins' ire. He explains, "I never had a big fight with him because I realized if I did *exactly* what he said, I would be a better dancer for it."

Even to those who weren't dancers, Robbins evoked fear. Edward J. Lewi, a current SPAC board member, handled public relations and marketing for the center in its early years. Although he was new to ballet and the performing arts in general, he became fast friends with Balanchine.

But with Robbins, who was never a regular presence at SPAC, Lewi tried to be on his best behavior. "Everybody knew when he was on SPAC grounds," he says. With the showing of "Goldberg Variations" approaching in 1970, Lewi's promotional instincts got the better of him, despite Robbins' strict admonitions.

"He told me he didn't want press, and if he saw any press he would embarrass me by stopping the performance and asking the press people to leave," recalls Lewi, who did, in fact, allow local and national reporters and critics to attend (along with the paying public). "I took a real chance, and I lucked out and it worked. But he knew, because as soon as he walked off, he said, 'You are lucky,' and went right by me."

Lewi remembers positive reviews though he himself missed the actual performance. "I was so shook up I couldn't even watch it," he says.

Actually, the reviews at SPAC and the following spring in New York were mixed. But looking backward over the entire Robbins catalog, "Goldberg" can now be seen as an important example of the choreographer challenging himself and his audience to wrestle with abstract structure and extended form. And as his first choreography to Bach, it foreshadows three of his final ballets, all acclaimed settings of Bach: "A Suite of Dances" (1994), "2 & 3 Part Inventions" (1994) and "Brandenburg" (1997).

For those lucky enough to have witnessed its birthing process, "Goldberg" remains deeply etched in the memory. Here's how another cast member, Bruce Wells, described it to author Greg Lawrence, in his Robbins' biography "Dance with Demons":

"We went on in our practice clothes, (while Robbins) stood on the side of the stage and he described what he was working on to the audience. And I do remember that being an incandescent night, because it was filled with raw, creative energy in a performance space, and the man was now saying things of course we had never heard. That was a thrilling, thrilling night – I remember we brought the house down and we were not really aware of the little jewel that we had (in 'Goldberg') until that happened."

CHAPTER 7
Making EMPAC

Up on the Hill:
The Experimental Media &
Performing Arts Center

NEWMUSICBOX, OCTOBER 2008

Just where is the intersection of art and science? To most of us, it's as small and instant a thing as snapping a shot with a digital camera or pressing down middle C on an electronic keyboard. Yet "At the Intersection of Art and Science" is the official descriptive slogan for something much much bigger – a mammoth new landmark in upstate New York and perhaps even in the future of the arts.

The place is EMPAC, the new Experimental Media and Performing Arts Center on the campus of Rensselaer Polytechnic Institute in Troy, New York, officially opening on Friday, October 3, 2008. More than six years in the making, it is a building measuring some 220,000 square feet and costing nearly $200 million. And those are dollars from earlier in the decade. According to Curtis R. Priem, an entrepreneur and RPI trustee who contributed $40 million to EMPAC, it would cost about $1 billion to launch a similar undertaking today, due to the surging costs in construction, concrete, cooper and the like.

EMPAC includes four performance spaces – a 1,200 seat concert hall, a 400 seat theatre with a seven-story fly space, and two flexible "black box" spaces measuring 3,500 and 2,500 square feet respectively – plus audio and video production suites, studios for resident artists, large glass enclosed atriums, a cafe and more. Not just an arts venue, EMPAC is wired into RPI's super computer – one of the newest and largest at any American university – and each of its large halls has been conceived and engineered to support advanced research in visualization, animation, simulation, acoustics, optics, and haptics (the study of touch). Designed by Grimshaw Architects of New York with acoustical consultation by Kirkegaard Associates of Chicago, EMPAC has advanced technologies and myriad applications said to be unparallel by any other single facility in the world.

As EMPAC's sleek glass building has risen out of a grassy bluff above downtown Troy, a major question has also arisen: Why is an engineering school opening an arts center? The answer lies at the heart of the tenure of RPI president Shirley Jackson, a physicist who chaired the U.S. Nuclear Regulatory Commission for four years under President Clinton. She took the reins of the 84-year-old institution in 1999 with the intent of positioning it as a leader for 21st century technologies.

In March 2001, Jackson secured a $360 million anonymous gift to the university, which at the time was the largest single contribution ever made to a school. About half of that money went to a center for research in biotechnology, which opened on campus a few years ago. The balance has gone toward EMPAC, which has been envisioned as a place for the development of new technologies in the arts and communication and also for fostering a new kind of thinking by RPI students.

"EMPAC is both a place and a program. It is a performing arts center, a research location and agenda, a hub of campus interaction, a channel for academic programs and more – a powerful combination for art, science and engineering," stated Jackson, to the RPI community earlier this year. "EMPAC will prepare our students for global leadership roles by exposing them to experiences which will foster innovative problems-solving, multicultural sophistication, intellectual agility, and the ability to see connections between and among disciplines across a broad intellectual front. With EMPAC our aim is create an intellectual community that did not before exist, and a cultural change at Rensselaer that will reverberate globally."

RPI is certainly not the first university dedicated to engineering and science to expand its culture and reach. In 1969, the Carnegie Institute of Technology merged with a neighboring humanities school to become Carnegie Mellon University.

"We could have followed the Carnegie Mellon model and taken the price of EMPAC and built a school of humanities and social sciences," says Samuel Heffner, chairman of the RPI board of trustees. "But this building is more than a concert hall. It's a true laboratory and a significant move forward not only for Rensselaer but for the concept of arts and technology. EMPAC will have a long-term effect on the future of Rensselaer and will change lives."

Grand rhetoric has certainly been flowing as EMPAC nears its opening; sometimes the language is even rather poetic.

"It's this bridge, or it's this river where arts and science and technology can come together and have a confluence and the highest levels of quality will meet under one roof," says Johannes Goebel, EMPAC's director. Goebel is a composer and was the founding director of the Institute for Music and Acoustics at the Zentrum für Kunst und Medientechnologie (ZKM) in Karlsruhe, Germany, having supervised the opening of its building in 1996. For a period during the 1990s, while still at ZKM, he co-directed Stanford University's Center for Computer Research in Music and Acoustics, where he was also a visiting composer.

Goebel's arrival at RPI in 2002 was certainly not the first time an artist was part of the university community. A small arts department was established in 1975, primarily as an opportunity for students to pick up some electives or participate in a performing group. In 1987, under the chairmanship of composer Neil Rolnick, the department expanded into an academic center offering the nation's first Master of Fine Arts program in "integrated electronic arts," wherein students developed technical skills that are applicable to multiple fields, such as music, video and gaming. A popular undergraduate degree program followed in 1996, and more recently RPI became one of the first institutions in the nation to establish a Ph.D. in electronic arts.

Under the banner iEAR (Integrated Electronic Arts at Rensselaer), RPI has been making public presentations of up to a dozen concerts, films, demonstrations and lectures annually and has also hosted artists in residence to work at its facilities for extended periods. Among the more notable musicians presented over the years are Philip Glass, John Zorn, Frederic Rzewski, and Laurie Anderson.

Most iEAR events have taken place in the modest auditorium of RPI's arts school, which seats a few hundred and seldom draws a full house. EMPAC, it's worth noting, is an independent entity within RPI. The arts department remains on the other side of campus in the grand old West Hall, which was built as a hospital during the Civil War era (and is said to be haunted).

So the arts do have some established roots at the university, but given the modest draw of iEAR presentations, another question arises:

Can RPI pack in audiences at EMPAC's many halls? And what impact will EMPAC have on the larger arts scene of New York's Capital Region, which also encompasses the cities of Albany, Schenectady, and Saratoga Springs and is a short drive from the cultural Mecca of the Massachusetts's Berkshire County.

Regarding the latter question, Goebel has stated that EMPAC will not duplicate or compete with any programming already happening in the region. But local audiences by definition have a limited amount of time and funds, if not a finite capacity for experimentation, as well.

The Albany Symphony Orchestra (which often performs at the Troy Savings Bank Music Hall, an acoustically acclaimed 19th century hall, also with 1,200 seats, located just a few blocks from EMPAC) has a long history of working with living American composers. Under the ebullient leadership of music director David Alan Miller, its audiences have become accustomed, if not always fully game, to the experience of hearing new works on nearly every program. And in recent years the local gallery scene has had an upsurge in shows by local artists. But otherwise, the region is no Manhattan or Berlin with crowds eager to hang out on the cutting edge.

Yet looked at from another perspective, EMPAC is the latest link in a chain of major new contemporary arts venues that dot the Hudson Valley and extend into New England. A tour of these facilities would start 60 miles north of Manhattan in Beacon where the Dia Foundation houses its massive modern art collection in a 1929 Nabisco factory. Dia: Beacon opened in 2003.

Up the Hudson River another 50 miles in the tiny town of Annandale-on-Hudson is the Fisher Center for the Performing Arts, a sparkling and curvaceous theatre complex designed by Frank Gehry, which also opened in 2003 and is located on the campus of Bard College.

The City of Troy and EMPAC are another 58 miles further north, and then 40 miles northeast and over a mountain pass is North Adams, Massachusetts and MASS MoCA, the center for new art, sculpture, and performance housed in 13 acres of former factory buildings, which opened in 1999. Each of these facilities represents a major new infusion of culture into a former industrial center, with the exception of the Fisher Center, which has enhanced an already vibrant artistic scene at Bard.

EMPAC has not waited for the completion of its building to start presenting events. Seeking to build its brand and engage local audiences, EMPAC has produced 50 different happenings since April 2004. Along with some lectures and film screenings, there have also been concerts with Anthony Braxton, So Percussion, and the Flux Quartet, as well as performances by Troika Ranch, Lone Twin, and Tere O'Connor Dance.

"EMPAC 360" was an outdoor performance and spectacle on the building's construction site – highlighted by dancers repelling on its walls – in September 2005 attended by more than 2,000 people and named by the Times Union as the arts event of the year. And last winter, lighting designer Jennifer Tipton bathed the construction site in color for about a month (one of the only non-theatrical projects in her long career).

While Goebel has been supervising the building's construction and the installation of its technologies, the events have been selected and produced by a three-member artistic team: Kathleen Forde, visual arts curator, Helene Lesterlin, dance curator, and Micah Silver, music curator. The EMPAC web site lists 27 other personnel, but Goebel has estimated that a staff of at least 40 or more will be needed to run the facility. If the current web site – one week before opening night – is any indication, they are scrambling to fill more than a dozen other positions, including box office manager, production technicians, web developer, master carpenter, video engineer and director of research, among others.

Up until now, most EMPAC events have taken place in out-of-the-way auditoriums and campus venues, but approximately 10,000 people have already attended an EMPAC presentation. That figure should easily be surpassed with the string of opening celebrations, which are spread over the first three weekends of October.

The kind of parallel advancement in both art and technology that EMPAC seems to be all about may be best displayed in "There Is Still Time... Brother," a new 20-minute feature film scheduled to play continuously in one of the large studio spaces during the first weekend of events. Commissioned by EMPAC and produced in association with the University of New South Wales and ZKM in Germany, where it premiered last December, it is a model of how the realization of an artistic concept can lead to technological breakthroughs.

The film was conceived, developed and performed by the Wooster Group, the influential SoHo-based theatre collective, and is shown on an extraordinary 360-degree screen. Unlike an IMAX film, which encompasses the viewer's peripheral vision, the screen of the Interactive Panoramic Cinema literally surrounds the viewer, measuring 40 feet in diameter and 15 feet high.

To get a feel for the film's warp-around environment, imagine a busy cafe or office with multiple conversations taking place between people sitting and standing, entering and exiting. The collage-like script, partly improvised, explores themes of war and media, with allusions to the 1959 nuclear holocaust film "On the Beach" and excerpts from Rosie O'Donnell's online blog, among many other widely varied references.

Rather than being a giant sensory overload, each screening of "There Is Still Time... Brother" is controlled – edited, one could even say – by a single viewer in a swivel chair. Wherever he or she points the chair at any given moment, the film is clear and the audio is full, while the rest of the screen is blurred and the sound muffled. Thus, it's impossible to grasp in one viewing every aspect of the piece and no experience of it is ever quite the same.

Though the IPA technology already existed, Goebel wanted to boost the quality of the sound for the new piece, in keeping with EMPAC's high standards for both audio and visual production. Typical cinema sound comes from either left or right, above or below the screen. Yet this can be inexact and confusing when the screen is a wrap-around. Enter Jonas Braasch, assistant professor in the architectural acoustics program at RPI.

"With the screen that size, it becomes very important that the sound comes exactly from the same direction as the visual," says Braasch. "In theatre production you record everything with microphones close to actors but your recording doesn't have any information about their location. We designed a system that would record the sound and take the data of where it's located."

Played back through an array of 32 speakers distributed on three levels behind a new permeable screen, the dialogue in "There Is Still Time... Brother" will seem almost as if the actors' voices are coming directly out of their mouths.

Braasch has written an article on his new microphone tracking system for the Computer Music Journal and is at work on a patent application. He foresees a number of other uses for the technology including for the synchronization of musical performances via the internet. Braasch came to Rensselaer in 2006 from McGill University in Montreal. EMPAC, he says, "is one of the few (electronic arts) centers that has the right balance of people involved in the arts and involved in engineering. That's very difficult to have, without one side dominating the other."

The creation of "There Is Still Time... Brother" also had an effect on its artistic team. According to Wooster Group producer Cynthia Hedstrom, EMPAC's commission reversed the troupe's normal approach to technology. "We tend to start with content and then find ways that technology can enhance it. Here we were starting with technology and finding content for it. That was unusual."

The Wooster Group's development process lasted several years but the film itself was shot in about a week. "Then, as soon as it was done, (artistic director) Elizabeth (LeCompte) says, 'Oh, I've got another idea (for a 360-degree film).'" Concludes Hedstrom, "It's fertile ground." And that might be said not just for the technology of "There Is Still Time... Brother," but perhaps for EMPAC itself.

INDEX

ABOUT THE AUTHOR

Joseph Dalton has covered the arts scene of New York's Capital Region for the Times Union since 2002, filing more than 800 stories to date. In addition to the kinds of profiles and features included in "Artists & Activists," he has also written extensive reviews of the Albany Symphony, Boston Symphony, Philadelphia Orchestra, New York City Ballet, and Glimmerglass Opera, as well as the Kirov Orchestra, Van Cliburn Piano Competition, Boston Early Music Festival, and Marlboro Music Festival. In 2004 he received the ASCAP Deems Taylor Award for music journalism and in 2005 he took a first place award from the New York State Associated Press for arts and entertainment writing. Dalton also contributes to Time Our New York, The Advocate, Opera News, American Record Guide and Symphony Magazine and the web sites New Music Box and Musical America. A veteran of the recording industry, Dalton began his career in A&R administration at CBS Masterworks/Sony Classical and was executive director for 10 years of Composers Recordings, Inc., the nation's first nonprofit classical recording company. At CRI he produced 300 CDs of contemporary American music, including two Grammy-nominated discs and first recordings of Academy Award-winner Tan Dun, and the Pulitzer Prize-winning composers Aaron Jay Kernis, Paul Moravec and David Lang, among many others. He has been a grants advisor to the New York State Council on the Arts, the New York State Music Fund, the Aaron Copland Fund for Music and the American Composers Forum. As a consultant to the Estate Project for Artists with AIDS, he led a three-year research initiative into the effects of the epidemic on American music that resulted in an on-line report and catalogue (www.ArtistsWithAIDS.org). Dalton lives in Troy, New York with his companion, the playwright Richard Morell, and their cats in an apartment full of locally produced art.

www.josephdalton.net